'In presenting how soccer life was [...] of those who took part in that fa[...] game a valuable service with this [...]

'The strength and the character of Shindler's book comes not from the memories of the 1964 Youth Cup players who had successful careers but from the tales of those who slipped away into obscurity . . . a warm, witty and sometimes unbearably sad tale'
Manchester Evening News

'A real insight into how cruel football can be'   *Zoo Weekly*

'A brilliant concept . . . This is a gripping story of sporting and social history told with great clarity and unflashy eloquence'   *The Times*

'This is the third book in the author's "Manchester football trilogy" – the others being *Manchester United Ruined My Life* and *Fathers, Sons and Football*, about the Summerbee family. This is the best of the lot . . . remarkable book'   *Sunday Times*

'A touching, epoch-evoking story of youthful dreams – some dashed, others fulfilled – from a compelling writer'   *Jack*

Colin Shindler was born and raised in Manchester. After graduating from Cambridge University, where he is now a part-time lecturer in history, he completed his PhD thesis on Hollywood and the Great Depression. He wrote the screenplay for the movie *Buster*, and has written and produced television series such as *Lovejoy*, *Madson* and *Wish Me Luck*. He won a BAFTA for his production of *A Little Princess*.

His first book, *Manchester United Ruined My Life*, became an immediate bestseller and was shortlisted for the William Hill Sports Book of the Year prize. His second non-fiction book, also a *Sunday Times* bestseller, was *Fathers, Sons and Football*. It told the story of three generations of the Summerbee family, all of whom had played professional football, from the 1930s to the present day.

GEORGE BEST
AND
21 OTHERS

Colin Shindler

headline

Also by Colin Shindler

Manchester United Ruined My Life
Fathers, Sons and Football

First published in 2004
by HEADLINE BOOK PUBLISHING

First published in paperback in 2005
by HEADLINE BOOK PUBLISHING

10 9 8 7 6 5 4 3 2 1

ISBN 0 7553 1154 X

1964 FA Youth Cup semi-final
programmes courtesy of Cliff Butler

Typeset in Cochin by
Letterpart Limited, Reigate, Surrey

Printed and bound in Great Britain by
Mackays of Chatham plc, Chatham, Kent

Headline's policy is to use papers that are natural, renewable and
recyclable products and made from wood grown in sustainable forests.
The logging and manufacturing processes are expected to conform to
the environmental regulations of the country of origin.

HEADLINE BOOK PUBLISHING
A division of Hodder Headline
338 Euston Road
LONDON NW1 3BH

www.headline.co.uk
www.hodderheadline.com

Dedication

This book is dedicated to my brother, Geoffrey Shindler, who patiently and kindly taught me everything I needed to know about life and art and sport. As a United fan, it was his idea that I started to support City, when I was three years old and unable to defend myself. I have remained constantly grateful to him.

Contents

Acknowledgments

My primary debt of gratitude is to the following players, who shared with me their memories of those matches and their subsequent lives: Glyn Pardoe, David Sadler, John Aston, Mike Doyle, David Connor, John Fitzpatrick, Alan Ogley, John Clay, Bobby Noble, Chris Jones, Dave Farrar, Phil Burrows, Alf Wood, Alan Duff, Jimmy Rimmer, Bobby McAlinden and Willie Anderson. John Buckley told me of the life and times of his friend, Dave Wild.

David Meek and Peter Gardner, the indispensable journalistic chroniclers of those famous times, were particularly helpful, as were Fred Eyre, who was a year ahead of my lads, and, at the *Manchester Evening News*, Pete Spencer, Lynn Prince and Paul Hince, who was a junior contemporary of the main actors. Michael Kennedy helped to paint a picture of Manchester's role in the history of journalism, just as Tony Wilson did for the music of the city.

The morning after a crushing home defeat, Jim Cassells kindly spent time telling me about the current Manchester City youth team, and Dave Bushell did the same at Manchester United. I appreciated Diana Law's help in arranging the latter meeting and, as ever, I have received nothing but courtesy and co-operation whenever I have contacted Manchester City. In particular, I would like to thank John Wardle, Alistair Mackintosh and Bernard Halford, as well as Sara Billington and Rebecca Firth in the administration office. Michael Grade's office kindly arranged for me to see the 2003 FA Youth Cup semi-final first leg at the Valley.

My thoughts on the games and the history of those times have benefited from constant discussions with committed friends on both sides of the fence, in particular Geoff Watts, Mike Summerbee and Ian McShane. Howard and Mandy Gruber and Marc and Caroline Conway provided much appreciated Mancunian hospitality.

My agent, Luigi Bonomi, has been an enthusiastic supporter of my trilogy of Manchester football books and his trenchant comments have always been perceptive and constructive. At Headline, this book has received its customary sterling support from my greatly valued editor, Ian Marshall, a loyal Red who has now persuaded his company to publish three books in which his club has been subjected to a barrage of Jewish jokes and literary references. This is professionalism of the highest order. For all the support I have received from Martin Neild, Kerr MacRae, Juliana Lessa and all the publicity and sales teams at Headline, I remain constantly grateful.

If anyone wants to know why there are no interviews with any of the current Manchester United youth team in this book, it's because the club's manager believes that any such discussion would have left them permanently corrupted. Phew! Close call there, Alex. I was planning to quote large chunks of romantic poetry at them!

On a happier note, I want to pay public tribute, once again, to my wife Lynn and my two children, Amy and David, who have been hopelessly infected with the Manchester City virus. Thanks to David Bernstein and Kevin Keegan, this need no longer be fatal.

MANCHESTER UNITED YOUTH
RED SHIRTS AND WHITE SHORTS

1
RIMMER

2
DUFF

3
NOBLE

4
McBRIDE

5
FARRAR

6
FITZPATRICK

7
ANDERSON

8
BEST

9
SADLER

10
KINSEY

11
ASTON

Referee :
K. DAGNALL,
(Bolton)

Linesmen :
F. Lassey (Red Flag)
H. P. Thomason (Yellow Flag)

11
BROWN

10
McALINDEN

9
JONES

8
PARDOE

7
FROST

6
BURROWS

5
WOOD

4
CLAY

3
WILD

2
DOYLE

1
OGLEY

MANCHESTER CITY YOUTH
BLUE SHIRTS AND WHITE SHORTS

Dramatis Personae

MANCHESTER UNITED
Red shirts, white shorts, red stockings
Black of purpose, evil of heart

Jimmy Rimmer
A very young goalkeeper with very long arms
Born Southport, 10 February 1948

Alan Duff
A right-back who used to be a left-winger
Born North Yorkshire, 24 January 1946

Bobby Noble
A fierce-tackling left-back and captain
Born Cheadle, 18 December 1945

Peter McBride
A Scottish right-half, known as Pinky
Born Motherwell, date of birth unknown

Dave Farrar
A centre-half and schoolboy international uninterested in football

Born Manchester, 7 April 1947

John Fitzpatrick
A Scottish left-half, known as Perky
Born Aberdeen, 18 August 1946

Willie Anderson
A right-winger, young and Scouse
Born Liverpool 24 January 1947

George Best
A tortured genius
Born Belfast, 22 May 1946

David Sadler
A centre-forward and ex-bank clerk
Born Yalding, Kent, 5 February 1946

Albert Kinsey
An inside-left, another Scouser
Born Liverpool, 19 September 1945

John Aston Jr
A speedy left-winger, son of youth team trainer
Born Manchester, 28 June 1947

MANCHESTER CITY

Sky blue shirts, white shorts, blue stockings

Pure as the driven snow, a band of noble heroes

Alan Ogley
A long-sighted goalkeeper, affectionately known as Mister Magoo
Born Barnsley, 4 February 1946

Mike Doyle
A right-half, mysteriously playing at right-back
Born Manchester, 25 November 1946

Dave Wild
A right-back, mysteriously playing at left-back
Born Stockport, 5 June 1946

John Clay
A scheming right-half
Born Stockport, 22 November 1946

Alf Wood
A slide-tackling centre-half and captain
Born Manchester, 25 October 1945

Phil Burrows
A full-back mysteriously playing at left-half
Born Stockport, 8 April 1946

Ronnie Frost
A right-winger
Place and date of birth unknown

Max Brown
Another right-winger
Place and date of birth unknown

Glyn Pardoe
An inside-forward and wunderkind, City's youngest ever debutant
Born Winsford, 1 June 1946

Chris Jones
A centre–forward and grammar school boy
Born Altrincham, 19 November 1946

Bobby McAlinden
An inside-forward and future best friend of George Best
Born Salford, 22 May 1946 (same day as George Best)

David Connor
An outside-left and future utility player and supersub
Born Manchester, 27 October 1945

Prologue

Who? Youth teams? Never heard of any of them. Well,
except George Best, obviously. And Mike Doyle and
David Sadler, didn't they play for England? Oh yes, John
Aston, great European Cup final for United. Oh, that's Glyn
Pardoe, is it? Shame what happened to him. And, oh yes,
John Fitzpatrick, dirty bugger wasn't he? And that one must
be Jimmy Rimmer, who went on to play for Arsenal, – or
was it Villa? But that's all. Oh, wait a minute, David Connor,
he was a supersub, wasn't he? And Bobby Noble, whatever
happened to him? He was going to be a big star at one time,
I remember. Actually, now I look at the photos and see the
names, I seem to recall quite a few of them.

And so you should. Seventeen players from the Manchester United and Manchester City youth teams of 1964, nine
from City, eight from United, went on to play for their first
teams, with varying degrees of success. That's a phenomenal
conversion rate. The only comparable statistic comes from
the United side of 1992, which boasted the talents of Beckham, Neville, Butt, Scholes and Robbie Savage, and the City
team of 1986, which produced White, Moulden, Hinchcliffe,
Lake, Redmond and Ian Brightwell. Both these teams won
the FA Youth Cup, but they never faced each other.

The teams of 1964 met over two legs in the semi-final of

1

the Youth Cup and the memory of those two matches and those twenty-two players have lasted a lifetime. This book charts my attempts to discover what has happened to them since those magical nights. Those players were only three or four years older than I was, which was another reason why I felt a close connection. If only the chief scout at Manchester City had seen me hit the bar with a rasping ten-yard drive for Kay House in a vital house match against Derby House I, too, might have been trotting out in a blue shirt to face the Red hordes – physics homework notwithstanding.

Mancunians have always loved their football teams, identified with their success and stuck with them in their fallow years (sometimes beyond the limits of reason). In April 1964, when City were in the second division and United were recovering from the shock of just avoiding relegation a year earlier, 50,000 people watched the youth teams play their two-legged tie. By comparison, when Manchester United played their home leg in the semi-final of the FA Youth Cup in 2003, just over 4,000 people turned up to the Theatre of Dreams. In April 1964, the average attendance at Maine Road for first-team football was 15,000. The first leg of the Youth Cup derby on 8 April 1964 drew an attendance of 29,706. It captured the imagination of the city and was a match every supporter wanted to see.

I was fourteen years old and have never forgotten the atmosphere of that night. In the fervour and intensity with which the game was played, it compared favourably with many first-team derbies. It was also a particularly special occasion because it was the semi-final of a knock-out tournament, and there was to be no return match in six months' time. City's relegation in May 1963 had deprived Manchester of its two annual derby matches for the first time since 1949, so the kids had a lot to live up to. It was our chance for revenge, but United felt they owned that FA Youth Cup.

They had won it for the first five years of its existence and they had no intention of surrendering it to anyone – especially City. Besides, they had George Best.

By then, everyone knew that Best was going to be a star. He had made his debut the previous September, but had been dropped immediately. However, following a Boxing Day defeat, he had been recalled and had set the first division alight. A few days after the first leg of the Youth Cup semi-final he made his international debut for Northern Ireland. He was expected to win the Cup by himself, but the City right-back, Mike Doyle, was determined he wouldn't do it at his expense. That night was the start of a mutual enmity that was to stretch across the rest of the decade and reach its apogee in the personal tragedy of Glyn Pardoe.

The George Best saga has, astonishingly, fascinated the public for forty years. From football prodigy in the mid-sixties, through successive metamorphoses as commercial superstar, sex symbol and celebrity runaway in the early seventies, to his 'retirement' at twenty-six; his subsequent, increasingly desperate comebacks, his failed relationships with women, the alcoholism that saw him imprisoned briefly and then caused his brush with death before a transplanted liver gave him the chance to start afresh, and the revelation that he has seemingly spurned it – throughout all these well-documented crises he has never forfeited the love, or at least the attention, of millions of people, many of whom never saw him play.

But there were twenty-one other players on the field that night in April 1964, and this book tells their stories as well as his. They are not as well known as Best's, but they are equally deserving of a public hearing, because these players, too, had their dreams and hopes, some of which were realised, most of which were not.

Although this story follows a specific group of players

from 1964 to 2004, in many ways it is a timeless tale, for no matter how much the game has changed, football continues to lure in talented youngsters and then toss them callously on the scrapheap if, in the opinion of one or two men, they don't make the grade.

As fans we continue to hope that we are spotting the next generation in action. That was certainly my feeling when I watched both City and United again in the 2003 FA Youth Cup. The dream regenerates itself no matter how often we know it will all end in tears, which is one of the many things that makes football so special to so many of us.

I remember a great many derby matches from the sixties – particularly the 3–1 City win at Old Trafford on the way to the championship in 1968 – but the 1964 Youth Cup semifinal is right up there with the best of them. It was a time of hope for me and the match seemed to shadow what was happening in my life. My mother had died eighteen months earlier and, although the two events can hardly be compared in their intensity, City were relegated that same season. It seemed as though a greater power than the Football Association or, indeed Bury Grammar School, had condemned me to a lifetime of misery.

By April 1964 the immediate pain of my mother's death, as well as the humiliation of relegation, was starting to fade. The Youth Cup tie seemed to echo this time of renewal. Derek Kevan and Jimmy Murray were banging in goals for the first team and after the O levels I was due to sit in June 1964, I would never have to open another physics book in my life. If City could beat United, even at this junior level, it would be a sign from above that my time of torment was drawing to a close.

No archive film exists to demonstrate the magic that captivated the 50,000 spectators who watched those matches, but it is etched on the mind in a way that no recording can replicate. However, even if they were able to show that match on television today, the camera simply wouldn't be able to communicate the excitement of that historic tie, especially the first leg.

Looking back on those games, at the photographs of those players, I am struck more than ever by the cruelty of the football business. These two exceptionally good teams played in the days when clubs expected to unearth, nurture and promote their own local talent, and they contained a fair number of players who were dyed-in-the wool supporters of the clubs they signed for, yet scarcely a single player left United or City a happy, fulfilled individual.

Best's demise has been all too painfully recounted any number of times, but this book reveals, too, the extent of the pain felt by David Sadler, that most honest and phlegmatic defender who served the United cause faithfully for eleven years and was denied a testimonial by his 'father figure', Matt Busby. Johnny Aston was so traumatised by his time at Old Trafford that from the day he was transferred to Luton Town he hasn't returned. He continues to support the club, as he did as a boy, but the scars are still too raw for 'closure' after thirty years.

David Connor has been unsuccessfully trying to persuade City to fulfil the promise they made in 1972 of a testimonial match. Alf Wood, Phil Burrows and Chris Jones are still resentful of the manner in which Malcolm Allison harried them out of Maine Road. Glyn Pardoe was forced into retirement as a player after George Best broke his leg in a derby match, but Pardoe returned as a coach. He was then scandalously sacked by Peter Swales after more than thirty years at Manchester City. And those are just the players of whom people have heard! Can you imagine what the less successful players have to say? Well, you need imagine no longer. Just keep turning these pages and all shall be revealed, much of it in the words of the players who played in those games.

There is something uniquely appealing about the promise of sporting youth. The hype surrounding Wayne Rooney in 2004 is evidence that it survives, even in today's celebrity-obsessed environment. The players I have talked to all have stories to tell of the promise of their own youth. You could see their eyes lighting up as they remembered with affection John Aston Sr and, especially, Jimmy Murphy and the days at The Cliff, or Johnny Hart and Dave Ewing as, in a desperate attempt to preserve their unbeaten record, they cheated in the head tennis games they played against their boys.

All those who lined up for the match at Old Trafford in front of 30,000 passionate fans must have felt that this was the start of their careers in football. They couldn't have failed to experience the nerves that had certainly grabbed hold of me and my group of City-supporting school friends as we watched anxiously from the Paddock at the side of the Stretford End. Losing that derby match was going to mean it would be murder at school in the morning – every bit as bad as losing a first-team derby match. You really don't want to live after a particularly important defeat. After all, why continue with life when all the future holds is the certainty of failure at O level physics? I needed City to win so badly that night.

This is a book about football, about football players and the development of the game, but I hope it succeeds in revealing the game in the context of its social history. Of course, there is a certain amount of nostalgia. I felt a connection to Mike Doyle and Glyn Pardoe that I will never feel for Nicolas Anelka or Sylvain Distin, much as I admire them. The visceral dislike I manufactured for John Fitz-patrick and Bobby Noble is entirely different from the feelings I have for Djemba-Djemba and Forlan. Frankly, I don't much care either for or about the current United team. I tend to turn off the television when they come on, but David Sadler and John Aston and George Best were as Red as Doyle and Pardoe were Blue – and I respected them for it.

The youth team was merely their first manifestation in the shirt they would wear with such distinction, for so long. It's not that Butt and Scholes don't have the same Manchester connection, but that their lifestyles are so remote from the rest of us that we can no longer identify with them in the same way, and I believe the game is all the poorer for it.

This book is also the story of a city of enormous historical fascination, the city of Manchester, and of its unique relationship with its football teams. For as those two youth teams were on the way up, the city itself was on the way down, struggling to adjust to a post-war, post-industrial world that preferred man-made fibres to honest Lancashire cotton. To a city in decline, its artistic and sporting heroes become disproportionately important, which is another reason why these youthful stars of the sixties have remained as important to me today as they were back in my schooldays.

I have always wondered what was it like to be a football player in that city in the sixties, the decade which climaxed in 1968 with United as champions of Europe and City as champions of England. I hope this book will convey those feelings. After all, it was thrilling just to be a spectator in those golden days – 'Bliss was it in that dawn to be alive/But to be young was very heaven' – until they kicked off and we were a goal down in four minutes.

CHAPTER ONE

_____

Naughty, Naughty Lads April 1964

I t was the best of times, it was the worst of times; it was the spring of hope, it was the winter of despair; it was the age of wisdom and Matt Busby, it was the age of foolishness and George Poyser. Manchester City were recognising that it was going to take at least another season in the second division to recover from the relegation they had suffered the previous year. Manchester United were looking to add the league championship and the European Cup-Winners' Cup to the FA Cup they had won the previous year.* Was it ever thus?

From the depths of the gloom that had begun to envelop the Blue half of Manchester came the glimmer of a light. As the 1963–64 season progressed, it became clear that, remarkably, Manchester City had been found in possession of a youth team of uncommon talent. It was perhaps less of a surprise to discover that Manchester United also boasted a youth team that season which was capable of winning the FA Youth Cup final for the first time since 1957 and the days of the Busby Babes. United had won it for the first five years of its existence and their inability to do so for the previous

* Note for directors of Manchester United plc: The FA Cup is an unsponsored knockout competition originated by the Football Association formerly of deep significance in English domestic football.

9

seven years had caused much soul-searching and gnashing of teeth at Old Trafford, where the trophy was regarded as United property and only on loan to other clubs who might have dared to win it.

After a bye in the first round, United hammered Barrow 14–1 in the second round and, after scraping past Blackpool 3–2 and gaining a more comfortable 2–0 victory over Sheffield United, the feeling grew that there was only one team capable of denying United their rightful inheritance. Intriguingly, they played only a couple of miles away. In early March 1964 both teams won their quarter-final matches. United exhibited considerable nervousness in their 3–2 win against a Wolverhampton Wanderers team inspired by Peter Knowles, who would shine briefly in their first team as a somewhat combative inside-forward, before retiring after becoming a Jehovah's Witness and being ordered off by a power even higher than the Football Association's disciplinary committee. In their quarter-final match City won thrillingly 4–3 at Elland Road against a Leeds team that included Peter Lorimer, David Harvey and Eddie Gray, players with whom many of them would cross swords on more exalted stages over the next ten years.

Everyone hoped that the draw would keep the two Manchester clubs apart so they could meet in the final, but it was not to be. Swindon Town played Arsenal in the other, quite meaningless semi-final encounter 200 miles away to the south, but from the end of March onwards the world of Manchester football became increasingly obsessed by the impending clash of the titans, some of whom had not yet started shaving.

Fate had cruelly denied Manchester football fans their traditional derby match entertainment for that season. More to the point, Denis Law and the referee had denied them the previous May when, in the most important derby to date,

Law had contentiously won a penalty six minutes from the end of a match in which City had outplayed United throughout, but scored just the one goal. Albert Quixall equalised from the penalty spot, thereby saving United from the very real prospect of relegation and condemning City to that fate; a fate which was mathematically confirmed three days later when they lost the last match of a miserable season 6–1 at West Ham.

Denis Law and Manchester City were to exact a terrible revenge on United eleven years later, but, in the spring of 1964, City fans were desperate to let the old enemy know they were still capable of hurting them and the Youth Cup offered the only realistic prospect of retribution. John Aston, the United left-winger, remembers growing up in a divided city, as a United supporter:

> City were always the enemy to me – the other team in Manchester. There were lots of City fans where I lived in Clayton, lots of my school pals were City fans. I remember 1963, that vital relegation match at Maine Road when United scrambled a draw, and coming out to play in the street the following evening. The City lads were there and I remember I was surprised that they'd actually come out. I thought they must have been devastated. I wouldn't have dared to show my face. I'd have had to stay indoors for forty-eight hours. Football was that important to me.

It was an attitude echoed by the other local lads, of whom there were plenty on both sides. The comments of Willie Anderson, the Liverpool-born United right-winger, are interesting:

> United v City was just another game to me. It was

11

United v Liverpool that was my derby match. I got a big kick out of playing against Liverpool, but City were just another team. The crowd was what made that game special for me, but for Bobby Noble and John Aston and maybe Dave Farrar it was a big derby match. All those schooldays of teasing City supporters and being teased by them. They didn't dare lose this game, so they were frothing at the mouth, but for me it was that huge crowd that made it so special.

Unlike today's youth sides, this was no random collection of unknown hopefuls. When a seventeen-year-old made his first-team debut in 1964, graves didn't stand tenantless and the sheeted dead certainly didn't squeak and gibber in the Roman streets as the media does now when Wayne Rooney, James Milner and their ilk appear for their senior sides. This was merely the normal progress of a talented young-ster. When those twenty-two players took to the field to play in this Youth Cup tie, no fewer than five of the City team and three from United had already played for their respective first teams. Indeed, Glyn Pardoe had famously made his debut at Maine Road against Birmingham City on 11 April 1962, when he was fifteen years and 315 days old, and George Best was about to make his first appearance for Northern Ireland. Each was the big white hope of his side and their careers were to be linked throughout the next eight and a half years, until the tragic events of December 1970.

Like the school system, eligibility for the Youth Cup was based on how old players were on 1 September of any given year. On the City side, Alf Wood and David Connor had been born in the autumn of 1945, just after the cut-off date of 1 September, so although they were both eighteen when the match was played their birthdays had fallen just the right side of the line. Albert Kinsey was the oldest player on the field and the United captain, Bobby Noble, had also been born in the last year of the Second World War. By contrast, Jimmy Rimmer was easily the youngest, having only just passed his sixteenth birthday when the teams ran out that cold April night.

These lads had grown up in that strange period of austerity after the war, in a provincial city which had lost its original commercial role in the world. They had all experienced some kind of deprivation, financial or emotional, and a surprisingly high proportion of them lost one parent before turning professional. Although the entire United side had signed associate professional forms, which made them groundstaff lads, Dave Wild, Chris Jones, Phil Burrows and David Connor were still amateurs – not amateurs in the sense that Colin Cowdrey or Peter May were amateur cricketers, but in the sense that Manchester City were not sure they were going to sign these kids to full-time professional forms and had therefore told them to get jobs and train as amateurs, financially compensated only by the refund of expenses in the shape of a ten shilling note – fifty pence in devalued decimal coinage.

United, by contrast, treated their Youth Cup team as if they were the first eleven and consciously went through the same match-day routine – a game of golf at Busby's club in Davyhulme, followed by an early dinner and then a coach to take them to Old Trafford through the ranks of the supporters. The players' relationship with the fans was akin to that of a collection of talented schoolkids. After all, these lads were only seventeen or so and even George wasn't a truly household name yet. When they appeared in the first team their arrival was greeted with disappointment, because it meant that Denis or Bobby or Nobby weren't playing. Here, however, they were the successors to the great Busby Babes and given their rightful due.

They had all been the best player in their school, the best player in their junior team, and the scouts had been knocking at the door (illegally in most cases) since the kids were nine or ten years old. With one exception, all these young players had ever wanted to do was become professional footballers. With most of them, it was impossible to tell who was going to make it. So much depended on factors that were not yet apparent – physical development, mental strength, family circumstances, the financial health of the club. As they lined up you could be pretty sure that George Best would certainly make it for United, and probably Bobby Noble and David Sadler. For City, you'd wager a small bet on the prodigy Glyn Pardoe and on John Clay and Alf Wood, mainstays of the half-back line, the one almost as skilful as George Best, the other a rugged defender whom England had already capped at youth level. For the rest, it was a fascinating open question. And that's why so many of us turned up that night.

It was a Youth Cup match, for heaven's sake, and not even the final of the competition at that, but the gate at Old Trafford for that first leg was a staggering 29,706. For the players who had yet to make their first-team debuts, it was the biggest crowd they had ever played in front of. Phil Burrows, the City left-half, remembers the day for more than the obvious reason:

On that day, 8 April, it was my eighteenth birthday. I did a full day's work [training to become a quantity surveyor] in Denton and then got the bus to Maine Road to meet the rest of the lads. I think we took the coach to Old Trafford and I was marking George Best in the evening – he was just about to make his international debut, at the same time as Pat Jennings. It was an electric atmosphere – you'd love to play like that every week.

Even at the age of seventeen, George Best was regarded as Manchester United's most potent weapon. Under normal circumstances he wouldn't have played. Indeed, United had progressed thus far without any contribution at all from Best, but with the scent of a highly prized Youth Cup trophy in his nostrils, Busby decided to gamble. With the possible exception of the rather dour Wigan-born John Pearson, who had previously played perfectly competently at inside-right during the run to the semi-finals, the other United players were delighted to see George. They knew the impact he could have on this vital match, as John Aston recalls:

> That semi-final was a huge game to me. They certainly felt that way at the club, but I don't think they'd ever seen City play. I mean, they wouldn't have had them watched the way they do today. But we had to bring George in and that meant we knew we were going to win. The problem with George was whether he'd be fit to play, because he was playing so many games he could easily have got crocked. It was a big boost to see George with you in the dressing room. We turned up at 3 or 4p.m. for a pre-match meal and talk. The match kicked off at 7.30p.m. and there was George, and it was like a shot in the arm.

From the kick-off, all twenty-two players launched themselves into the action – and each other – and the pace never slowed for the entire ninety minutes. With both sides suffering from an unending adrenaline rush, the fouls came thick and fast and Mr Ken Dagnall, the referee from Bolton, seemed an ineffectual and almost irrelevant figure.

Although the primary purpose of the youth team coaches was to deliver mature players to the first team, this derby match had its traditional impact on both training staffs. Jimmy Murphy, the United assistant manager, and John Aston Sr, the youth team trainer, had both been around Old Trafford since the end of the war, Aston as a full-back in Busby's first great side and Murphy as Busby's invaluable deputy, the man who had kept the club going when Busby was on a life-support machine in the Rechts der Isar Hospital in Munich. They knew City were the enemy and whipped up their charges with unusual emotional rhetoric. 'They shall not pass' was Jimmy Murphy's much-vaunted expression, but left-back Bobby Noble remembers a more significant phrase, whispered in his ear just before he led his team out: 'Remember, son, they can't run anywhere without ankles.' The player Noble was marking that night, City right-winger, Ronnie Frost, was soon to recognise the truth of this observation.

On the other side of the passageway, in the away team dressing room, the normally mild Johnny Hart and the big Scotsman Dave Ewing were urging on their charges in similar fashion. Both had been regular players for City in the previous decade and both remembered the scars of the derby match defeats more than the glory of the victories (of which there were a few, so enough of the sarcasm, thank you). They were both determined that the youngsters in the pale blue shirts realised the importance of their heritage, though in reality such had been the build-up that it was impossible for them to trot out on to the pitch feeling anything other than that they were carrying the fate of the entire nation on their slender shoulders.

Within a few minutes, the pattern of the game was set. Alan Ogley, the City goalkeeper, has only one memory of that night – wave upon wave of red shirts descending on his goal at pace. That isn't surprising. From the kick-off, it was apparent that the two United wingers, Willie Anderson and John Aston Jr, had the beating of the City full-backs, Mike Doyle and Dave Wild, and Ogley was soon facing a barrage of dangerous crosses. Picking up the very first one, Albert Kinsey nipped in front of the City defence and slid the ball home. There were no prawn sandwiches to still the roar that acclaimed this early blow. The red scarves waved and you would have sworn you were at a grown-up derby match.

The United wingers continued to torture the City full-backs. City right-half, John Clay, one of the big successes of the night, can still remember wondering, '… why Doyley was playing at right back, because I thought John Aston might run him ragged. Dave Wild was playing left-back and Dave Wild was a right-footer who had played at full-back and Dave Wild couldn't kick for toffee with his left foot. It was a disastrous tactical mistake, because John Aston tore us to pieces.'

Before half-time, Glyn Pardoe managed to bundle in an equaliser, though: 'I remember I had a real battle with those two Scottish wing-halves – John Fitzpatrick and Peter McBride. I was brought down a few times, but I managed to score at Old Trafford. It was a left-footer on the left-hand side of the box, which hit the bar and came down over the line and came back out again.' Glyn undersells himself somewhat. Before he had unleashed that venomous shot against the underside of the bar he had left three United defenders in his wake. It was the only moment when realism matched expectation for the City supporters. Thereafter, despite the fierce competition in the middle of the pitch, United continued to pull away as two more goals from Albert Kinsey and one from David Sadler eventually gave the home team a somewhat flattering 4–1 victory on the night.

Sadler had become involved in a bruising encounter with

Alf Wood: 'I marked David Sadler in that match. He never challenged particularly ruggedly, because I used to attack attackers, but he had tremendous confidence in what he could do – a bit like Ken Wagstaff years later at Hull. David Sadler's composure in the box was tremendous. Even inside the penalty area with everyone sliding in all over.' Although Bobby Noble sorted out the City right-winger, Ronnie Frost, fairly swiftly on the other flank, Alan Duff was struggling to close down the City outside left: 'David Connor always gave me a difficult game – he was quick and small and wiry, always a battle against him. You needed to intercept the ball and stop it getting to him. I kicked him over the touchline, and for some players that would be enough, but Dave Connor never gave in and came back for more.'

Clay and Burrows fought desperately to keep their side in the game and with more composed finishing from Glyn and Chris Jones, the tie might have turned out very differently. However, with a quarter of an hour left and the score at 3–1, City captain and centre-half, Alf Wood, decided it was time for decisive leadership: 'When we were 3–1 down, I drove myself further forward to try and get a goal back, but they got another one to make it 4–1 when I was stranded upfield. I got a real bollocking off everyone for that, but if we'd pulled it back to 3–2 we'd have a real chance at Maine Road. They had players up front who could be penetrative. We didn't.'

Next day, the players eagerly read the newspaper reports. Seeing their names in print was still something of a thrill. They hadn't yet experienced the full horror of a roasting in the press and all the reports emphasised the quality displayed by the youngsters. The condemnation was reserved not for the players who had made mistakes, but for the overheated nature of the contest. In the *Daily Express*, the headline over Bill Fryer's report was 'Naughty, Naughty Lads', and even

David Meek, in the *Manchester Evening News*, issued a plea for calmer heads in the second leg, with 'Play It Cooler, Boys' his considered response. Back in the dressing rooms there was no such equivocation. It was a derby match, for heaven's sake. What did the namby-pamby newspapers expect? They were playing for their careers in front of nearly 30,000 fans. Just like the first team regulars, they couldn't help but be affected by the passion engendered by such an occasion, and it was no wonder the crunching tackles went flying in all over the pitch.

As the final whistle blew for the end of that first leg, Jimmy Murphy's boys were thrilled to have won such a convincing victory against the local enemy and regarded the dirty play as nothing more than healthy competition. There wasn't a word of complaint from the City dressing room. Doyle and Wood, in particular, were quite capable of dishing out the necessary physical retaliation and had the scoreline been reversed, it is unlikely that United would have complained either. However, their defence was tougher and their attack more incisive, and though City had played some attractive football, they rarely threatened Rimmer's goal.

At 4–1 after ninety minutes, the result of the tie seemed a foregone conclusion to the losing supporters, but the City players managed to persuade themselves that the second leg, twelve days later, need not be the formal procession the scoreline suggested. To the City players who had been outscored but by no means outplayed, one of the comforting features of the first leg was that the much-vaunted George Best phenomenon had made little impact on the game, although that might well have been due to the fact that this was the fourth match George had played in the past week.

Max Brown, who had played on the left wing before David Connor had taken over his place there, came into the side to replace fellow Stockport Boys team-mate, Ron Frost, who had been badly injured in a tackle with Bobby Noble, yet another graduate of the talented Stockport Boys academy. Presumably, Jimmy Murphy's parting words on the subject of ankles were still turning over in Bobby Noble's brain as Frost was brought down, clutching his ankle.

Brown for Frost was the only change on either side as City came out into the familiar atmosphere of Maine Road on a filthy, sodden Moss Side night. They believed that if they could get an early goal, backed by a large and vociferous crowd, they could still cause United some anxieties – and the plan nearly came off. More than 20,000 fans came to the rotting iron hulk of a stadium, which was over 5,000 more than the attendance for either of the previous two first-team home games. John Clay points out wryly: 'If we'd been in the first team we'd have been on crowd bonus money, so to make it up to us the club took us to the Palace Theatre to watch a pantomime or something.'

In the days before Kevin Keegan, Manchester City were not renowned as a club that looked for the grand gesture. If it wasn't as electric an atmosphere as it had been in the first leg at Old Trafford, it was nonetheless enough to generate the expected partisan support. For John Aston and the other local United boys it was a trip into enemy territory: 'I'd played for Manchester Schoolboys at Maine Road against Birmingham Schoolboys, but it was like a foreign country. United was my home and City was the enemy. Maine Road was older than Old Trafford. It was draughty, slightly poorer.' Nonetheless, over the two legs, John Aston gave an outstanding performance, as Alan Ogley is quick to acknowledge: 'Before the start of the second leg I thought we could win it. I know I needed to keep a clean sheet, but it didn't happen. United had more experienced players than we did – Best, Sadler, Noble. And they had wonderful wingers – if there was one key player it was John Aston.'

The first goal came after eighteen minutes and was scored by either Mike Doyle or Alf Wood, depending on whose testimony you wish to believe. Unfortunately, it went into the City goal. Ogley blocked a shot from Sadler, but the ball ran loose in the penalty area. In the frantic scramble that followed, Wood half-cleared it off the line, but it hit Mike Doyle and rebounded into the goal. In *Blessed*, the most recent of his (auto)biographical outpourings, George has written unflatteringly about Mike Doyle, his carefully cultivated dislike of United and particularly his 'crowing about how they were going to humiliate us'. It was certainly true that even at the age of seventeen Doyle was happy to let the world know of his Blue allegiance. The mild-mannered Alan Duff, the United right-back that night, remembers Doyle's part in cranking up the intensity: 'The semi against City was such a big game. It was so important to win. I'd played against City reserves and A and B teams, but this was something different. You couldn't get anyone Bluer than Mike Doyle and whenever you played against Doyle it was always, "Fuckin' Red bastards".'

Best's book gives a clear indication of the mutual enmity between Doyle and himself, which was to increase down the years, culminating in the tragic events surrounding Glyn Pardoe's broken leg in a derby match in December 1970. However splenetic Mike Doyle can be on the subject of Manchester United, he is ready, though, to pay tribute to the gulf in class between the two teams over the course of that semi-final: 'In that Youth Cup game itself they completely outplayed us – simple as that. They had a lot more players to choose from than we had. We probably had two subs and the rest of them were the amateurs who played at Urmston. All the Old Trafford lot were apprentices – they could probably have fielded two sides.'

One was sufficient for the job. Again, Glyn Pardoe

equalised before half-time, but if City thought they could overcome a three-goal deficit in the last forty-five minutes, goals from Best and Sadler soon disillusioned them. Three minutes into the second half the overstretched City defence gave David Sadler too much time to turn on the ball in the penalty area and he put United ahead again on the night. Inaccurate recall aside, George Best had a wonderful game in that second leg and proceeded to display the full range of his talents as he scored three minutes after Sadler's goal to put United 7–2 ahead on aggregate and seal victory.

John Clay and some of the other City players had already played against Best at junior level:

The only real memory I've got of those two games was of Bestie. He went to United the same month I went to City – July 1962 – and then we played them in the B team and so on. I remember we got him in a corner, two of us, and he just turned and left us both for dead. He was just incredible. The United lads said even their most seasoned pros couldn't get the ball off Bestie.

David Connor remembers that this was no less than what they had all expected:

George wasn't that influential when we played at Old Trafford, but he then did a John Aston when we came back to Maine Road, because he tore us apart. In the first match all the talk was about George, because of who he was. Before the game Johnny Hart said to me to make sure that I came back and helped out. I did, but I found myself playing more in my own half than I did in the opposing half. That was because there was so much flank play to do with United.

Alf Wood, too, was sceptical about Best's impact in the first leg: 'Bestie could get past anyone he wanted to whenever he really wanted it. He was one of the all-time greats, but he did an awful lot of nothing at the edge of the box. He wasn't as good a winger certainly as Neil Young.'

He didn't need to be, though. Not that night. To their credit, although they would have been forgiven if their heads had dropped after that deeply frustrating own goal, City never stopped trying and spirited goals from Glyn Pardoe and Bobby McAlinden reduced the arrears, giving the home crowd something to cheer at last. The goals came in rapid succession and caused significant tremors in the United defence, although David Sadler scored again before the end to earn United a 4–3 win on the night.

John Aston, out on the left wing, saw with alarm that United's wing halves were starting to panic:

We had Johnny Fitzpatrick and Peter McBride, two Scotsmen, playing at half-back. We used to call them Pinky and Perky. I remember George turning round and laughing at them saying, 'Look at those two – they're panicking and there's only five minutes to go.' And I was actually counting on the wing and I was having a panic, too, because when it went to 4–3 I thought we'd won the first game 4–3 as well, so I thought it was now 8–6! It shows you what pressure does to you. Then when we kicked off again I realised we'd won the first leg 4–1, and we weren't two goals up, we were four goals up and it was over. But I do remember thinking it was 8–6. I was laughing with George at Pinky and Perky, but there was 20,000 City fans going mad and the ball's coming back from the net to the centre circle and they've scored two goals very fast and I'm trying to add up.

Before his arithmetical brain was taxed too greatly the final whistle blew and the first great derby in the lives of this young collection of players was over. Alan Ogley knew that the defence had been too porous – 'The problem with Phil Burrows was that he wasn't strong enough and the problem with Alf was that he wasn't quite tall enough, though you couldn't fault his attitude' – but he still felt sick to his stomach, just the way supporters feel after losing a derby game.

United had triumphed, but there was a general recognition that the gulf in class between the two teams was not that great and could probably be accounted for in the person of George Best. There was, too, a feeling that if United had the better players, City had the better team. City had competed hard in both legs, particularly in midfield, where John Clay promised to be a star of the future. Given the wretched state of the first team and the current gulf in status between the two neighbours, it was at least something for hard-pressed City supporters to cling to. Maybe not next year (1965) or the year after, but when the seventeen-year-olds were twenty or twenty-one, the future for City might be bright once more. Little did we know quite what 1968 would bring – to both sets of supporters.

United had been treading water since Munich and Matt Busby's overriding ambition was to win the European Cup, almost as an act of expiation for the guilt he had suffered since he had returned from his lengthy stay in the Munich hospital. However, the club now had a youth team more talented than any since the days of the Busby Babes and it was almost a foregone conclusion that they would triumph over Swindon Town, whom they were now due to meet in the final – but the two legs of this unique derby match were effectively the real final.

Even in the aftermath of a bitterly fought contest, there

was still room for old-world courtesy, as John Aston recalls:

> I came out of the dressing room, dead chuffed we'd
> won and all that, and it was much more open than it
> was at Old Trafford, where it was private, but at
> Maine Road it wasn't and it felt slightly odd and
> hostile; and there, waiting for me with his arms out-
> stretched, was Albert Alexander, the City chairman.
> And he took my hands and said, 'Congratulations.
> Well done, Johnny. Well played.' And I could see he
> really meant it. Anyway, I was sixteen and I didn't
> know how to take it, so I just looked at my feet and I
> did a little shuffle and I muttered, 'Thanks very much.'
> You know at the end of the game when players shake
> hands and they say, 'well done,' and they don't mean
> it, because they've just been beaten, but it's a courtesy,
> a ritual you have to go through? Well, this little old
> man, he really did mean it. It was such a wonderful
> sporting gesture and I've never forgotten it.

The first derby battle was over. There would be plenty more
to come in the years ahead, but not for all of the players. It
was unreasonable to believe that all twenty-two of them
would meet again at Maine Road or Old Trafford in a first
division contest in, say, 1968. From that collection of bright
young hopefuls there would inevitably be casualties, but
who?

CHAPTER TWO

The Way to Old Trafford 1945–62

'Since the war' – it was a phrase we heard all the time in the fifties, usually in the context of everything having gone to pot 'since the war'. The Second World War had been the finest hour of the British Commonwealth and its Empire and any exhortation to further effort always referred to the Dunkirk spirit, which was strange to those who saw Dunkirk as an evacuation rather than a glorious victory.

In moral terms, however, it was a 'good' war in which Britain had stood alone against the might of Hitler's armed forces for more than a year before the German invasion of Russia. It had also obeyed the primary rules of classical drama with a first act of ignorance, followed by a second act of terrifying defeat, culminating in a final act of total victory. Fascism was destroyed in Italy, Germany and the Far East. Democracy had survived its fiercest threat. The British Empire emerged politically intact, but economically bankrupt, and Pax Americana was the inevitable consequence.

The war had drained Britain's coffers to such an extent that the world's most famous economist, John Maynard Keynes, was delegated by the prime minister, Clement Attlee, to approach the Americans for money. Harry Truman had recently been sworn in as president, following the death of Franklin D Roosevelt in April 1945, and when Churchill lost the khaki election in the summer of that year it was the end of the old Anglo-American alliance that the Anglophile Roosevelt and the half-American Churchill had created with such success – neither Truman nor his economic advisers saw much purpose in subsidising Britain and its outdated imperial possessions.

Attlee believed he had been elected to introduce the sweeping social reforms of Labour Party policy – nationalisation of the railways and the coal mines, the Beveridge proposals on unemployment insurance and social security, the creation of a national health service. All this, of course, cost money which Britain no longer had and Keynes had nothing to bargain with except the historical fact that Britain had saved the world from Fascism for twelve months on her own. The Americans were unimpressed and Keynes returned home with his tail between his legs, the offer of a large interest-bearing loan from Washington and the certain knowledge that the dollar had now replaced the pound as the symbol of international currency.

The war against Japan might have been won by the devastation caused by the atomic bombs dropped at Hiroshima and Nagasaki in August 1945, but the rest of the world now lived in the permanent shadow of the hydrogen bomb and the Cold War made the possibility of world annihilation by mutually assured destruction a constant, hysterical presence.

Britain might have contributed a significant amount to the development of the Manhattan Project, as Oppenheimer's venture was called, but it emerged from the Potsdam conference, at which Truman had told Attlee and Stalin of its success, as the least important of the three Allies. 'I did not become the King's First Minister to preside over the liquidation of the British Empire,' Churchill had gruffly informed Roosevelt, when the latter wanted to know Churchill's post-war plans for the colonies. Indeed he didn't, but his immediate successor did.

In the fifties, it was still possible to repeat, without being jeered at, Cecil Rhodes' famous phrase that to have been born an Englishman was to have won first prize in the lottery of life (you just had to ignore the warning signs that this wasn't quite the case, which became more and more apparent after the debacle of Suez in November 1956). British children sat in school classrooms whose wall maps showed the world as defiantly pink, even as British troops were being evacuated from their former colonial territories, but in reality our parents had emerged from the deprivation of war to discover the deprivation of the age of austerity, the looming possibility of another war against the encroaching power of international Communism and a world made fearful by the discovery of 'the bomb'.

It was a changed world, but not one our parents rushed to acknowledge. They had sacrificed. It was important that their children knew how much they had sacrificed and that those children should grow up in a similar spirit of selfless-ness, which is why none of us were allowed the sweets we wanted until they came off the ration. Still, tell that to the young people of today ...

The working-class footballer of the sixties grew up in a deferential society in which, like his parents before him, he 'knew his place'. In this rigid social hierarchy, women were subordinate to men and children to their parents. The national anthem was played in cinemas and theatres before or after each night's entertainment, although bolder sections of the movie audience would walk out as soon as it started, which would never have happened before 1939. The anthem, like the union flag before it was appropriated by football hooligans and the makers of kitsch underwear, was an object of veneration. Politicians, the church and the royal family were all afforded the greatest respect by a world that knew neither Jeremy Paxman nor Rory Bremner. Doctors could pontificate in hospitals and surgeries without fear of physical violence. It was a world in which teachers rather than their pupils held the weapons of mass destruction, even if they were usually a cane or a worn-out plimsoll. Flick knives were the most potent teenage armaments and these tended to be used mostly when slashing the seats on the upper decks of double-decker buses, out of sight of the conductor. There was an almost unquestioning respect for family, education, government, the law and religion. In short, it was a long time ago.

The world of football was also stratified along social lines. Nobody wanted to run a football club for the money that could be made out of it. Money wasn't important, but prestige and power were. Football was still the glory game that bred heroes, not the arena for conspicuous consumption that feeds on its own media hype. The only large car in the car park belonged to the chairman and players still knew what the inside of a bus looked like. It was the era of the maximum wage and contractual serfdom. The talented youths who chose football over cricket or other sports didn't do so because the financial rewards were disproportionately large, and indeed football and county cricket clubs encouraged players who were good enough to play both sports professionally to do so.

Managers were former players who invariably hadn't been able to save anything from their careers and still lived from one weekly pay packet in a sticky brown envelope to the next, usually in a small terraced house owned by the club. They, like their trainers, were just grateful to be allowed to continue to earn a wage from the game they loved. Trainers, those tracksuited men who sprinted on to the field when summoned by the referee to attend an injured player, were most unlikely to have any medical knowledge. Who can forget the sight of Laurie Barnett trying to 'fix' Bert Trautmann's broken neck in the 1956 Cup final with the application of a sponge dipped in a bucket of cold water? The players themselves were on a lower level and the juniors or apprentices led an existence that most managements thought scarcely worth acknowledging, except for that brief moment when their signature as a schoolboy might be sought by a rival club.

John Aston's early experiences with the club he supported are illuminating, but by no means atypical. His father, also John Aston, was a key figure in the first Manchester United side assembled by Matt Busby, the team that won the FA Cup in 1948 and the league championship in 1951–52. Between 1946 and 1954 he played 282 games for United and scored thirty goals, an astonishingly high figure for a full-back, partly explained by his versatility as a substitute centre-forward. The first sight John had of his father at work was a game which his mother took him to and which ended badly for his father, when he broke his arm just before half-time. In the second half he re-appeared with his arm in a sling and played at outside-right, with Johnny Berry dropping back to fill in at full-back. In the days before substitutes, it was not uncommon to find the wing positions occupied by a series of hobbling, disabled players whose mere presence on the field, even in such a limited capacity, was deemed more beneficial to the club than their total absence. What it did to the player's injury was a complete irrelevance. Mrs and Master Aston, sitting up in the main stand, would hardly have been comforted by the service John was continuing to give Manchester United, even when clearly in pain. John Aston Jr recalls:

Nobody had a car in those days and Dad needed two of the other players to help him get dressed, he was in that much pain. Anyway, he's staggering out of the door after the match and someone says to him, 'Where are you going, Johnny?' and he says, 'I'm going to Ancoats to get my arm set.' The physio, who had just started but was still there when I was there, was a guy called Ted Dalton. He was a bit of character, but he was a social climber – that was the type of bloke he was – and he insisted that my dad should stay behind to see 'Mr So-and-so' – Dad couldn't remember his name. The fact that he was a 'Mr' meant he was a surgeon. Anyway, Ted took Dad home to his house – Ted had a car – and Ted and his family sat down to their evening meal. Meanwhile, Dad was feeling terrible, because his arm was broken, but he was told, 'Mr So-and-so will be round soon.' Anyway, it gets to around 7 o'clock in the evening and my dad gets up and says, 'I'm going, Ted. I can't stand the pain any longer.' At which point Mr So-and-so turns up in a tuxedo, because he's been at a formal dinner. My dad could smell the alcohol on his breath. Anyway, he sets my dad's arm and buggers it up. That was the sort of treatment you got at Manchester United in those days. You didn't have medicals then – if you could make steam on the mirror you were fit. That was the first game I remember going to. I must have come home on the bus with my mother afterwards. Because of what happened in that game fifty years ago, my dad still has pain in that arm and can't rotate it properly to this day.

This first ghastly experience didn't put off the younger Aston, though, and he continued to make progress through the ranks of schools soccer, playing for Manchester Boys and then graduating to Lancashire Boys:

I was probably the best lad in my year at school, though I was small for my age and United had reservations about me because of my lack of weight, but they let me train with them as an amateur for twelve months, training on Tuesday and Thursday evenings. After about twelve months I got a bit cheesed off. I'd had the odd game in the fourth team but I wasn't getting anywhere. They spelt my name in the programme as 'Acton'. I left school at sixteen and began work in a garage. Had I not been a footballer, I don't know what I would have done. My dad, who was the trainer at United, could see I was getting cheesed off, so he had a word with Harry Cooke, who was the chief scout for Everton. I played one match for Everton B team at Bury on the Saturday and afterwards Everton immediately offered to sign me as an apprentice. My father went into Old Trafford on the Sunday and told Busby, because they all went in the day after to chat about the game the previous day. Anyway, Busby got me down on the Monday and signed me for United. It took that sort of prompting from another club, but I would certainly have signed for Everton if United hadn't come in that fast.

It is ironic that the son of the United youth team trainer only just made it on to the books, because United prided themselves on having the best developed scouting system of any club in the Football League. Major Frank Buckley, the manager at Wolverhampton Wanderers, was probably the first to pay careful attention to the development of a youth policy, but Busby was more of a visionary and set out to transform the way the whole club played its football, so that the youngsters were trained in the Busby way from the moment they set foot inside Old Trafford. Jimmy Murphy and John Aston Sr were loyal and uncomplaining lieutenants. The key figure, however, was the chief scout Joe Armstrong who, ironically, had begun his career at Manchester City. David Meek, who reported on United affairs for the *Manchester Evening News* for forty years, believes Busby's poaching of Armstrong and the attraction of their shared religion was a significant factor in United's thriving youth policy:

> When Busby tried to take boys from his favourite Celtic Catholic background, the parents always wanted to know how the boys would be looked after, and Joe was a staunch Catholic who would always promise these parents they would go to mass. You needed someone to swear at the kids on the field, but someone like that would have been no good at persuading the parents to let their boys leave home and play professional football. Not that they were all Catholics, but it was a major factor.

Right-back Alan Duff was a Catholic and recalls the fact there seemed to be lots of 'left-footers' on the staff at United. He went to Sacred Heart Secondary School in Redcar, where he started as an inside-forward. Right-winger Willie Anderson, on the other hand, grew up in the religious polyglot society of Liverpool: 'I went to a Protestant school but lots of my friends were Catholics. When we picked teams it would frequently be Catholics v Protestants. There was no trouble. It wasn't like Belfast or Glasgow.'

It wasn't as if Busby and Armstrong only sought Catholics, as was abundantly clear when Bob Bishop, the Northern Ireland scout, sent over the Protestant George Best from

Belfast. It must have had something to do with Best's ability to play football. However, there is no question that Busby had a predilection for Celtic-born Catholics like himself and, under his stewardship, United always contained a high proportion of such players.

Signing schoolboys was a highly competitive and ethically dubious occupation even then, as Willie Anderson's story illuminates:

> I was a big Liverpool supporter as a kid. There was a guy called Alan A'Court who played outside-left for them and he used to come to our school and coach us. I was all lined up to go to Liverpool when I went off to Old Trafford to play for Lancashire Schoolboys. I must have had a good game because the next day Joe Armstrong and John Aston Sr showed up at our house. They arrived in a car, which was big news in our street at that time. They knocked at the door, and my dad wasn't back from work yet, and they said they'd come back when he came home. They came back in an hour. My dad was a porter in the big fruit and veg market in Liverpool. He wasn't a big football supporter, but he knew all about United and he seemed impressed with Joe Armstrong and John Aston, so I agreed to go to United that night because I didn't know if Liverpool were planning to sign me. I used to watch my friends playing for Liverpool A and B teams and later I met Bill Shankly, who used to come up to me with that broad Scottish accent and say, 'How are you doing, son? How's it going at United? You should never have gone there. You should have come and played for us.'

It appears that signing a promising lad to deprive the local team of him was by no means uncommon. Just as Busby whisked Anderson away from Liverpool under the nose of Bill Shankly, so centre-half Dave Farrar was signed, it was widely felt, because he was the England Schoolboy centre-half and if United didn't take him City almost certainly would, and they might regret the fact. Farrar was in a particularly strong position because, unlike every person whose name appears in this book, he made it quite clear to everyone that, despite being exceptionally good at it, he didn't much care for football:

I was never mad for a ball. I went to Nicholls Street Secondary Modern School in Ardwick, on the corner of Devonshire Street and Hyde Road. The headmaster there was very keen on football and I was picked to play for the East area. I was a defensive wing-half then. I failed the eleven-plus, but that didn't worry me, because I come from this inner city area and all I wanted to do was to be with my mates and take a trade when I left school (though until I was fourteen or so obviously all I wanted to be was a professional footballer). By the time I left school I was that sick of football ... I looked old. At fifteen I could go into a pub without a problem and my mates were older, too. That was the age when I just wanted to stop playing football. I played for Manchester Boys when I was thirteen – I was at least a year too young. Alf Wood was playing, I remember, so I must have been full-back or wing-half, and I think David Connor played for us, too.

Now, I'd been playing football every Saturday and I know everybody loves it, but I was probably getting distracted with my mates, who were seventeen and eighteen and they were earning. So I went to the headmaster and I said I didn't want to play any more. He was on the committee of Manchester Boys and really keen and he said, 'Why, lad?' I said, 'I've just had enough.' He said, 'You've got the England Schoolboys trials coming up. Will you just do them for me? If you make it, play, and if you don't, that's fine, don't worry about it.' So I went to the trial and I was sat in an English class one day and the headmaster walks in and asks for me. He takes me outside for a word and he says, 'I'm sorry to have to tell you but you've been picked to play for England.'

You can imagine the disappointment etched on Dave Farrar's face as he heard the sickening news, which was soon transmitted to Old Trafford. Dave's domestic circumstances, although by no means unique, nevertheless were of such a nature that they helped determine his response to the prospect of a life in football. He was raised as an only child in the concrete urban jungle of West Gorton. When he was eight years old his father died of cancer, a slow painful process that the young boy dealt with by teaching himself to kick with his left foot. His mother had always worked, but now the family income was cut by over half and the pressure on her was intolerable:

She had to work even before my dad died. She worked in a machinist's shop and did all the pressing, but there was also piece work. I was a latchkey kid. I came home from school and I lit the fire. My mum got back from work, made the tea, then she had to go out to work in a pub to earn the money to keep us going. My mum got so exhausted by what she was doing that she was hospitalised, too. I must have been about twelve then.

Perhaps other youngsters would have seen a career in football as the perfect opportunity to escape the poverty and hardship of such a life, but Dave Farrar never felt that way, although he was undoubtedly delighted by the chance to play for his country at such a tender age:

> That last year it seemed like I was never in school. I was always playing a match somewhere, but I had no intention of becoming a professional footballer and I wouldn't let a scout in the house. I just wanted to be like my mates and work in the building trade. When the scouts started knocking I tried to get my mother to turn them away. I just didn't want to know about going to a club, but there was a friend who lived nearby and he was a Bolton scout, and there were scouts knocking on the door all the time when I was still at school. Technically that was still illegal.

Nevertheless, Joe Armstrong got in by wooing Mrs Farrar and taking her to watch her son playing for his country. Dave was tempted to sign for Bolton, because of the neighbour who worked for the Wanderers, but he settled for United, despite having been a City supporter as a little boy when his uncle and late father had taken him to Maine Road. City belatedly made an offer for him, but his mother refused them entrance. It appeared that they claimed they would have come earlier, but were anxious not to do the wrong thing since Dave didn't have a father. United paid Mrs Farrar £200, although, as Dave points out, without bitterness: 'Another lad who'd played for England would have got £2,000, because his dad was a businessman, and there was only me and my mum and they took advantage. That was their point – 200 quid was a fortune to my mum.'"

Twenty years later, Granada TV's *World in Action* team

made a programme about Louis Edwards and his nefarious dealings as chairman of Manchester United. They tracked down Dave, who was living in Urmston at the time. 'They pestered me and wouldn't leave me alone – the researcher, the producer, everyone. They wanted me to back up everything they already knew – under-the-counter payments for signing on ... They wanted me to sign a paper, but I wouldn't do it. I got 200 quid for signing for United.' Dave's wariness of the football world wasn't new, though, because two decades earlier he had refused to sign the full-time apprentice professional contract, too:

> I wanted a trade as well, so United got me a job as an apprentice plumber through a building firm that they used, so I could always get time off for training and games during the week. I was paid £3 for plumbing and maybe £6 or £7 by United. I stuck at the plumbing for about six months but I realised it wasn't going to work. I had to make a choice, so I asked them to go back in. Training was only Tuesdays and Thursdays at the Cliff. Busby came down to one session when they were making the decision whether or not to sign me to a full-time professional contract. I think I might have met him once or twice before, but I knew it was a big deal him coming down to watch me. Anyway, they took me on as an apprentice professional and I really enjoyed the training, especially when we did it with the first team.

Willie Anderson was another who was suspicious of football's ability to provide him with a decent living and who wanted something more substantial than United's initial offer:

> I was always worried that I'd never make it as a

professional soccer player, so I told them I was determined to have an apprenticeship, meaning I hoped they'd fix me up part-time as an apprentice mechanic or apprentice toolmaker, but they thought I wanted to be an apprentice professional and they said, 'OK. No problem.' They paid me seven quid a week as an apprentice professional and I was living away from home for the first time. I guess my Mum cried when I left home, but my family was a typical Liverpool one that never really showed its feelings. For those first few weeks I was really homesick, because when the season ended in May everyone left and went home, but I had to stay there at the ground.

Anderson had left school at Easter and moved down the East Lancs Road to Manchester. The social dislocation was difficult. After all, he was only fifteen years old and Manchester was culturally very different from Liverpool. It was much easier for the boys who could continue to live at home while taking their first faltering steps in the professional game.

Just up the A565 in Southport, Jimmy Rimmer was showing signs of being the outstanding goalkeeper in the county. He played for Lancashire Boys, where he was spotted by the former player, Joe McBride, and his cause was taken up by Harry Boyle, who played left-back for Southport, who were then in the fourth division. Len Newcombe, the Southport manager, was also convinced of Jimmy's talent and began an assiduous courtship of the boy's parents – with a box of chocolates. It wasn't exactly the proverbial washing machine or, as we shall see later, the car that Don Revie believed was the way to a parent's heart, but it was probably the best Southport could manage as they desperately clung on to their Football League status. However, Joe McBride was part of Busby's far-flung Scottish family and word of

Rimmer's progress soon filtered through to Old Trafford.

Mr Rimmer Sr was a builder who was determined that his son would join him in the building trade. Len Newcombe offered to make Jimmy the very first apprentice professional in the history of Southport Football Club, but Mr Rimmer was unmoved. Indeed, so determined was he that Jimmy should follow him into the building trade that not only did he get Jimmy fixed up to learn the art and craft of bricklaying, but he also had a letterhead printed that proudly proclaimed 'Rimmer & Son'. The 'son', however, had different ideas and pointed out that his hands were meant to catch a ball not lay bricks. He demanded that his name be removed from the letterhead as soon as the call came in from Old Trafford. Mrs Rimmer was quietly thrilled, but Mr Rimmer had no truck with the idea of football as a living. Besides, Jimmy was a Burnley fan. What exactly was the attraction of Manchester United? It's a question many of us still ask on a daily basis.

Bobby Noble had the advantage of advice from a father who had played for Stockport County, but had retired from the game and was working as an engineer in Burnage. Like the rest of the youth team he eventually captained, Bobby made rapid strides through the school system and was soon a fixture in the Cheadle Boys side, initially as a workhorse inside-forward, before being pushed back to wing-half in his second year by the coach, Ken Miller. He was never left-footed, although he was eventually to make his mark as a left-back, following the same progress as the right-footed Glyn Pardoe. On leaving Broadway School in Cheadle, Bobby was offered associate professional terms by both City and United. City guaranteed him £8 a week, but United offered only £5. His father left the ultimate choice to him and he made a perfectly rational decision, particularly when he persuaded United to match City's wages:

City were going nowhere at the time and I felt that if I didn't make it at Old Trafford I could always come down and go to Maine Road. I thought I was on £8 a week, because when I got to Old Trafford I found that I was in the A team every week, but I was only on £4 10s take home pay and there was a lad called Mick Box who was on eight quid, even though he was in the B team every week. So I complained to Joe Armstrong and I was given £8 a week.

What has so far been apparent has been the absence of Matt Busby. Even George Best had little to do with Busby at first. Indeed, it was the very neglect demonstrated by the club which caused the young Irishman and his fellow countryman, Eric McMordie, to flee back to Belfast within forty-eight hours of arriving in Manchester for the first time. It is a well-known story, of course, but oddly it never appears to attract any opprobrium. In most clubs the absence of the manager in the lives of the groundstaff lads would hardly be remarkable, particularly when the manager had such admirable deputies as Joe Armstrong, John Aston Sr and Jimmy Murphy. However, the mythology of Manchester United has always laid excessive emphasis on the innovative pastoral care aspect of its youth team, so it is interesting when digging beyond the authorised version to discover that the system was just as flawed as that of most other clubs.

If Busby's personal involvement in the signing of the youngsters is the mark one should use to gauge how interested the club really was in them, then the one player on that youth side Busby was desperate to sign was neither George Best nor Bobby Noble but David Sadler. It is hard even for United supporters to get too enthusiastic about Sadler, possibly because he carried himself with such extraordinary composure, rarely demonstrating the sort of emotion the crowd loves to see. When the 'baby-faced assassin', Ole Gunnar Solskjaer, cynically chopped down a Newcastle United forward as he advanced on goal in a match United were desperate to win but couldn't, he trotted off, scarcely waiting for the inevitable red card, and was greeted by a standing ovation from the crowd. This was never David Sadler's way.

Sadler grew up in Yalding, a hop-growing village in Kent usually seen on the television news every winter when it floods. His father was the tenant-landlord of a pub, but his mother had died of a brain haemorrhage when David was only eight and his sister even younger – further evidence of the frighteningly high number of one-parent families among our twenty two players. When Busby and Murphy motored down to Kent to persuade Mr Sadler to let his son travel to Manchester, look round the town and sign associate profes-sional forms, it was as if two dignitaries had arrived from another planet:

It was a big event for the village, as you can imagine. My dad's pub had a forecourt, so Matt and Jimmy parked their car there. They came in and talked to me and my dad for however long it took. I remember the talks finished quite late and they were staying in London. They'd driven down that afternoon. By this time news of their arrival had spread in the village and there were quite a lot of local people around to see the famous Matt Busby. Anyway, they came out of the pub, got into the car, waved to the villagers and, of course, the car wouldn't start. It was extremely embarrassing.

This was the winter of 1962–63, the famous big freeze when lots of cars failed to start, no matter how famous their owners. Sadler was a much sought-after property. He had been on the fringes of the England Schoolboys side, but hadn't made it into the team – his place being taken by Glyn Pardoe. Growing up in a village of some 1,500 souls in the heart of the Kent countryside, the nearest professional clubs were Gillingham or Crystal Palace, which weren't exactly local, and he rarely saw professional football. Although as a boy he had trained at Selhurst Park and at Tottenham, he saw most of his non-school action in senior amateur football in Maidstone. Amateur football, which had been very strong in the ten years after the end of the war, when Wembley was annually filled with 100,000 supporters for the FA Amateur Cup final, was a declining force in the early sixties. Its last two significant outposts were in the northeast (Crook Town and Bishop Auckland) and in a small pocket south and east of London (Maidstone and Walthamstow).

It was a very different world from the hard, poverty-scarred working-class suburbs of Manchester, Glasgow or Belfast, whence most of the two teams originated. Sadler was a bright young lad and he and his father could see there were options in life beyond football as a career. Until United got involved, he intended to stay on in the sixth form at Maidstone Tech and perhaps go on to teach PE. He passed the thirteen-plus rather than the eleven-plus and went from Oldborough Manor Secondary School in Maidstone to the Tech. Apart from his talent, what was outstanding about Sadler as an early teenager was his size; he was already quite mature at the age of fourteen, playing for the Under-15s at the age of thirteen. He also played cricket for Kent Schools, ran for the county's athletics team and seemed destined to progress to Loughborough and train as a PE teacher.

However, there were problems for Sadler both at home and at school. After the death of his wife, the pressure of looking after his two children began to have an impact on Mr

Sadler and his health started to suffer. During the key summer months, this was particularly unfortunate. There were five pubs in Yalding and they all relied on the profits made during the hop-picking season, when the London-based hop-pickers came down with their kids for the summer holidays. They stayed in the hop huts, as they were called by the locals, which were, at best, nothing more than four brick walls and a corrugated iron roof. They'd pick hops and fruit in the day and drink in the pubs at night. The pubs were all full for those six to eight weeks of the summer, but it was a small community and they'd all struggle for business thereafter: 'There was a bit of conflict with my father because I'd always want to be out, playing sport, and he became quite unwell and he wanted me to help. It's a hard life being a publican and I hated it, because I just wanted to play sport. We had some conflict on that one.'

As the biggest and most talented player in which-ever team he played for, David was inevitably chosen as centre-forward, and as a big, strong, talented lad in that most glamorous of positions, he scored enough goals to attract the attention of the scouts, which didn't please his school:

There was a PE teacher, John Smith, at Maidstone Tech, who was very encouraging, very supportive. But then I had a bit of run-in with the school, because at that time Under-15s football was very competitive. You had Under-11s, Under-12s and so on up to Under-16s at school level, as well as at county level. You either stayed on to do A levels or you left school, but in terms of sport after the age of fifteen it just faded away. There was no competitive football after that. At school, after it was decided I'd stay, they only had friendly matches against other schools.

Sadler was asked to go to Maidstone United, who then played in the Isthmian League. It was senior amateur football, the equivalent of today's non-league football, and so at the age of fifteen he was playing in senior men's football:

> They were all wary at first, but once I'd proved I could handle myself physically and could score goals, what did they care? The school wasn't happy, because there was a conflict of interests – they wanted me to play for the school, even though it was non-competitive. After the run-in, I subsequently left the school and went to work in the Westminster Bank, because the bank manager was on the board of Maidstone United. That would be in the equivalent of my first year in the sixth form. I was quite well qualified to work there – I had half a dozen O levels. I could now play for Maidstone on a regular basis. I then got picked quite quickly to play for England Amateurs, and I was scoring regularly, so clubs were really paying attention. I'd been to trials and summer camps and all that. Arsenal seemed very grand and cold. I remember the marble halls. It wasn't warm like West Ham was. I think George Swindin was the manager.

It was by no means a formality that just because Manchester United came a-calling, his signature would follow on the dotted line:

> I nearly signed for Wolves. They'd made enquiries and they had Bill Slater at centre-half, and he'd been an amateur international and taught PE, and become a pro and played for England. I remember meeting Stan Cullis. I played for a representative team, England

Amateurs against The Army, something like that, and I
met Slater and Cullis and they were a top side. I didn't
really have a team in mind.

However, the siren call from Old Trafford eventually proved
too strong. Sadler's prolific scoring attracted the attention of
Joe Armstrong, who asked the young giant what he was
planning to do, and that was when Sadler began to think
seriously in terms of football as a career:

> Soon afterwards I met Jimmy Murphy, and as
> young lads, what with the Busby Babes and Munich,
> and the history of young players getting into the
> United team and so on, everyone felt something for
> United, because of what had happened. Anyway,
> they approached me and I talked it over with my
> dad and we agreed that I'd sign for United. There
> was a little bit of financial inducement, but it went to
> my dad. I signed amateur forms for United, so I
> could work on in the bank. I could have gone to
> United there and then, as a sixteen-year-old appren-
> tice, but we decided I'd sign amateur forms in
> October 1962, stay as an amateur and play for
> Maidstone, and sign professional on my seventeenth
> birthday in February 1963.

The financial inducements seemed to vary slightly from
player to player. It's hard to be definitive because not only
was the amount affected by how good the player was and
how keen the competition from rival clubs was, but also such
matters were never discussed in front of the children. At the
age of sixteen or so, they were generally so excited to be
signed to a contract by Manchester United that they showed
no interest in negotiating a new washing machine, believing,

like all teenagers, that dirty clothes are dropped on the bedroom floor and then simply appear, miraculously clean and folded, on the edge of the bed a few days later.

In fact, David Sadler's financial situation for the next few months was more advantageous than any of his future colleagues on the youth team, despite playing as a so-called 'amateur':

> I got paid as an amateur – brown envelopes in the boots I'm afraid. I was getting as much from playing for Maidstone as I was from working as a junior in the bank – £5 for football and £5 or £6 from the bank. Maidstone had had a poor side for a few seasons, so they went to London and got this chap called Harry Hill to be the manager, and he attracted London players. I was just a local boy playing with all these Londoners, who came down to train and play in the matches. The London boys certainly weren't travelling to Maidstone just for the love of football. It was a fair bit of money if you played twice a week. I gave the money to my dad – it was the way it was. I wasn't resentful. After all, my sister, Sally, was still at school.

Mr Sadler Sr's deep suspicion of Manchester and its urban ways was probably a big help in the contract talks. As in all such negotiations, the more reluctant the parent to let his son go to Old Trafford, the stronger his bargaining position, but most fathers were so overwhelmed by the prospect of their sons playing for Manchester United that they were putty in the hands of Joe Armstrong. Right-back Alan Duff was a typical victim. Although he grew up in the North Riding, for whom he played as a schoolboy, and supported his local club, Middlesbrough, Duff's father had been born in Manchester and was a passionate Manchester United supporter, a fact he mistakenly revealed to Joe Armstrong early in negotiations. No wonder the Duffs thought Joe was so wonderful with the parents.

It was his father who had taken the young Alan Duff to Middlesbrough matches, where he recalls arriving as early as 1.15p.m. for a 3p.m. kick-off and never paying an entrance fee, as he was invariably lifted over the turnstiles. He saw Lindy Delapenha, one of the very first black players to make his mark on the English game, and the first stirrings of a prolific goalscorer called Brian Clough, before he moved to Sunderland. However, his father's influence was never far away and he recalls hearing the news of the Munich air crash in the local scout hut and becoming obsessed, like the rest of the country in February 1958, with Duncan Edwards' two-week but ultimately unsuccessful fight for life. It was his father, too, who made a habit of taking his son to the beach at Redcar, removing his right boot and encouraging him to kick with his left foot. It is a story that stands comparison with Dave Farrar's tale of how he taught himself to kick with his left foot when his father lay dying in hospital. Alan believes that his father had played football in the army with John Aston Sr and, although he never confessed to doing so, his father must have written to his old army colleague and asked him to see his son in action.

Alan is the first to admit he was fortunate to wind up on the books at Old Trafford. Following the encouragement of his Scottish PE teacher, Bill Turley, he played for the North Riding Schoolboys, then Yorkshire Schoolboys, although the trial for the latter was a disaster. However, his school received a letter informing them of Duff's selection for Yorkshire Schoolboys at outside-left, which came as a big surprise to a right-footed boy who had never played on the wing in his life:

But I was in. Anyway, we played Lancashire and we got hammered – Albert Kinsey was playing for Lancs and I ended up playing at left-half. That's how Albert remembered me. We played Northumberland at Blyth Spartans' ground and had four games altogether. United asked me to go for a trial though they didn't ask me to sign, and so did Arsenal, but I didn't fancy them. My local team, Middlesbrough, had shown a slight interest, as had Sunderland, but the draw of Manchester United, plus the fact that I had relatives there and my dad wanted me to go there, was decisive. My mum wanted me to go to Boro and stay at home.

One reason why teams like Middlesbrough, Stockport County and Barnsley remained uncompetitive was the poor performance of their scouting system. They seemed to rely on boys (or their schools and/or parents) writing in for trials. The fact that Stockport Boys produced so many fine players for the two Manchester clubs should really have been cause for great concern in the boardroom at Edgeley Park. The fifteen-year-old Alan Duff supported his local club, Middlesbrough, but the club had shown scant interest in him, so he happily crossed the Pennines and went to live with his relatives in Manchester for the duration of his four-week trial in April 1961.

Easter seems to have been a popular time to sign these lads. Alan Duff left school on the Friday when they broke up for the Easter holidays of 1961 and began his trial for United on the following Monday. Willie Anderson went through a similar, but even more haphazard process, the following year:

I was fifteen when I signed apprentice professional forms, right around Easter 1962, because I went back

50

to school after the Easter holidays and told them I was leaving. They were all amazed because it was Manchester United, but I'd been the best player in the school. The Lancashire Boys match was a real fluke, because I got the dates wrong and I never made it to the ground. Then I was playing for Huyton Boys against Bootle Boys and the coach came up to me after the game and asked why I hadn't gone to the trial, and it was only then I realised I'd got the weeks mixed up. Anyway, they picked me for the Lancashire Boys squad over that Easter break. I used to be a striker and a right-half, but when I came on for the first time for Lancashire Boys they asked me to play wide on the right and that's where United used me.

Alan Duff's trial had been equally successful:

At the end of the four-week period they offered me a contract as apprentice pro – I think I was on seven quid a week, out of which I had to pay for digs, so I paid my auntie three or four quid. At the end of the trial period I came home with the contract after playing with the B team. I walked home and when I got in I found Bob Dennison there, the manager of Middlesbrough, who were in the second division. I remember taking the contract out of my pocket and showing him and he shook my hand and wished me all the best. They were a bit slow off the mark. I got a new suit from United as an incentive. The better players, I know, got a lot more. As a fifteen-year-old who's just been given a contract by United, I'd have paid them. I'm sure my parents got something out of the deal, but because my dad was so keen for me to go there, they probably gave him very little.

Despite being in their late fifties today, most of these ex-players admit to knowing almost nothing of what transpired in the talks between Joe Armstrong and/or Manchester United FC and their parents, and what little knowledge they do have is now invariably second-hand and coloured by rumours of what others got. However, such was the close relationship between Dave Farrar and his mother, and such the parlous state of their financial circumstances, that £200 sounds pretty accurate. Bobby Noble, though, is still cross about what he regards as exploitation by United: 'Both my parents worked. My mother had two jobs, cleaning in pubs in Stockport and so on. Albert Kinsey got a big signing-on fee – £1,000 I believe – but my parents got nothing except the standard £10 signing-on fee.'

Albert Kinsey is currently somewhere in Australia and unable to confirm or deny Bobby's tale, but the real inducement was probably nearer to that offered to Mrs Farrar. United were never a particularly munificent or generous club and Busby believed strongly that the honour of playing for Manchester United should outweigh any petty financial considerations. He'd played for peanuts, so why should modern kids be any different? It was Busby's firm belief that the players should be paying the club for the honour of pulling on that wonderful red shirt, but it's unlikely that the agent of Rio Ferdinand or Roy Keane would subscribe to this philosophy today.

We shall see later how opinions about Busby varied, but it's clear that he liked David Sadler from the start, and that the feeling was mutual. Sadler was mature for his age and, as Matt took a strong dislike to players who were too fond of the ladies or alcohol, it was soon apparent that, in that talented youth team, David Sadler was going to present him with the fewest problems – unlike Best and Noble:

Matt seemed like a very wise old man to me as a
sixteen-year-old. He said all the right things as far as
my father was concerned, [such as] I'd be really well
looked after, and that was important, because I'd
never been much further than Maidstone in my life –
perhaps to London on the odd occasion. London was
regarded as a naughty city, but Manchester was in
another country.

Busby arranged for Sadler to spend a week at Old Trafford
with the young centre-half Wilf Tranter as his guide. He
trained with the lads and Wilf showed him around the club
and the town and took him to the cinema. At least the cinema
was warm, for this was February 1963 and the country was
in the grip of that great freeze. After the 1–0 away win at
Craven Cottage on Boxing Day, the United first team didn't
play again until they drew 1–1 at home to Blackpool in the
last week of February. It was frustrating to be invited up to
play for Manchester United, then to be left kicking his heels
and flapping his arms – in short, anything to keep warm.

Eventually, when the big freeze thawed and the country
had recovered from the inevitable floods that followed, football started again on mud-heap pitches. The hard going
suited Sadler's bustling style of play, and he scored in
matches for the A and B teams, but couldn't prevent the
youth team from being knocked out of the FA Youth Cup in
Sheffield. Only Alan Duff, Bobby Noble, George Best and
Albert Kinsey survived to make it into the Cup-winning team
the following season. Phil Chisnall, Ian Moir and Jimmy
Nicholson, promising youth team graduates, were already
nineteen or twenty and hence no longer eligible.

The period when Sadler arrived was an awkward one for
the club. The previous season United had finished a feeble
fifteenth in the first division and, despite a promising Cup run

which saw United slip past Aston Villa, Chelsea, Coventry and Southampton, almost all by single-goal margins, the 1962–63 league season was turning out to be even worse. Notwithstanding twenty-three goals in his first season by record signing Denis Law, and nineteen from the reliable David Herd, Busby's team was struggling to avoid relegation. Although Leyton Orient, enjoying a surprising single season stay in the top division, were favourites for a quick return to obscurity, the accompanying position seemed likely to be occupied by Birmingham City, Manchester City or Manchester United.

Even signing Pat Crerand from Celtic in February, for £56,000, an act which was to bear fruit in future years, could not arrest the slide and four successive defeats in March 1963 placed the team's first division status in great jeopardy. Because of the big freeze, the return derby match at Maine Road wasn't played until the middle of May. If United lost it, they would almost certainly go down, and not even an appearance in the FA Cup final against Leicester City would be much comfort when weighed against such a trauma. After nine minutes of the most important derby match in living memory, Bobby Charlton lost the ball in midfield. It was whipped out wide to Joe Hayes and quickly transferred inside to Peter Dobing, who slipped it into the path of the prolific goalscorer, Alex Harley, whose first-time shot crashed past David Gaskell in the United goal to put City ahead. Watching nervously in the main stand, the United youth team in the making exchanged nervous glances. Would it be better for their careers if United were relegated? Somehow, looking at Matt Busby's grim visage, they doubted it.

They were, however, learning just what it was that made derby matches so special. Going down the tunnel at half-time, fortunate to be only 1–0 down after a second

Harley goal was ruled out by a highly contentious offside decision, Crerand threw a punch and laid out David Wagstaffe, with whom he had been booked just before the whistle had blown. 'Did you hit Wagstaffe?' asked the unsighted Busby of his latest recruit. 'Me? No!' replied the indignant Crerand, desperately hoping Busby couldn't see his grazed knuckles. Busby accepted the denial and passed on to more important matters. United were closer to the humiliation of relegation than at any point in Busby's long and distinguished career at United. If they lost this match and had to languish in the second division, they would be less of an attraction for the talented local youths of the future.

Fortunately for United, Wagstaffe's brain must still have been affected by the contact with Crerand's fist. Six minutes from the end of a game City had dominated, and with United seemingly devoid of any creative ideas (the United forward line read Quixall, Giles, Herd, Law and Charlton), the befuddled City left-winger sent an unnecessary back pass towards Harry Dowd from thirty yards out. Denis Law, who, on his return to the Maine Road ground he had graced two years earlier, had been frustratingly anonymous as far as United fans were concerned, sprinted after it. Dowd dived at his feet and knocked the ball away for a corner, but Law fell over the recumbent goalkeeper's body. The referee pointed to the spot. Aware of how much now depended on the outcome of the penalty, the more nervous United players looked steadfastly at the Platt Lane stand as Albert Quixall tucked the spot kick into the net at the scoreboard end. Not since Gavrilo Princip had assassinated the Archduke Franz Ferdinand at Sarajevo in 1914 had one shot caused quite so much widespread misery. Three days later, City lost 6–1 at West Ham and their fate was sealed. United beat Leyton Orient 3–1 at home on the same day and the destinies of the two clubs – and of those twenty-two boys who were to take the field against each other eleven months later – were set.

CHAPTER THREE

The Way to Maine
Road
1945–62

In the immediate post-war years, Manchester, like the country, had lost an empire and not yet found a role. In the late nineteenth century it was proverbially remarked that what Manchester said today the world would say tomorrow. By 1945, Manchester had been reduced to a mute acceptance of the fact that its cotton industry was dwindling and consequently the world no longer cared much what Manchester said.

Before the Clean Air Act of 1957, Manchester was a monochromatic town. Soot from the thousands of belching industrial and domestic chimneys coated the buildings. Everything was black and grey except, you could say, the sky blue shirts of Manchester City and the blood red shirts of Manchester United. The two teams seemed to provide the only colour in a city that had never valued aesthetics – particularly if they had to be paid for.

The town hall in Albert Square, designed by Alfred Waterhouse in the 1860s, and the original university buildings are singularly lacking in the extraordinary neo-Gothic flair that permeated other Victorian edifices, such as St Pancras Station in London or Keble College Oxford. When Manchester reached for the fantastical in the early 1930s, it created only the grandiose tastelessness of the Central

Library, a hideous edifice, bearing no relation to the buildings around it, which appears to have been the product of a mind that confused St Peter's Square, Manchester, with St Peter's in Rome. In fact, I always thought it looked as though a Catholic wedding planner of some wealth, but no taste, had decided to bake a gigantic wedding cake in the shape of the Vatican.

Manchester has existed since Roman times, the evidence for which is, or at least used to be, a pile of bricks in a goods yard at the southern end of Deansgate, and was a larger, more important town than many which had sent two representatives to Parliament before the Great Reform Act of 1832. This discrimination, of course, later fuelled the belief that blatant southern bias was why the England cricket selectors never picked Harry Pilling and why Mike Summerbee only won eight England caps.

It is entirely typical of Manchester that, when it was necessary to build a home for the best provincial orchestra in Britain, it constructed the Free Trade Hall on Peter Street, another structure of no recognisable architectural merit whatsoever, but one dedicated to a noble idea rather than simply memorialising a rich patron or yet another monarch. It also stood on St Peter's Fields, the site of the 1819 Peterloo Massacre, which had been another sign to the England selectors, this time those who sat in Westminster rather than St John's Wood, that Manchester was cultivating a dissenting power base.

Even in its declining years, before the recent regeneration, Manchester never wanted to be, or even to imitate, London. If you didn't care for Manchester it certainly wasn't going to spend much time, or any cash, worrying about it. The Duomo in Florence or the Giralda in Seville were the symbols of other cities' wealth, but Manchester costed aesthetics and found them too expensive. Sidney Bernstein didn't waste money designing a temple when he came to erect a suitable home in Quay Street for his Granada Television, but it's ironic that the city which contains the lavish splendours of the Alhambra should give its name to a company that became notorious for cost-cutting measures. Mind you, Bernstein put his money into programmes and the people who made them, and in so doing created the best television company, for its size, in the history of the industry.

Manchester had its own daily newspaper, the *Manchester Guardian*, which we read partly for the guarantee of its reports on local sporting matches, but also because it was a well-written paper with a well-justified international reputation. Until long after our two youth teams had matured and left football as active participants, Manchester was the alternative to Fleet Street, a complementary centre of journalistic activity. The performances of the Halle Orchestra and the productions at the Opera House or the Palace Theatre became important because the Manchester-based newspapers wrote about them. Manchester University didn't want to be Oxford or Cambridge and became the paradigm of a provincial university, one blessedly free of influence from the Anglican church. In the early years of the twentieth century, the days when Rutherford was in his prime, Manchester University had few rivals in terms of intellectual distinction.

Manchester's strength came from the cotton towns of its hinterland, the resourcefulness of John Kay and Richard Arkwright and Samuel Crompton and their successors, whose invention and entrepreneurship created the cotton industry at whose centre stood Manchester, otherwise known as 'Cottonopolis'. After the industrialisation of cotton manufacture, Lancashire became responsible for 90 per cent of all the cotton made in England, and cotton accounted for nearly 50 per cent of national exports. The burghers of Manchester shipped cotton to India and China and owned mills in

Austria, Russia and South America, and, when the Manchester Ship Canal opened, linking the city to the Irish Sea, Manchester became a world port. In its nineteenth century glory years, Manchester's power and prestige were such that no one there cared what people 180 miles away in the south-eastern corner of the country thought, because, from the top of the city's tallest building, you could see an entire world.

Manchester's leisure activities were equally self-contained. If you wanted the sea, cheap and vulgar Blackpool was less than fifty miles away, the more genteel atmosphere of Lytham St Annes or Southport a similar distance. If you wanted the countryside, there were the vast expanses of the Lancashire moors or the rugged beauty of the Peak District to the south. The scenic majesty of the Lake District was only eighty miles north and, although the mountains and the coast of north Wales were technically in another country, they were still adjacent to Lancashire and, if only to spite the insufferable pomposity of Yorkshire folk, a journey into north Wales meant you didn't have to cross the Pennines to get there. More to the point you didn't have to go south of a line that stretched from Glossop to Buxton to have access to everything that men needed and desired.

This was the Manchester our two youth teams were born into. The problem was that Manchester was changing in the fifties and sixties and losing its distinctiveness. This stemmed, of course, from the decline of the cotton industry, which in turn produced the death of Cottonopolis. In Victorian times, as the industry expanded, the ensuing population boom had led to a proliferation of inadequate housing. The disastrous Depression, which scarred the inter-war years, intensified these conditions and, when the bombs started to fall on Manchester and Salford in 1940, it appeared that the Luftwaffe was a better agent of slum clearance and social change than the local council or government housing departments.

The fifties spawned a unique phenomenon – the teenager. In previous generations there had been a direct switch from child to adult, but the creeping prosperity of the fifties permitted the emergence of a new socio-economic group, whose spending power created a teenage culture, one heavily influenced by America. In 1955 Glen Ford and Sidney Poitier starred in *The Blackboard Jungle*, a film about a crisis school in a deprived urban area, but its claim to fame was the impact of its title music – 'Rock Around The Clock' sung by Bill Haley and the Comets. This caused such widespread disturbances throughout Britain – young people were seen jiving in the aisles! – that many local councils banned it as likely to incite a riot. The song was so popular that the following year a film called *Rock Around The Clock* was released, just as the cult of Elvis Presley was emerging. No local council could legislate this new music out of the shops and the heads of young people, however much they might have wished to do so.

In 1956 the Royal Court Theatre in London produced John Osborne's play *Look Back in Anger*, which is generally regarded as one of the first signs of major change in the moribund state of British theatre of the time. In a short space of time, this new trend led to the emergence of Wesker, Storey, Delaney, Arden and Pinter as new playwrights with new authorial voices and, inevitably, to a new breed of actor to whom, as Albert Finney demonstrated in *Saturday Night and Sunday Morning* (1960) and Tom Courtenay proved in *The Loneliness of the Long Distance Runner* (1962), a northern accent was no longer a bar to film stardom.

Manchester and the northwest started receiving ITV programmes when Granada Television began transmitting in 1956. Unlike the BBC, which was still broadcasting according to the Reithian principles of education, information and entertainment, ITV interpreted 'public service television' somewhat differently and viewers watched imported American series and the new adverts with fascination. Britain was undergoing a gradual process of 'Americanisation', by which was meant it was succumbing to the brash standardised mass culture of commercial television, popular music, advertising and the growing economic importance of the teenagers who consumed it.

Also in 1956, Britain embarked on its last and most disastrous imperial adventure, when it invaded Suez in response to the nationalisation of the canal by Nasser – only to be humiliatingly sent packing by the outraged President Eisenhower, who had not been forewarned of the collusion between Britain, France and Israel. Here was incontrovertible confirmation of the shift in world political power away from the nineteenth century Pax Britannica. The opposition to the Suez invasion in this country had been vociferous and it contributed greatly to the new sense of disillusionment with traditional figures of authority. Schoolteachers, policemen, politicians, and eventually the royal family, all suffered varying degrees of public contempt as British society groaned under the pressure of seismic change. Dissent, from the late fifties, was the new conformity but, predictably considering the nature of the game's administrators, football resisted as long as it could.

The football clubs which our youth teams joined in the early sixties had not, in essence, altered since the days before the First World War when most of them were established. The power rested entirely with the clubs and the players were indentured serfs until 1961, when the maximum wage, which then stood at £20 a week, was abolished. The iniquitous retain-and-transfer system, however, still kept the players at the mercy of their clubs, no matter what the weekly wage they had managed to secure for themselves, and it was 1963 before

Mr Justice Wilberforce declared the system illegal, after the Professional Footballers' Association and Newcastle United had fought a lengthy, bitter and costly legal action over the transfer of George Eastham to Arsenal.

This, of course, all went on above the heads of the youth team, though its consequences were to have a direct bearing on their future careers. At the age of nine, however, Mike Doyle's legendary combativeness was clearly still in the nascent stage as he wrote to the *Manchester Evening News*: 'I try very hard at school, but still am not very good at arithmetic. I am good at all kinds of sports and I could become a professional footballer. I would like that very much. If I can't do that I would like to become a PT instructor. Besides earning a good wage, I would enjoy doing my job as well, which I think is very important.'

Although many of the stories the players have to tell illuminate the role that pure luck and mere chance played in their lives, it is interesting to note that Harry Godwin, later to be City's chief scout, must have kept that letter on file for five years, because on 24 April 1961 he wrote from his home in Higher Blackley to Mike's parents, on Manchester City headed notepaper, in exquisite copperplate handwriting (he wrote with a ruler underneath the line), a letter that still occupies pride of place at the front of the bulging Doyle scrapbook. It read:

Dear Mr & Mrs Doyle,
    Please find the attached clipping, one of two reasons for my visit to your home, the other being to find out how Michael was playing after his unfortunate accident. [Mike can't remember the accident but he assumes he must have fallen off his bike, although the dates suggest it could be the result of the clash with Alf Wood mentioned below.]

Having satisfied myself on both points, may I thank you for making me so welcome. As for Michael, tell him not to worry about this little set back. He'll be as right as rain in no time. By the time next August comes along his leg will be stronger than ever for what could be a very eventful season for him.

If in the future I can be helpful in realising the fifth line of the clipping [the desire to become a professional footballer] you can count on my support. However there is every probability that I will be in your area in the next few weeks. If so, I will pop in and have a chat.

Until then,
Best wishes
Yours sincerely,
Harry Godwin

Mike Doyle has always proudly proclaimed his support for the Manchester City team he graced for so long, although during the course of research for this book honesty compels me to state that at least two witnesses to Mike Doyle's early childhood days maintain that Mike exhibited Red tendencies. I find it difficult to believe, if only because neither of the witnesses could explain how such a radical transformation could then have taken place. What is certain is that Mike's father, a policeman called Tom, was a City fan. Indeed, his whole family and everyone on the street where they lived were City fans. His grandparents lived a hundred yards from Kippax Street, which is why the story of how Mike got to Maine Road is not as straightforward as you might imagine.

Charlie Gee, who was a part-time scout and friend of Tom Doyle, followed Mike's progress after he failed the eleven-plus and went off to secondary school. It was not a particularly traumatic moment because, as his letter to the

Evening News two years previously had stated, all he was ever interested in was playing football:

> I used to train, going running even as an eleven-, twelve-year-old. One weekend, Phil Burrows was at a school called Reddish and I was at a school called Fir Tree. Reddish School was top dog in local schools football and we had to play them, and we were frightened to death, because of their reputation. We lived in a police house then and Fir Tree was only 300 yards away and that's where we played them. We beat them 4–0.

By the age of thirteen, Doyle was playing in the Stockport Boys side that included future City signings John Clay, Geoff Howard, Stan Goddard, Dave Wild, Ronnie Frost and Phil Burrows, as well as Bobby Noble. Not surprisingly, it was good enough to win the Cheshire Cup, which they took away from the previous champions Mid-Cheshire, and for the first time ever they beat Manchester Boys at Edgeley Park. Alf Wood was playing centre-forward and broke Doyle's ankle that day, which may be the reason the two never really got on. Just before Mike was due to leave school, Charlie Gee came to the house and asked Mike what his future plans were:

> I think I must have been very naïve then, because all you do is listen to your parents. Even at that age I knew I was going to end up at City, but not long after a scout from Stoke came knocking. I had no idea they'd even been watching me. He said he'd like to take me and my parents and show us round the ground and see the training facilities, so we went and we got picked up in a big old Jaguar and they offered

my mum a fridge and a washing machine. I could see my dad was just totally pan-faced, but my mother, now I think back, she must have been tempted, because at that time all we had was a washing tub and a scrubbing board. My dad said casually, 'What do you think?' I said, 'I don't know. Will I have to move away?' and he said, 'Yes, you'll have to go and live in digs,' so straight away I said no.

Tom Doyle's dearest wish was clearly to watch his son play for Manchester City but, though Stoke had been seen off, a much more serious danger soon came knocking. In 1961, Burnley were the league champions, having won the trophy in spectacular fashion by beating City 2–1 in front of 66,000 people at Maine Road the previous May. Their strength lay in their successful production of home-grown players who had passed through their excellent youth system:

A chap came from Burnley and he took us up there and their setup was fantastic. They took us to a Cup game between Burnley and Everton. Everton were top of the league at that time, but Burnley beat them 2–1. After the match, all the players were elated and [first team full-back] Alex Elder put his arm round me and introduced me to everyone. We got back home and my dad asked me the same thing. Now this time I was really impressed, because they had four pitches that looked as smooth as a putting green, but I asked the same question: 'Where would I have to live?' He said, 'Digs.'

It was the perfect escape route for the increasingly anxious Tom Doyle, and Chelsea, Arsenal and West Ham were dispatched the same way. Then came the call he must have dreaded:

> In the end I had an offer from Manchester United. I didn't want to go to London, but I wouldn't have to if I went to United. I had a chat with Joe Armstrong and he took me down to the Cliff. I knew about United, because Phil Burrows and me used to go to Old Trafford one Saturday and Maine Road the other Saturday. That's what we did – City one week, United the next week. I didn't like the atmosphere at the Cliff – it might have been because it was in Salford and there was nothing to look at – so then Charlie Gee came round and said, 'If you're good enough, you'll make it.' That's what I did. I signed on for City as an apprentice pro at £7 10s a week plus luncheon vouchers. To be honest, at the end of the day there was only ever one place I was going to go, provided they came in for me.

It must have been an enormous relief to Tom when his son finally signed apprentice professional forms at Maine Road.

Alf Wood concedes that there was indeed a certain amount of distance between Doyle and himself: 'I do know that Mike Doyle thinks that when I played for Manchester Boys against his Stockport Boys side, apparently I broke his ankle, and that's why we were never particularly friendly.'

When Alf led the team out that night at Old Trafford, it is likely that he would have been thought of as a certainty to become a first team regular at Maine Road, having made his first division debut the previous season. His way to Maine Road had been atypically smooth:

> I was born in Macclesfield, but grew up in a pre-fab

in Blackley, and then we got a council house in Wythenshawe. Dad was an engineer in Altrincham. In his later life, my dad travelled the world, maintaining or installing machines in New Zealand, Canada, Russia, everywhere. When I passed the eleven-plus and went to Chorlton Grammar, my mum took on a job as a cook in a secondary modern school. My headmaster threatened that if I didn't start doing my homework properly he wouldn't let me have the time off on Friday afternoons to join up with Manchester Boys in London or Bristol or wherever.

The grammar school headmaster's threats were almost traditional. It was much less likely that a secondary modern teacher would react in the same way. Somehow, if a grammar school boy wanted to become a footballer, it was seen as a betrayal of the educational system which had been designed to root such nonsense out of him. Frankly, if a secondary modern school leaver wanted to play football for a living, well, it was no worse than digging ditches and in an era of almost full employment it would provide a job for another unskilled labourer. His father was proud of the fact that Alf had passed the eleven-plus and, as was the pattern in those days, when memories of the Depression were still painfully clear, wanted to ensure that his son had a proper job with a trade. Football, which was of short duration, was not the career most parents would have chosen for their academically gifted children. The decision was almost made for him by the O level examiners, who failed Alf in five of the eight subjects he took. He passed commerce, maths and English and his way was clear to begin his career as a footballer at Manchester City – after his father had dealt with the scouts from Blackburn Rovers, Bolton Wanderers and, most resistibly, Southport.

After leaving school, Alf was permitted to sign amateur forms with City, but his parents were so concerned that he had a trade at his fingertips that he began work as an electrical engineer, rebuilding Manchester Piccadilly Station, until, after ten months, the contract was completed and he was laid off. Meanwhile, he was spending Tuesday and Thursday nights with Johnny Hart, Dave Ewing and the rest down at Chassen Road in Urmston:

> I said to Dad it was daft. I was earning a shilling and a ha'penny an hour – that was £2 2s 6d a week – and City were offering me £8 a week as an apprentice pro. Stan Goddard was one of the other groundstaff boys (he died at twenty-two I think), [with] Glyn Pardoe, Fred Eyre and Ken Fletcher, and then the following year Howard, Doyle, Clay and Frost came. I was only there for a year because I signed full-time pro forms at eighteen.

In contrast to the relatively smooth transitions of Doyle and Wood, those of centre-forward Chris Jones and outside-left David Connor were fraught with disappointment and anxiety. Chris was brought up in a terraced house in Altrincham:

> My uncle lived at number five and my dad lived at number seven. I was brought up with my uncle, who still lives there today. I was the middle of five children. My father looked after the two youngest after the family split and my uncle Bill took the three oldest – Elaine, Hilary and me. We never knew what happened to my mother. I was about two or three years old when she left, but we never knew the real reason.

Chris becomes another in the lengthening list of the sons of one-parent families. He claims not to have been brilliant academically, but neither was it a surprise when he passed the eleven-plus. There were three grammar schools in the area where he lived – Altrincham, Sale and Lymm. Sale played rugby rather than football, so that was rejected, and Chris became a pupil at Lymm Grammar School:

> I played for the school, but no scouts ever came to watch, and I was wondering why I hadn't been discovered. I was captain of the school team, but even though I played for Sale Boys nobody picked me up from there and I never got picked for Cheshire Boys. I slipped through the net – I think today the system is better organised. Oddly enough, there was another lad who played for City, who lived on the same road – a full-back called Peter Leigh. Eventually I asked him how to get a trial at a professional club. I always wanted to be a professional footballer and he was the one who told me about a trial taking place at Chassen Road in Urmston.

Peter Leigh had made his debut for Manchester City in April 1960 in the defeat by Bolton Wanderers. The *Manchester Evening News* had written perceptively that Leigh '... could look back at his debut with some satisfaction. He put up a sterling performance, was cool throughout and obviously has a tremendous future.' That future was with Crewe Alexandra, for whom he made over 500 appearances. Nevertheless, Leigh's current position on the staff at Maine Road was the stuff of dreams as fifteen-year-old Chris Jones made his way to Urmston, one Saturday in June 1962, just one hopeful amongst the 150 lads of a similar age who turned up at Chassen Road with their own lovingly nurtured dreams of glory. Even with a convinced sense of his own destiny, it was clearly a daunting prospect for young Jones:

> I got there and I could see this chap writing down names in a notebook and putting them in positions. Now I was a goalscorer at school, but I could play on the wing. I was good at the basics – get the ball, pass it and move, or cross the ball and if I get a chance I'll have a shot. I liked to play outside-left so I could improve my left foot. I looked at the list and saw there were far too many centre-forwards, but only three right-wingers. So when Johnny Hart asked me where I played I said right-wing.

It was an intelligent move from the grammar school lad, but it didn't seem to have paid off. An announcement was made that there would be a final trial at the end of the day and that's when the apprentices would be coming along. They would include John Clay, Mike Doyle and Bobby McAlinden, all of whom had signed apprentice professional forms by this time:

> I played my first match, but nobody said anything, so as the afternoon wore on I thought that was it and I got changed back. My uncle said, 'Shall we leave?' and I said, 'I think I'll just watch this final game,' which was coming on in a few minutes. We leaned on the fence near a lady who was always watching City games and a chap who turned out to be Harry Godwin came by and she asked him if he'd found anybody. Harry said, 'I have, love, yes. I've found him and lost him.' She said, 'Who's that then?' He said, 'A lad called Jones.' I put my hand up and said, 'Do you mean Chris Jones?' He said, 'Yes.' I said, 'I'm Chris Jones' and he said, 'What are you doing changed

already? You're in this game.' So I changed quickly and ran out and joined them on the right wing. The moment I really remember is in the dressing room afterwards, when Johnny Hart said he wanted some people to come back and train with the apprentices on Tuesdays and Thursdays and my name was on it and so was Dave Connor's. Terrifying it was, when they read the names out and you thought you were being let go, but it was the others who had to leave.

David Connor has an identical recollection of the agonising reading of the lists. To hopeful but fatalistic teenagers it must have been like the women in the First World War who gathered round the lists of killed and wounded to see if their son's or husband's name was on them. To lads like Jones and Connor, growing up in an era of relative peace and prosperity, the death of that dream of a life as a professional footballer was utterly traumatic. Although he might be given another chance at a different club, it was nevertheless rare that a boy would succeed at another professional club having been rejected by his first choice. That was why they were convinced they were going to make it, even though the system appeared to them to have been devised to crush their spirits. Chris Jones recalls the agonising summer of 1962:

I used to come back from school to the house in Altrincham, then get another bus to Stretford, then another one to Flixton, in order to get to Urmston for 6.15p.m. The training would be about two hours, but I wasn't signed to anything and my mates kept saying that City were just stringing me along and they'd drop me in the end, but I kept persevering and persevering throughout that summer. Then came a time at the end of August when I was supposed to go on holiday. I told Harry Godwin, who just said I should go on the holiday as arranged and come back to Urmston afterwards and carry on training. I was still too frightened to ask if they were going to sign me to anything, and the longer this went on my mates were telling me City were stringing me along.

All the lads were painfully aware who had been signed to associate professional forms and who was still left dangling. The security and the status that the contract conferred were what they all craved so desperately. As the summer wore on and the first-team professionals returned for training, Chris Jones reached bursting point: 'I couldn't stand the suspense any longer. I said to Harry Godwin, "Harry, what's going to happen to me?" "Oh, Chris, yes, we've decided to sign you to amateur forms." I don't think my feet touched the ground all the way home.'

It was what Chris and his family wanted, but it wasn't what the school wanted and Chris experienced much of what Alf Wood complained about, even though he had played for the school every Saturday morning. Just before the first trial, Chris had sat his O levels and when the new season began he discovered that he had passed in the five subjects which were deemed necessary to begin life in the sixth form and make university a logical conclusion of his education.

However, once City had collected his signature on the amateur forms, the club naturally assumed that Jones would be available to play as selected for the B team or the A team in the Lancashire League. Chris was desperate to play, despite some of the less than glamorous grounds he had to play on, because the A and B sides were rarely permitted to play on the first-team pitches. He recalls a particular mud heap of a pitch at Blackpool, out beyond Squires Gate, as Bloomfield Road was preserved for the senior side.

It was therefore a significant moment when he made his debut at Maine Road, against Bolton Wanderers, for a Manchester City reserve side containing the great Bert Trautmann in goal. To his great joy Chris scored the equalising goal for City that day in a 1–1 draw. The school was not impressed. To play in the game he had to pull out of a match against another local school. The school and its star centre-forward were on a collision course. After a game against Blackburn in which Chris scored again and played well, Johnny Hart switched him to centre-forward. He was now starting to develop physically, which was a vital prerequisite if he was eventually be offered professional terms. The prospect of signing those forms for City had become an obsession for Jones:

I [should have] signed for City one smoggy Tuesday evening in early December 1962. I took the electric train into Oxford Road Station and then got the 76 bus to Lloyd Street and worked my way like a blind man along Claremont Road, because it was such a peasouper you couldn't see a hand in front of your face. I was just so desperate that if I didn't get to Maine Road that night they'd have changed their minds in the morning. I crawled up to the old players' entrance. There was one light above the door shedding no illumination whatsoever. I knocked on this door and nothing happened. Eventually, Dave Ewing came and opened it and said, 'What do you want, son?' I said, 'I've come to train.' 'Oh there's nothing happening tonight. Come back on Thursday.' I staggered back from the door, worked my back down Lloyd Street, hoping to find a bus, and bumped into Harry Godwin, and he was the one who said, 'Oh, don't worry, wait till Thursday and we'll sign you then.' I was desperate for him to say, 'No, come on. we'll do it now.' I had to go back home and tell everyone that I hadn't signed.

As requested, he went back in on the Thursday to sign the forms and met for the first time the manager, Les McDowall, and his assistant, George Poyser. The young players were kept away from the first-team management and their business was conducted with Harry Godwin, the scout, Johnny Hart and Dick Nielssen, who were in charge of their training at Urmston, and the occasional supervision from the first-team trainer, Jimmy Meadows. Johnny Hart was regarded as something of a soft touch, who found it difficult to say 'no'. Jimmy Meadows, whose career as a potential international full-back was ended by a devastating knee injury in the 1955 FA Cup final, when City lost 3–1 to Newcastle United, was much more of an old-fashioned disciplinarian and the boys knew that if Jimmy was there, the evening would begin with a mandatory and spirit-crushing twelve laps of the pitch. Ironically, almost as soon as he had signed the coveted amateur forms, the great freeze of the 1962–63 winter began and Chris played almost no football until March 1963.

Amateur forms were clearly a rung below the associate professional forms that they all longed for, the forms that told the world that the boy was now a professional footballer, being paid money by a first division club to play football. As the favoured recipients of the club's bounty, these apprentices tended to assume an air of grandeur when confronted with the boys in their age group who were still only amateurs or even worse, unsigned. Chris Jones struck up an instant friendship with John Clay, but was immediately at loggerheads with Mike Doyle, who called him a grammar school twat. Chris could comfort himself with the fact that the first part was true enough and that, as an amateur, he could still follow the path of conventional scholastic achievement – sixth form in the grammar school and then university – but in truth it wasn't much of a riposte to the constant taunts from Mike Doyle; and, besides, like the rest of them, all he wanted to do was to play professional football. The attraction of the relative freedom offered by life in the sixth form at school was wearing thin.

David Connor remembers the reading of the lists of retained names as the most frightening moment of the week:

> Every Tuesday and Thursday it always seemed like there were new faces. When we were done and had got changed, Johnny Hart would come in and start shouting out names, 'Wilson, Thomas ...' and so on. And we soon realised that these lads who were called out stayed behind and were told they weren't wanted any more. To the rest of us he'd say, 'OK, everyone else, see you on Thursday.' We never saw the lads again whose names were called out, and that was scary, because you were only a fifteen-year-old.

David Connor was born an only child and brought up in Gorton, close to Dave Farrar, but when he was about eight his family moved to the green-belt suburb of Wythenshawe, which was developing as an overspill from the slums. Up to the age of nine he had never played on grass. The boots in which he used to play football had bars on the soles instead of studs, because they used to play on shale on the rec in Gorton. Shortly after moving to the planner's urban paradise of Wythenshawe, he went to a school called Oldwood Juniors, where he had a trial for the Under-11s and can still remember the thrill of playing for the first time on the lush grass of summer time. St Thomas School, which he had been attending in Gorton, was a relic from the Victorian age, with its toilets out in the yard, but Oldwood was a modern airy building, full of windows and built of glass and steel. During the trial, Connor was slipping all over the place and the teacher came over and said, 'Where's your studs, boy?' A puzzled Connor could only shrug helplessly and point to the bars on the soles of his feet. There was no point having studs on football boots in Gorton. There was no grass.

The move to Wythenshawe and the new school were blessings for David Connor, who soon played his way into the junior team but wishes, with typical modesty, to make it clear that he wasn't the best player and really only played because he loved the game and his friends were in the team. This modesty haunted him in his professional career and was responsible for problems which arose later. Of all the players, he was one of the few to doubt his talent at the highest level. As a schoolboy, however, he demonstrated a well-regarded versatility, which also dogged his later career. After the age of eleven, he was promoted to Oldwood Senior School, where he also played for the cricket team and then captained the Manchester Boys basketball team and also represented Cheshire in athletics. He was one of a group of eight lads who all did the same things together and who had the inestimable advantage of having the support and encourage-ment of a number of sport-obsessed, dedicated teachers.

David's father had been a moulder, making moulds for railways when they lived in Gorton, but that trade just disappeared with the changes in manufacturing industry already visible across the land. When the family moved to Wythenshawe, Mr Connor Sr started to work at Manchester airport, where he stayed for more than twenty-five years:

He was working there when Ringway terminal was just a shed. He did everything, worked on cargoes, everything – a good utility player – that's where it started. My mum was one of five sisters and all of them and their parents were in the rag trade. My mum was a dressmaker, another sister was a seamstress and so on. My mum had a bad heart which got steadily worse and she died in her early forties. I was about fifteen and had just gone to City when she died, but she'd been ill and she was on tablets for the last ten years of her life. Now she could have a heart transplant, but not then. I was very close to her and when she died I was devastated. My dad was very strict, an old-fashioned Victorian type of father, and I was an only child. At school I'd run home for lunch, because my mum worked at home and she'd always make potato hash for dinner, so I'd have that and then run back to school again in half an hour, so I could get in a quick game of football in the yard before lessons started again. My mum was a marvellous lady. Ironically, because she had a bad heart, she always worried about my running.

It was David Connor's selfless, non-stop running that eventually turned him into the Forrest Gump of Manchester City. He followed the traditional path of playing first for the local area team, Manchester South, and then Manchester Boys, where he played at outside-left, because the inside-forward positions which he favoured were already taken. In the infamous match against Stockport Boys in which Alf Wood broke Mike Doyle's ankle, Connor played against John Clay, Bobby Noble and Mike Doyle, but unlike them there was no offer of associate professional terms. He simply had to persevere if he was to realise his dream:

On a Saturday, when I was about fourteen or fifteen, if I wasn't playing for the school I played for an all-age team up in Altrincham. That was the best thing that ever happened to me. The older players used to look after me. We got to a couple of finals and I scored a couple of goals. I felt slightly embarrassed, because they took me to the pub afterwards and I used to sit quietly in the corner. The manager even used to pay me my bus fare. There were no cars or anything then. Anyway, one of the scouts wrote to my dad to see if I wanted to come training with City, but Joe Armstrong also came and offered me a trial at the Cliff. My mum's family were all big United fans, apart from my grandad, who had a wooden leg – he'd lost it in the First World War – and he used to work on the barges. Anyway, grandad was City-mad [author's note: it's not clear exactly how the wooden leg influenced his support for Manchester City]. I went to Maine Road more often than Old Trafford, because my grandma used to pay me one shilling and sixpence to take my grandad to City. We had to be there an hour before the game started because of his peg leg and we used to stand by the crush barrier at the old scoreboard end at Maine Road, so he could lean on it. At the end of the game we had to wait for half an hour, because it was so difficult to walk down the steps with that peg leg. Anyway, he thought I was City-daft like him, but really it was because my gran gave me that one and six. Also, they wouldn't allow us kids to sit on those crush barriers at Old Trafford, but at Maine Road I'd sit on it and my grandad would hold me. The crowds were bigger at Old Trafford, and that frightened me a bit as a little lad, and Maine Road was only one bus ride away from Gorton.

If Chris Jones' fate was determined by leaning on the fence

as Harry Godwin spoke to a woman about the missing boy Jones, David Connor's path to Maine Road was even more fortuitous. He had received a letter from City informing him of the day he had to be at Maine Road, where a coach would take him and the other hopeful triallists to the pitch at Chassen Road in Urmston. Unfortunately, the day of the Manchester City trial turned out to be the same day as the United trial, arranged by Joe Armstrong. It was an impossible position for a teenager, with a United-mad family and a City-mad grandfather with one leg:

Even going out through the front door I didn't know if I was going to the Cliff or to Maine Road. I knew that if I went to United I had to get a bus to Piccadilly, walk down to Deansgate and get a bus from Victoria Bus Station to Broughton, where the Cliff was. So the same bus would take me from home to Maine Road or to Piccadilly for United. When I looked in my pocket I only had one and threepence and it was ninepence to get to Maine Road. So that was why I went to Maine Road, where I was picked up by a lovely man called Johnny Hart, who looked after me for many, many years. So I've now got sixpence left. Anyway, I played in this trial at Urmston, and it was worrying, because there were kids coming on and off all the time and you could never be sure who was doing well. But at the end, Johnny comes over and says, 'David, we'd like you to come training with us every Tuesday and Thursday evening.'

In the summer of 1961, when this brief but significant conversation took place, Connor had just left school and taken a job in an accountant's office in the centre of Manchester. He had done well at Oldwood Senior School and left with nine O levels and two A levels. He had also been made head boy, but now his attention was focused on reconciling the desire to play professional football with the need to learn a trade:

> I worked during the day, then every Tuesday and Thursday, as soon as we'd finished, I used to rush like mad to Central Station, where the G Mex is now, and get the six o'clock train down to Urmston, where we started training between 6.30 and 6.45p.m. Then we'd train, it seemed all night, because the last train went from Urmston around 10.20p.m., which got you back into Manchester. By the time I got into town I'd missed the last regular bus, so I had to get the all-night bus, which came after about fifty minutes, so I never got back to Wythenshawe till about quarter to one in the morning. I was absolutely shattered and I then had to walk the last 200 yards home, where my mum had my tea ready – at one o'clock in the morning! She insisted I ate it. I did that routine for quite a while.

Maybe it was his day job training as an accountant that enabled David to realise early on that the odds were not in his favour. Apart from Alf Wood, the local Wythenshawe hero, nobody he knew from his area had ever been signed by either City or United:

> I didn't like being an accountant, because I always wanted to play sport. I earned two quid a week I think, but by the time I'd spent my bus fares and dinner money I think my mum ended up supporting me in this job. The crunch came when I got picked for Lancashire Under-18s, to play Durham, and to this

day I don't know how that happened. Anyway, the game was at Deepdale in Preston. I think Howard Kendall was playing for us. Don't forget I was still an amateur with City at that stage and another club could give seven days' notice and then sign you. My dad had a Ford Anglia with three gears and he took me to Preston – there was no motorway in those days and it was thirty miles of nightmare fog over Belmont. We could only go 25mph at top speed and in that fog you couldn't see across the road. I had me head out of the window, looking for the verge, and we were still in the car when the game kicked off. I don't know what I was doing there. There was no one else from City there.

As in all good British comedy films of the period, when the fog lifted, the Connors, in their trusty Ford Anglia, found themselves going round and round a roundabout, followed by a police car. The Connors explained the situation and were thereupon given an impressive police escort to the ground, though it should be admitted that they were only half a mile away at the time. Mr Connor let his son off at the players' entrance, then parked the car before finding his seat in the stand. Meanwhile, downstairs, his son was still getting changed when the players came in for half-time. David didn't recognise any of his team-mates, who all came from the local clubs of Preston, Blackburn and Burnley. The half-time score was a depressing 3–0 to Durham:

> I heard someone say, 'We'd better put him on, then,' meaning me, so some poor lad was dragged off and I trotted out for the start of the second half. It was still a bad night and the ground was really heavy, but I was fit and fresh and within a minute of the restart I

crossed from the left and the centre-forward headed it in. My dad's in the stand and people are saying, 'Who's this lad who's just come on?' and my dad says nothing. Then we get a corner on the right and I'm on the edge of the area and it comes straight at me, so I just volley it and it goes right in the corner. So now they're getting very excited in the stand and me dad still doesn't own up. Now I'm going past their full-back at will and I get in another cross and the centre-forward heads it in and it's 3–3. Up in the stand me dad tells them the name is Connor and, to cut a long story short, we ended up winning 4–3. It was one of those days when everything comes off.

Rather in the manner that John Aston Jr was signed in a somewhat ungracious I-suppose-we'd-better-sign-him-to-make-sure-Everton-don't way, so David Connor soon realised that news of his triumph in the fog at Preston had clearly filtered back to the city of Manchester and provoked a similar reaction:

On the next Tuesday I go for training at Urmston and I knew there was something funny going on because we started with a game – no training. And they brought the apprentices down – players like John Clay. Dave Wild was marking me and he had the reputation that he would kick you to death. Years later, when Dave Wild was a referee, we talked about that night and he told me that Johnny Hart had said to him before the game started, 'Hit David Connor hard in the first few minutes.' It was just to see my reaction. Anyway, I gave Dave a bit of a runaround and for the first time ever – and I mean *ever* – I thought to myself in the dressing room afterwards,

'Oh well, at least I'll be coming back on Thursday.'
Then Johnny Hart starts on the list of names –
'Thompson, Wilson ...' and so on – and then he says
'Connor!' I couldn't believe it. 'The rest of you, thank
you, but get dressed and leave.' I was devastated. It
was all over. So then Johnny Hart comes over and
sees me looking shell-shocked, sloping off with the
other rejects. He says, 'Tadger what are you doing?'
because he'd given me the nickname of Tadger. 'Now
look, on Thursday ...' I say, 'I won't be coming on
Thursday.' He says, 'Why not?' I say that he called
my name out. He says, 'No! Your name wasn't called
because of that. It was because I wanted you to bring
your dad down on Thursday. Mr Poyser was here this
evening and he wants to meet him.' The whole game
was arranged for his benefit, because after that game
at Preston four teams put seven days' notice in. If
City hadn't signed me by then, they could approach
me. I didn't know about it. I think Preston, Burnley
and Blackburn and someone else had all asked to
approach me, because I was still an amateur.

Accompanied by his loyal father, Connor made the trip back
to Chassen Road on the Thursday evening. He clearly did
enough to impress, because they offered him the munificent
sum of £7 a week. Compared to the £2 and a few coppers he
was earning in the accountant's office it was riches indeed.
Mr Connor Sr could see no reason why his only son, David,
should not take the gamble and dedicate himself to the now
very real possibility of a life in professional football.

When David took the field against United in April 1964
he did so as an outside-left. Playing behind him at left-half
that night was Phil Burrows, who had joined the club before
David Connor as a left-winger. Clearly the management

rated him less highly than Chris Jones, because he lost his place due to a family holiday. David Connor recalls:

> We had a B team game and he was picked before me, but when the team was announced he went and told Johnny Hart that he was going on holiday that weekend. Now Johnny Hart looked at him and said, 'You're a foolish lad. You should have took your holidays before the season started.' This was the middle of September and that's how all this started, because Phil never got back in as a winger.

Phil Burrows was yet another graduate of the Stockport school system. His primary school was very successful in football, cricket and swimming, and Phil had already won a collection of junior Stockport trophies. He moved effortlessly through the ranks, alongside the other lads who were shortly to find their way to Maine Road and Old Trafford:

> John Clay played for two years for Stockport Boys and Mike Doyle was born the same year as me, but after September, so he was classed as the next school year. Clay, Doyle, Wild, Noble and myself all played for the same Stockport Boys side. We won the Cheshire Cup, beating Birkenhead Boys in the final, and we also got to the final of the Manchester County Cup – I think we played Stretford Boys at Old Trafford.

Like Bobby Noble, his father (and indeed his grandfather) had played for Stockport County:

> My father played in the longest ever game. County played Doncaster in 1946 in the first season after the end of the war. They played for 206 minutes. It was

85

rumoured that people came to watch the game, went home, had their tea and came back to watch the end of the game. My father and grandfather each had a trade, because the money wasn't there. In 1939 my dad got into the first team and was just about to start negotiations for a professional contract when war broke out. He went off to France and had to be evacuated. He was a pattern maker, like a joiner, working with wood, and then he was involved in the war effort here, making big frames for metal castings. His best friend at County was Harry Stott, who was Paul Warhurst's grandfather. My mother and his wife were best friends. The women went to Stockport County to watch them play against United in a war-time game and neither of them ran out. Then United ran out and they were playing for United. He even scored for United in that match. He played five games for United in that 1940–41 season, mostly as a winger, but he got injured and his career finished quite young.

Like David Connor, Phil's first schoolboy allegiance was to United and the first faltering steps were taken with the usual caprice: 'At our local theatre there was a play on and it was about football, but this guy had a huge red and white rosette and I wanted it. And after the show, my parents went backstage, and he gave it me. The next Saturday United were at home, so I went with the rosette and that's how I became a United supporter.'

This is why children should be kept away from the rogues and vagabonds of show business. To cement the allegiance, his mother started knitting a red pullover with black and white figures on it. The besotted Phil would 'wash up, go to the shops, do anything just as long as she was knitting'. The mid-fifties were a good time to be a United supporter. United won the league in 1956 and 1957 and narrowly missed out on the coveted double (in the days when it was a more significant achievement than it is today) when they lost unluckily in the 1957 FA Cup final against Aston Villa:

My team was the Busby Babes. I loved them. I remember I came home from school around five o'clock on 6 February 1958 – I was nearly twelve. I'd just started at the secondary modern and I went home with a lad called Dave Laycock, who was a very good friend of Mike Doyle, and every hour we'd go in to hear the latest bulletin. We could scarcely play. Then the next morning we saw those photos of the wrecked plane on the runway.

I was really a football supporter with allegiances to United, because I'd seen them play – everyone had to be Blue or Red and I was Red. Dennis Fidler [a Stockport lad who had been on the books at both City and United] had a chip shop directly opposite our house in Reddish. I went in one night. I think United were playing Leeds and he asked if I was going to the game that night. I explained that I couldn't afford it and he gave me the money.

I used to sing in the local choir and on Saturdays I would go and put my football kit on, go to the church for nine o'clock choir practice, get the bus to the park, play football, go home for lunch, get on a bus again to Manchester, run to Oxford Street Station, get off at Warwick Road, then I used to love weaving at pace, through the crowds. I played in the morning and if the match was away from home I'd be late getting to Old Trafford and it was always full, so I couldn't see a thing, but the crowd would pass you down to the front.

For all his United allegiance, the first scout to come calling at the Burrows' house was Colin McDonald from Bury, who signed Phil on schoolboy terms at the age of fifteen, but at the end of that season Harry Godwin saw him in a local match and the race was on. Harry, as we have seen, could be very persuasive, but at the time Bury held the whip hand, until they picked Phil for Bury Youth and played him in the last game of the season, in which Phil damaged his Achilles tendon – a really serious injury:

> I was on crutches for a number of weeks and Bury never even bothered to contact me. A lad called Dave Roberts, a full-back, brought me home and I had to go to hospital next day, where they said the leg was broken. They put the leg in a plaster cast, then they looked at the X-rays again and decided it wasn't broken, so they cut off the cast and that was absolute agony. Both sides of my ankle were black with bruising. When Harry came to see me I had strapping on the ankle, but by the following season I was fit to go training. I'd had enough of Bury and I went off to Chassen Road in Urmston, every Tuesday and Thursday night. I was living in Reddish at the time, so I had to get the bus into Manchester, walk across town to get the train from Central Station to Urmston, and get home at God knows what time. These days you have to ferry everyone in a minibus. Not then.

The more assiduous of the parents in this story were very concerned that their sons learn a trade apart from football, which was not regarded as a serious profession. When Phil Burrows left school, he immediately started work in Denton as a trainee quantity surveyor, but there is no doubt that his heart was in his football, despite playing only ten minutes of his first game for the Manchester City B side on the left wing, before substituting in goal. David Downes, who had graduated from the Stockport Boys team the year before him, was injured and Phil, all five feet seven inches of him, was summoned to take his place. A few weeks later he played his first game against Manchester United. It left an indelible impression: 'We kicked off, we lost possession, and this little skinny, dark-haired kid got hold of it, went round everyone and stuck it in the net. We kicked off again and the skinny kid got possession, went round everyone and scored. We lost 6–0 I think, but it was over in the first couple of minutes. That was my first ever encounter with George Best.'

If George Best was the great star of the United youth team in the early sixties, then Glyn Pardoe was probably City's equivalent. Like the rest of the boys on both sides, Glyn had been the best player in his school, where he played centre-half but still managed to score four goals every game. His versatility, however, was soon apparent as he also played inside-forward for Mid-Cheshire and centre-forward for Cheshire and England Schoolboys. His overwhelming superiority was the result of a combination of his natural skill and, most important, physical maturity. Like David Sadler, he could muscle other youngsters off the ball and was a daunting physical presence in the penalty area.

The key to understanding Pardoe is his family background in the village of Winsford in Cheshire. His father worked in a tailor's cutting shop and, although they encouraged Glyn in his ambition, his parents were just as unsure as those of the other boys about whether he would be able to earn a living in such a precarious trade. What eased their minds was the progress of Glyn's cousin, Alan Oakes. Glyn's mother and Alan Oakes's mother were sisters. As an only child, Glyn was close to Alan's family, who lived at the other end of Winsford, and although Alan was four years older and had made his debut for Manchester City when Glyn was only thirteen, Alan's brother Terry was just six months older and the boys grew up together in a close and supportive family.

Most City supporters of a certain age think of Oakes and Pardoe as two of the home-grown foundations on which the Mercer/Allison team was built. It comes as something of a surprise, therefore, to learn that Pardoe's path to Maine Road was by no means straightforward:

> I was earmarked for Everton. They used to pick me up on a Saturday and take me to Goodison with my parents for every home game. Johnny Carey was the manager then, but Harry Catterick took over and I didn't fancy him one bit. John Carey was a really nice, pipe-smoking gentleman, but Catterick struck me as being a grumpy old bugger. Anyway, George Poyser used to mither me to death to come to City and, in the end, because our Alan was there, I decided to go to Maine Road.

Liverpool was a reasonable commuting distance from Winsford, but travelling to Manchester wasn't easy. It was the matches he played for his school and then Mid-Cheshire, his local area team, followed by the full Cheshire Schoolboy sides which brought Glyn to the attention of the Everton and Liverpool scouts. His outstanding potential was soon spotted and he was selected for an England Schoolboys side which included Johnny Sissons, the West Ham United left-winger, and Alan Ogley, his future team-mate at Manchester City. Howard Kendall was in the squad, but he didn't make the team. Of all the youngsters he met on England duty, the one who made the biggest impression on Glyn was a young lad called Doug Prosser, who had all the skills imaginable at that age, but he never progressed. It is simply impossible to be sure at sixteen who will make a regular first-team player at the age of twenty-one.

Despite the persistent courting of George Poyser and the comfort that cousin Alan was doing well at Maine Road, life for the teenage prodigy bore no resemblance to the pampered seclusion in which today's talented teenagers are cocooned:

> I would catch the twenty past seven bus in the morning from the bus stop in Winsford, then get the eleven minutes past eight train from Northwich to Manchester, then jump on the first bus I could get from Central Station to Maine Road. We'd have to go out to Urmston on Tuesdays and Thursdays as well. So I trained Monday morning and afternoon, Tuesday morning and afternoon, then I had to get the bus to Central Station and catch the train to Urmston. So on Tuesdays and Thursdays I'd leave home at ten past seven and I wouldn't get home till nearly midnight.

Despite his rapid rise to first-team celebrity, Glyn was still the same shy lad and neither felt nor behaved like a star. Of course, had he done so there were plenty of people around to remind him of the reality of his lowly status. On 11 April 1962, amid a blaze of publicity, Glyn made his first-team debut at centre-forward as Manchester City's youngest ever player. A crowd of nearly 22,000 gathered to watch Glyn perform rather anonymously in a 4–1 home defeat by Birmingham City. It was a meaningless match in that City had been knocked out of the FA Cup at Everton in January and there were only five more matches of a dull league campaign left to play. City finished twelfth, so the debut of Glyn Pardoe was the most interesting event of the second half of the season in Moss Side, but his team-mates ensured that he wasn't going to get a swollen head:

The day I made my debut was a normal day as an apprentice and I remember that Bert [Trautmann] wanted to take me for lunch, but Jimmy Meadows, who was the first-team trainer, said, 'No. He's not going for any lunch. He's still got his work to do. He's got boots to clean.' In the dressing room before the game they were all my mates – 'Come on, son, you can do this, you can do that' – but come Monday morning I had to knock on the door before I could go into the dressing room. If you walked in without knocking they'd say, 'What do you think you're doing, son? Get out and knock.' So you'd go out and shut the door and then knock and this time nobody would answer you. So you'd just walk away. I was just an apprentice. It was the early seventies before that all changed.

John Clay was only six months younger than Glyn and was therefore a colleague in the Cheshire Boys side of their time. Dave Wild, who had followed John through the Stockport schools and Stockport Boys teams, failed to graduate to Cheshire Boys, although he joined them all on Tuesday and Thursday nights down at Chassen Road, Urmston. Dave started at North Reddish Primary School and from there he went to Reddish Vale Secondary Modern, which he left after two years when he passed his thirteen-plus. He, along with Mike Doyle, John Clay, Ron Frost, Max Brown and Bobby Noble, played for a man called Frank Aspinall, who ran at least three different junior teams in the Stockport area. The key team was called Westbourne Rangers and they played their games on Houldsworth Park. As Mike Doyle says, 'If you got into Westbourne Rangers that was it – you were the bees' knees. We won everything.' Frank Aspinall clearly had a good relationship with Harry Godwin, because so many of those twelve- and thirteen-year-olds ended up playing in the Youth Cup for City five years later.

Dave Wild was one of those who graduated to the City B team and then to the A team, but there his progress stalled. He was the only one of the City Youth Cup team never to be offered a professional contract. His father, Jack Wild, was a bus driver and, like many other fathers, had no belief in the security of a life in football. When it was apparent that no professional contract was to be forthcoming, it hurt Dave Wild badly, but his father had been desperate for his son to learn a trade. Dave went to work for Crossley Engineering at Openshaw as a wages clerk, while maintaining his attend-ance on Tuesday and Thursday nights at Chassen Road, hoping for the call that never came.

His team-mate in that Stockport Boys side, John Clay, had an altogether smoother ride through his apprentice years. John was close to an England Schoolboys cap, but never quite made it into the team. It was, though he obviously didn't know it at the time, a symbol of the frustrations he was to experience over the course of his career at Maine Road. He was born in Offerton, a district of Stockport, south of Manchester. His father owned and ran a bakery and confectionery business. John went to the local primary school, which was called Bank Lane, where he was inevitably appointed captain of the foot-ball team. He passed the eleven-plus examination to go the grammar school, of which there were two in Stockport. The choice was between the slightly superior Stockport School and the more conventional Stockport Grammar School. They were both excellent single sex schools, virtually opposite one another on the main road. At the grammar school they didn't play football – only rugby and other minority sports such as hockey and lacrosse – so initially John Clay looked like devel-oping into a fine stand-off half. However, after school, games of football with a tennis ball soon broke out:

The back garden of the house we lived in at Offerton backed on to Woodbank Park, so we took the railings down and there you stayed, after school or in the holidays; it was literally nine in the morning till nine o'clock at night. There were some good players there – a lad called Dave Maloney, who now runs a pub in Offerton, but he scored a thousand goals in local amateur football. I played against him when I was in the City A team and he was playing for Stockport Reserves. I scored four times past him that day. Anyway, in the second year, when we were now allowed to play football officially, I got into the school team and then I got called by Ken Miller, who was running Stockport Boys, who played at Kingsway in Cheadle. When I was twelve I was playing for the Under-13 or Under-14s, but this sort of thing was frowned on at grammar school. We took it all seriously at Stockport Boys, where we went training every Tuesday and Thursday. I was an inside-forward or wing-half and Mike Doyle played behind me at full-back. In the trial match I was up against Bobby Noble. Bob was the captain of Stockport Boys and also played for England Boys. He was a hard lad, was Bobby.

Nobody who ever played with or against Bobby Noble ever varied this judgement. It was an eye-opener for John Clay in more ways than one:

Don't forget I went to Stockport School and most of the other lads on the Stockport Boys team were probably all from secondary moderns, which were co-ed. I remember going into a shop with them and these lads virtually emptied the place of chocolates and cigarettes. There were a couple of old people there looking on and I was absolutely amazed. We used to go into Boots in Stockport and there'd be pictures all the way up the stairs and every time we went in there'd be another one missing.

Having fought his way through the eleven-plus exam, John was set to take a full complement of O levels, but somehow football kept breaking through. From the star-studded Stockport Boys side, John was invited to play for Cheshire Boys, alongside Glyn Pardoe. The captain was Bobby Noble again. Apart from being the toughest tackler, Bobby was a natural shouter on the field and, as such, was invited to assume the captaincy. John Clay's parents understood all about the attractions of football, but they insisted that John stay in school and take his O levels in the summer of 1962. That last year in the fifth form was a time of constant distraction, as it was for all the boys who were desperate to leave and start their careers as apprentice professional footballers:

My last year at school it got a bit difficult because I'd had approaches from eleven clubs altogether. All the big northwest clubs came in for me, plus Arsenal, and I frequently wish I'd gone there – it could all have turned out differently, certainly with the injuries and everything. Arsenal were very keen to sign me and I sometimes wonder what would have happened if I'd taken the plunge and moved away from home.

Very few boys did. Mike Doyle's anxiety about moving to Burnley was typical, as to a certain extent was the blinding homesickness that afflicted George Best and Eric McMordie the moment they arrived in Manchester and were left to fend for themselves.

John did make one trip to London at this time, but it wasn't enough to convince him of the merits of living there. He had already played in one international trial at Edgeley Park, but he hadn't had a particularly good game. The London-based selectors wanted to have another look at him and decided to call him into the squad for a game against East Ham Boys to be played at Upton Park. It was not a happy experience:

> I travelled down on the day, and in those days the train took a long time, so it was straight off the train and straight to the ground and on to the pitch. Again, I didn't do myself justice, so I didn't get a cap in the end. You get a badge for an international trial and a cap for playing for your country. I was really disappointed not to get a cap. Bobby Noble had played for England the year before, but hardly anybody from Stockport Boys had done that.

In between revising for O levels, John and his parents were having to fight off the attention of the scouts, particularly the Manchester United chief scout:

> Joe Armstrong came to our house every single night – I mean he camped on our doorstep. Every time we opened the door he was there. I found out later that if I'd signed for United we'd have got a washing machine and a television set, but from City we got absolutely nothing. We weren't that well off, but my dad resisted all those bribes and things from United. He was determined I should play for City. Don't forget the two teams were reasonably comparable at that point.

I find it comforting that naked prejudice by the fathers of

John Clay and Mike Doyle would eventually see their sons safely ensconced in pale blue shirts. For Mr Clay, who had been a City supporter all his life, the fact was that the bakery and confectionery shop he ran on Hall Street in Offerton meant that he was working every Saturday. It was the busiest day of the week, so he couldn't get away, but Uncle Joe, who lived next door, was deputed to take John to watch football. Unfortunately, Uncle Joe supported United, so John was exposed at a dangerously early age to the Red menace:

> This was just pre-Munich. I remember seeing Jimmy Greaves, who was a big favourite of mine, playing for Chelsea at Old Trafford. We were in the Stretford End and they passed the kids down to the front. I remember watching him closely during the knock-up and seeing the ball whistle into the net, but probably my favourite player was Eddie Colman and I used to model myself on him. I was more interested in the football that the United team played than I was in supporting the club. I was only about eight or nine years old, so I was no fanatic, even though I liked going with Uncle Joe to United. My dad and my brother were City fans and when I got a bit older I could go to Maine Road by myself and stand on the Kippax. Stockport and all round there is a pretty big City-supporting area. By the time I signed for City I was a Blue. I always stood by a crush barrier about ten to fifteen rows from the front of the Kippax and my mates from school and football all arranged to meet there.

Just as Mike Doyle gave his father kittens when he looked round the Burnley training facilities and was very impressed by them, so John Clay was also tempted by Burnley and

Everton, much to his dad's anxiety:

> I did, out of courtesy, go to Burnley and Everton.
> Burnley, in particular, had a good reputation for their
> youth policy. They were the league champions at the
> time [1960] and they had a special pitch for training.
> Everton also had a really good first team, with Alex
> Young and Jimmy Gabriel [they were to win the
> league in 1963], and they had a good youth policy,
> too, but I was always going to end up at Maine Road.

To the relief of his father, and with his flirtation with Eddie
Colman consigned to the attic of childish memories, John
eventually signed for City as an apprentice professional in
July 1962. Three weeks later he learned that he had passed O
levels in maths, physics, English language, French and history. His mother then wanted him to go into the sixth form,
but his father pointed with relief to the contract their son had
signed with City. As a sop to his mother, John began an
applied maths A level course, attending college one day a
week. Maths had been his best subject at school and it would
have been his route to university, but it was impossible to
maintain the requisite standard while polishing boots, sweeping the terraces and playing football at the same time. In
addition, when he was injured, he had to go to the ground for
treatment, rather than to college for applied maths instruc-
tion, and so the attempt to maintain some kind of academic
progress eventually fizzled out. Besides, it's unlikely that
Mike Doyle, Bobby McAlinden and the other apprentices
would have been too impressed. The management also knew
that success in football required total commitment and it was
never going to be compatible with an A level in applied maths.

McAlinden was an impish, creative, goal-scoring, pre-
dominantly left-footed inside-forward, of Irish immigrant

extraction, who was born on exactly the same day as George Best, in Belfast. Ironically, Bobby was born in Salford, the home of Manchester United's local support, but his entire family were dyed-in-the-wool City supporters. As a boy, Bobby didn't miss a City game (home or away) for four seasons. He grew up in the heavily Irish district of Delph and went to primary school at St Clements in Salford and then to Broughton Secondary Modern, near the Cliff. Impervious to the attraction of an A level in additional maths, Bobby McAlinden never wanted to do anything other than play football: 'I played for the school and went for trials with Salford Boys and played for them for two years from the age of thirteen. There was one really good player a few years before my time, a right-back called Albert Goulding. He went from Salford Boys to Bolton Wanderers, but he broke his leg and that finished his career.'

Ironically, despite the depth of the family's support for City, Bobby's first move was to Villa Park:

When I was twelve I had scouts from lots of clubs. Villa came first, then Wolves and City and United, Burnley and Bolton, but I ended up going to Villa. My dad took me to Wolves, but I preferred Villa. I should have gone to United – they and Burnley had the best youth systems – but I went to Villa because they were the first team to come for me and both my dad and me liked the scout. I liked what I saw – good training, good digs and so on – but I was a fifteen-year-old kid from Salford and I got really homesick and I came home and went to City. In the brief time I was at Villa, I became very friendly with George Graham, and we've been good friends ever since. I finished up playing against him in America, when he was playing for California Surf and I was playing for the LA Aztecs.

When the homesick teenager returned to Salford, his father contacted Manchester City. Bobby played in the mandatory trial game at Urmston, but Johnny Hart was clearly impressed, because Bobby was signed to associate professional forms faster than anyone except Alf Wood and Glyn Pardoe. Compared to the anxieties of David Connor and Chris Jones, Bobby's path to the City first team seemed remarkably smooth. His fellow apprentices were Mike Doyle (with whom he doesn't appear to have had an argument, making him almost unique), Ron Frost and John Clay.

Despite its proximity to Old Trafford, McAlinden's upbringing in Salford made him a recognisably local youth. Indeed, unlike United, who included two Scotsmen and an Irishman in their team, from the evidence of the Manchester City Youth Cup team of 1964, it appears that City didn't have a scouting system outside Manchester. Glyn Pardoe was known because of his rapid progress in the Cheshire schoolboy sides and, of course, his relationship to Alan Oakes. The only real foreigner in that City youth side was the goalkeeper, Alan Ogley, who came from that distant land across the Pennines.

Alan played for Barnsley Boys for three years, starting at the age of twelve, though he wasn't particularly tall for a potential goalkeeper. In fact, neither he nor Harry Dowd, with whom he alternated in the City goal for four years, commanded the penalty area with their physical presence, but we are now so used to the Schmeichel/James figures in goal it's a surprise to find that in the sixties such giant figures were rare. Ogley got his first chance because the goalkeeper for the Barnsley Under-14 side, Alan Hill, who later went on to play for Rotherham and Nottingham Forest, injured his shoulder playing for Barnsley Boys in the semi-final of the English Shield. A few days later, the Barnsley Boys Under-14 team were in the semi-final of the Yorkshire Cup and the twelve-year-old Ogley got the call to come and play for them. Barnsley won the Yorkshire Shield that year and Alan found himself on the ladder to stardom, playing for Yorkshire and subsequently for England at Under-15 level, with Glyn Pardoe and Albert Kinsey.

He also played cricket for England, both at schoolboy and youth level, and remains, uniquely, the only such 'double' international. His cricket career was nipped in the bud when his county told him, in no uncertain terms, that if he wanted to play cricket for Yorkshire and walk with the deities he had better forget all about this footballing nonsense. It was the start of the Close-Trueman-Illingworth-inspired Yorkshire domination of the County Championship and they could afford to be blasé. It was inconceivable in 1962 that the seemingly endless supply of raw, native-born talent would dry up, but the county soon came to regret its cavalier treatment of such a gifted young sportsman as Alan Ogley.

It wasn't long before the scouts came calling. Knowing that the great Bert Trautmann was approaching the end of his magnificent career, Manchester City, in the shape of George Poyser and Fred Tilson, were looking for a long-term replacement and settled on the young Yorkshire lad. Technically, scouts were not supposed to approach boys until they had left school, but it was a custom honoured more in the breach than in the observance. Certainly it meant nothing to Don Revie, who had just taken over at neighbouring Leeds United, who were then a mediocre second division outfit. On the groundstaff, however, were Eddie Gray and Peter Lorimer, and the new manager was able to discern the first green shoots of recovery. Revie decided that Ogley was to be his goalkeeper of the future. Alan, on the other hand, was unimpressed by the smooth talk of the scouts:

> I wanted to go and play for Barnsley. They were my team and I never missed a game, not since I was eight years old. The only time I missed a game was if I was playing away with Barnsley Boys and I couldn't get back in time. It was the club I always wanted to play for, and that's where I went, and inside eight months I was playing in the first team, in the autumn and winter of 1962, at the age of sixteen, because Alan Hill was injured.

Alan Hill's injuries were a recurring theme of Alan Ogley's early career. He played nine games for Barnsley, making his debut against Bristol Rovers at Eastville, where he had the game of his young life. By now he had grown a little and was five feet eleven inches and eleven stone in weight. Although Alan Hill regained his place in the first team when he had recovered from his injury, Barnsley had no doubts about signing Ogley to full professional forms when he reached his seventeenth birthday, in February 1963. As an apprentice he had been paid £7 a week and £1 appearance money, but as a full-time professional his wages were instantly doubled. Even on his apprentice pay, he had kept only £2 and given his mother £5. When he reached the dizzy heights of £14 a week, his mother insisted that she still wanted just £5. Alan was happy to give her whatever she asked for, but knew it was the unselfishness of his parents that had given him the start he wanted, because Don Revie had briefly made life very awkward in the Ogley household:

Don Revie offered my dad £5,000 and put a car at the bottom of the street and told my dad the car was his if I signed for Leeds. My dad just told Revie, 'Look, you can put whatever you like in front of me, but I'm going with what the lad says.' My dad earned eighteen quid a week down the pit. To my dad, five thousand quid was the world. I said to my dad I wanted time to think about it and Leeds said, 'OK, just give us a ring when you're ready.' I was sat in the house one day and I wasn't saying anything and my mum says, 'What's the matter?' I said, 'I don't know what to do.' She said, 'Do you want to go to Leeds or what?' I said, 'No, I want to go to Barnsley.' She said, 'That's OK,' and she put her coat on and went out to the phone box at the top of the road, because we didn't have a phone in the house, and she told Don Revie I wasn't going there. And that was it.

At the end of the 1962–63 season, which was the first year of the two-year apprentice course for Doyle, Clay and some of the others, City approached Barnsley for the signature of their young reserve team goalkeeper. Poyser had adopted the same persistent approach with Ogley as he had with Glyn Pardoe and his parents. In both cases it was successful, although Alan had displayed no desire to leave Barnsley. As a young professional, as opposed to an apprentice, he didn't have to go to the ground at Oakwell every day, so that once the season was over he was effectively on holiday. When the approach from Manchester City resulted in a formal offer, the club decided it was about time they let the player concerned know what was going on:

Johnny Steele was the manager and he came round to

103

the house saying they'd had an offer from Manchester City – I think that offer had been on the table for two years. I think City had left it there knowing they would come in for me as soon I signed pro forms. I'd turned them down as a schoolboy. It was a Friday in July and I was watching the Edgbaston Test match on television [England beat the West Indies by 217 runs] and the Barnsley manager said they'd accepted the offer and it was up to me, and that they wanted to meet me and my dad at Maine Road immediately.

The summer of 1963 was not a good time to be visiting Maine Road for the first time. The last home match had been the contentious 1–1 draw with United, the sickening realisation of relegation hung over the place like a noxious gas and the club was still licking its wounds before starting life in the second division:

> The place was like a morgue. That front is daunting. The glass is so thick. George Poyser was there to meet us and he put his cards on the table, saying that Harry Dowd was still their number one choice and I'd have to work to get into the side, plus, of course, Bert Trautmann was still there. Trauty was a big attraction in me going there. There were three great keepers to me as a kid. [There was] Lev Yashin – I saw him at Sheffield Wednesday in 1958 when he was playing for Red Star and he was dressed all in black and I thought that's what I want to be – and there was a goalkeeper called Dominguez, who played for Real Madrid at that time.

After Alan had signed for the club he met the chairman, who started to explain about the great traditions of Manchester

City. The history of the proud club fallen on hard times, however, made less of an impact on the seventeen-year-old than an inspired piece of public relations:

> The chairman said to my dad, 'Have you had the day off work?' My dad said, 'No, I don't work Saturdays.' But the chairman forced a hundred quid on my dad to cover him for the money he would have lost on his shift. That was a fortune to my dad, and I was on thirty-five quid a week then. Poyser said everyone in the first-team squad was on the same money after the abolition of the maximum wage. To be honest, I'd have been happy with twenty. He also said I'd have to fight for my place with Harry Dowd, but that was no problem.

At the age of seventeen, Alan Ogley was leaving the tight mining community of Barnsley in south Yorkshire and travelling across the Pennines into the foreign and possibly hostile territory of Manchester. He was the only one of that City youth team who wasn't able to live at home and, as we have seen with some of the others, it took some courage to make this move at such a tender age and at a time when English society was nowhere near as mobile as it is now. Although City knew that the lad would have to move into digs, it was discovered that nobody had made any arrangements and, although pre-season training was due to start the following Monday, it was thought that he would have to remain in Barnsley for a further two weeks until accommodation had been sorted out. In fact, Alan was so keen to get going with his new club that he insisted on starting with everyone else and, even though he had to move into the Beech Lawn Hotel in Dudley Road, the other side of Princess Parkway, near the Jewish Hospital, City graciously agreed to pay the hotel expenses. In retrospect, it should have been a clue as to the ramshackle nature of the administration of the club, who had just splashed out £8,000, a record transfer fee for a seventeen-year-old goalkeeper. In football, as in life, we tend to believe what we want to believe.

CHAPTER FOUR

First Love
1963–64

According to Philip Larkin, 'Sexual intercourse began in 1963/between the Lady Chatterley ban and the Beatles' first LP.' It was indeed an extraordinary year; a year which, in retrospect, historians have identified as the central hinge between one kind of Britain and the next. It wasn't just that many of the cultural phenomena which we loosely term 'the sixties' began in this year, but also that so many events of significance seemed to take place in both Britain and the world in the space of a few months.

In January 1963, Hugh Gaitskell, the leader of the Labour Party, fell ill and died quite suddenly, to be replaced by Harold Wilson, who was to dominate the political land-scape for the next thirteen years. Gaitskell performed an identical role between the time of Attlee and that of Wilson as John Smith did between the end of the old Labour Party under Foot and Kinnock and the emergence of the Blairite New Labour. Wilson made Labour electable again after thirteen years of what became familiarly known as 'Tory misrule'. Those of us born in the years soon after the end of the war had only really known life under a Conservative government, in same the way that those born after the mid-seventies did until 1997. In October 1963, Harold Mac-millan's health collapsed and as he entered hospital he resigned as prime minister. As the in-fighting raged, the Tory party effectively broke itself up and, by selecting the four-teenth Earl of Home as Macmillan's successor, the Tories brought to an end two hundred years of patrician Conservative leadership. When they regained power, it was under the grammar school graduates, Heath and Thatcher.

Macmillan's grasp on office had been grievously weakened by the effects of what came to be known as the Profumo Affair. The salacious press reports of the affair between the eponymous minister for war and a stunning-looking young woman of easy virtue seemed, at a stroke, to end the time-honoured deference due to cabinet ministers. The nation gawped at each successive revelation of depravity. The first murmurings began as the big freeze was about to start its thaw. The cautious but excited babble then rose to a tumultuous roar as Profumo admitted he had lied to the House of Commons when he stated there had been no 'impropriety' with Christine Keeler and he resigned at the start of June. Lying about government policy and spending plans is, of course, just politics, but lying about sexual relations with an attractive young woman is a resignation matter – or was.

Call girls, orgies in Mayfair and Cliveden involving, so it was rumoured, nine High Court judges, with one member of the cabinet waiting table in a slave's outfit bearing the notice, 'If my services offend please whip me,' another allegedly discovered *in flagrante delicto* in Richmond Park, the extraordinary linking of a West Indian immigrant hoodlum, a cabinet minister, a Russian attaché, spy rings and a society osteopath who provided the girls for those orgies – it all mixed together in the public mind. When the Commons debated the Profumo Affair, people queued for three days and nights for tickets to the Public Gallery, as if for the men's singles final at Wimbledon. When Lord Denning published his report on the whole unsavoury episode in the autumn of

1963, a crowd estimated at several thousand waited all night outside the Government Publications Office in Kingsway to be among the first to read it. They were not disappointed. It was the first government report to become a bestseller.

A week after osteopath Stephen Ward committed suicide rather than face the inevitable jail term a spiteful Establishment was preparing for him, the front pages were suddenly taken over by news of the greatest peacetime robbery in history. £2.5 million was stolen from the Royal Mail train. For the first time since the days of King John and the Sheriff of Nottingham, the instinctive sympathies of the majority of the country were on the side of the robbers. The audacity of the robbery, its scale and the fact that the victims appeared to be faceless, profit-seeking, exploitative bankers (with the exception of the driver who was coshed) all conspired to create a groundswell of public applause. It seemed to the beleaguered Establishment that orderly obeisant Britain was getting out of hand. When some of the robbers were convicted in early 1964, the court handed down prison sentences of thirty years. This was a vindictive punishment that made robbery a greater offence than murder, but it was symptomatic of a belief that Britain was changing and that the populace needed to see that the rulers of the country were still in charge. They weren't.

In March 1963, the polemical book *Honest to God* was published. It seemed to sweep aside the entire framework of the traditional teaching of the Anglican Church and became an instant bestseller. What was surprising was that it wasn't written by a defrocked priest or an angry atheist, but by the Bishop of Woolwich. That same month, Dr Beeching produced his long-awaited report on the railways, which effectively ended the transport system that had dominated Britain for 130 years. Half the stations and a third of the country's railway tracks were to be closed. It was official recognition that we had moved into the age of the motor car and the motorway. This was the new Britain, in which our young footballers were growing up, and 1963 was the year in which many of them were to make their first team debuts. Where were they on 22 November 1963 when President Kennedy was assassinated? Well it was a Friday lunchtime in Dallas, so the likelihood is that they were staring at the back page of the *Manchester Evening News*, wondering why the manager hadn't picked them.

The first thing Alan Ogley did after signing for Manchester City was to go back to Barnsley and propose marriage to his girl friend, Diane, whom he had met two years previously outside Oakwell. It was a shrewd move. The regular weekends back in Barnsley and the prospect of marriage did much to stabilise his life in a deeply insecure profession, keeping him out of the sort of trouble that habitually accompanies footballers with too much money and time on their hands. It also pleased the club, who liked to see potentially wild young men settling down as early as possible. (Keith Fletcher, the Essex cricket captain, believed that Derek Pringle's engagement helped to curb his young all-rounder of his propensity to bowl too many no-balls, but you'll have to ask Keith Fletcher exactly why, because I don't know.) When Alan Ogley returned to Maine Road it was by bus, which was slightly unfortunate because, nostalgia aside, the public transport system forty years ago was as inept as it is today:

> I walked in the ground, first day, late, because the bus from Barnsley was late. When I arrived there were lots of photographers there waiting for me. City had paid eight grand for me, a record for a goalie there. Johnny Hart met me in the tunnel – he became like my father, him and Dave Ewing. Johnny gave me my

gear and I got stripped in the reserve team dressing room and we got down to work straight away. I was a bit surprised. I'd been in the England international youth team, I was this record transfer fee, and I expected to be with the big boys, but I wasn't. Still, it was easier at City – apprentices didn't have to shin up the floodlights and replace the bulbs like we had to at Barnsley. First bloke to greet me when I got outside was Bert Trautmann.

Trautmann was on borrowed time. He had been sent off the previous September in a 6–1 defeat at home to West Ham United and played only four more times as the club slid towards the relegation trapdoor. Now Ogley was number two to Harry Dowd and Trautmann knew that, for all his achievements over the previous thirteen years, there was no room for him at the club. He played three games over Easter in 1964 and then bade his farewell in one of the best recalled testimonial games of all time. His generosity to Alan Ogley was very much in the character of the man. Towards Mike Doyle he wasn't quite so forgiving.

He had encountered the young Doyle for the first time on the Monday morning after the first match of the 1962–63 season, which City had lost at Wolverhampton by the humiliating score of 8–1. 'Hello, Bert,' the Stockport newcomer called out to him. 'How's the back?' This jokey reference to the number of times Trautmann had had to stoop to pick the ball out of the back of the net found no cheery reply. Trautmann had a somewhat Teutonic response to the light-hearted banter of the dressing room, despite being (or possibly because he was) the butt of a constant stream of 'Who won the war?' jokes. He might have to take it from Roy Paul or Ken Barnes, but he certainly didn't have to take it from Mike Doyle, whom he picked up with one hand, bashed against the wall of the dressing room and tried to hang by his collar from one of the pegs.

Ogley was to make his first-team debut in February 1964 and was the third of the City youth team to reach that mark. Glyn Pardoe had been the first, at the end of the 1961–62 season, and Alf Wood had been the second, over Easter 1963. Most of the apprentices were mercifully spared the general gloom that descended over the club as the 1962–63 season wore on. Doyle, Clay, Burrows and McAlinden could all clean the boots, sweep the terraces, go training, play snooker and turn out in the Lancashire League or the Central League without being greatly affected by the malaise that was paralysing the first team. The irony was that the closer they were to the first team, the more likely they were to be dragged into the depression that consumed players and supporters alike as the prospect of relegation loomed ever nearer. However, for the record, that year's youth team was just as inept as the first team. In December 1962, after a bye in round one, they were leading Sunderland through a Mike Doyle goal in round two of the FA Youth Cup when the weather caused the game to be abandoned. A week later, in the rearranged match, they were comprehensively outplayed and lost 0–4.

The defeat failed to put too much of a damper on the lads' spirits, though. John Clay recalls the lifestyle of the apprentices with some nostalgia:

The other apprentices were Doyle, Ronnie Frost and a lad called Geoff Howard, who lived above a fish and chip shop on the road going into Stockport – it's a Chinese now. There was also Bobby McAlinden, who was a bit of a gambler and became a big friend of George Best. That first season as an apprentice I was in plaster for two months. I started on £7 a week.

Laurie Barnett was the physio, Johnny Hart was the youth-team trainer and Jimmy Meadows was the first-team trainer. We had to sweep up, clean the boots, clean the dressing rooms and then we could go to town at lunchtimes, because we got paid in luncheon vouchers. That's where we met the United lads – people like Best and Sadler – because we played against them in lots of A and B and reserve team games and we all went to the Plaza when it was opened from twelve till two. That was where Dave Lee Travis and Jimmy Savile started. It was where the Odeon cinema stands today, but we went for lunch to the UCP on the corner of Whitworth Street and Oxford Road. We got luncheon vouchers, which were worth three bob, and the three-course lunch was three and three, so we had to pay the additional threepence. The Plaza was where I met my first wife, because she worked round the corner. We've since divorced.

Most of the apprentices lived this kind of lifestyle, although the amateurs like David Connor and Phil Burrows still had day jobs to go to. Glyn Pardoe and Alan Oakes, the country cousins as they were known, took their pleasures in their own way. Glyn remembers:

When I got into the first team I was on really good money, maybe £20 or £30 a week. I used to save most of it and that's why I could afford a car before I was eighteen. Mind you, I never went anywhere in it. Our idea of a night out was going to the Memorial Hall in Northwich – that cost us £1 each to get in. They all came there – the Beatles, the Stones, Billy J Kramer, Cilla Black, Gerry and the Pacemakers – before they were famous. Every Saturday a different group, that was our sort of night out, and during the week we'd go to the pictures. I was always away from Manchester. It suited my character.

There is something endearingly naive about the image of the United and City apprentices eating beans and chips together at the UCP cafe and listening to Jimmy Savile at the Plaza in their drainpipe trousers and winklepicker shoes. After lunch the two sets of lads would drift back to their respective training grounds, where it could be painful work, as John Clay recalls:

> We used to go the gyms then and we'd take on Dave Ewing and Jimmy Meadows and Johnny Hart, so it would be three against six at skittle ball, and they used to kick lumps out of you. We played with a hard plastic ball and, even though we'd whack it as hard as we could, if the ball hit them they wouldn't react, but if that ball hit one of us on the bare leg, it felt like your leg was broken.

Everyone remembers those games of skittle ball and head tennis against the coaches who would do anything to win. It certainly had the desired effect on Mike Doyle, who won a national competition at the game, beating Billy Bremner and Peter Lorimer in the final. His partner, ironically, was Neil Young, who is now remembered for never willingly heading the ball at all. The lads' professional lives revolved around Hart and Ewing and, to a lesser extent, the trainer Jimmy Meadows. McDowall and Poyser were distant figures. Glyn Pardoe confirms that Les McDowall was 'very quiet – almost invisible' and Mike Doyle thought they were solicitors when he met them on the day he signed forms at Maine Road.

They were always dressed in suits. None of the youngsters had much time for either McDowall or Poyser, believing them both to be out of touch with the players and, in Poyser's case particularly, to be grossly incompetent in the manager's job.

Given the atmosphere in the first-team dressing room and the endless trail of poor results, it's interesting to note how the groundstaff boys viewed the top players. Although the City crowd were disillusioned with the football they saw displayed by the first team, the apprentices all commented on the amazing skills of Joe Hayes, Roy Cheetham, David Shawcross and the rest. To be mixing with Trautmann and Harley on a daily basis, even though the club was on its way down, was a big thrill for the young lads, especially when their own self-worth was reinforced by the attitude of their friends and neighbours when they got home.

In the 1962–63 season, Alex Harley scored a remarkable twenty-three goals in forty league games in a failing cause, but what the apprentices remember is something the public never saw. Glyn Pardoe, who was only an occasional first-teamer that year, can still recall the flashy, brand new, blue Zodiac Harley owned, but what drove him crazy was Harley's privileged training routine: 'When we were lapping the pitch he'd be in the penalty area practising shooting – he'd smash it in the net one end, then run down the other and smash it in the net down there. We were running our cobblers off and he did nothing.' Mike Doyle confirms the fact that Harley was permitted to train by himself, but also has a strong memory of Harley coming in on a Tuesday morning, having flown off to Spain for two days to work on his sun tan.

Apart from Glyn, Alf Wood was the only other member of the youth side to make a breakthrough into first-team football in the relegation season. Bill Leivers, who had been a competent if unspectacular right-back for nearly ten years at Maine Road, had played most of that 1962–63 season as the regular centre-half. He was the latest in a long line of incompetents to attempt to fill the gap left by Dave Ewing, who had been such a stalwart of the successful Cup-winning side of the fifties, but who lost his form, then his place and was finally transferred to Crewe Alexandra in July 1962, before returning to help out with the youth side. By the middle of October 1962, City had conceded thirty-six goals in fourteen games. After the big freeze finally thawed at the end of March 1963, City were trapped in a relegation dog fight with Leyton Orient, Birmingham City and Manchester United.

On Good Friday, Leivers was injured in a 1–0 win over Nottingham Forest, so the following day reserve centre-half, Mike Batty, replaced him for the match at home to fellow strugglers Bolton Wanderers, which City also won 2–1. Batty limped off at the end of that one, so with the third of the Easter games due in two days' time, Les McDowall had no choice but to bring in Alf for his first-team debut. The return match at Nottingham Forest on Easter Monday night was drawn 1–1, with the prolific Alex Harley scoring the equaliser to give City an unusually productive holiday period with five points out of a possible six. Alf lasted only that one game before Leivers regained his place for a surprising 3–2 win away at Arsenal. Unfortunately, that was the end of City's triumphal march towards the mirage of survival. They lost the next five games, before beating Spurs at home in front of a full house, to set up the vital relegation derby with United.

Two of those five games featured Alf Wood. The first was a 3–0 home defeat by Blackpool, for whom Ray Charnley scored a hat trick, and the last was a 3–1 defeat at Villa Park, where Wood took a knock on his ankle and spent most of the game at outside-right, forcing Joe Hayes back into midfield. Alf recovered from the gloom of relegation quicker than anyone, because he was picked to play for England in the European Youth Championships, so he knew his star was continuing to rise:

> We went first on a tour to play Spain in Spain and then we went over to Tenerife to play there. Then it was the actual championship in Amsterdam. I scored the equaliser against Poland which kept us in the championship. I was still playing centre-half at this stage with Dave Sadler at centre-forward and Howard Kendall at right-half. We beat Ireland 5–1, which was very enjoyable, but then I got sent off against Austria in the semi-final. I went up for a corner and the ball went off one of their players for another corner, so I went to get the ball, but then I saw the ref was pointing for a goal kick, so I threw the ball back over my head so I could run back and defend, but the ref came over and booked me. Twenty minutes later I went up for a high goal kick with their centre-forward. I got to the ball first and headed it back and then the referee sent me off. The guy didn't get hurt or dive around – they didn't in those days.

It was Denis Follows from the Football Association who, later that night in the hotel, explained to a distraught Alf that apparently all the other semi-finalists had already had a player sent off so someone from the England side had to go to even it up. It was also Denis Follows whose smooth talking ensured a medal, which could otherwise have been withheld due to the sending-off, for young Alf.

The 1963–64 season started for Alf in the best possible way, with the newly promoted manager, George Poyser, preferring him for the centre-half position over Bill Leivers and Mike Batty. There is always the belief in August, when the sun is out (even in Manchester), that relegation is a blessing in disguise and that the team relegated in May is the most likely to be promoted back at the first attempt. There is more basis for this belief in today's money-fixated world, but in August 1963 it was perfectly possible to believe that a team comprising battle-hardened first division veterans such as Harry Dowd, George Hannah, Joe Hayes, Cliff Sear and Bobby Kennedy, with the promise of youthful wingers Neil Young and David Wagstaffe, as well as Alf and Glyn and the others, would provide the perfect combination for a fresh start. In front of 21,822 hopeful, optimistic supporters, City lost 0–2 at home to Portsmouth. For the second game of the season, away at Cardiff, Alf was dropped and didn't play again until the last day of November.

The real sensation on that first day of the 1963–64 season was to be found across the city. Their triumph at Wembley at the end of May and their narrow avoidance of relegation had convinced the Old Trafford faithful that the good times were about to roll again. Unfortunately, they played Everton in the Charity Shield on 17 August and lost 4–0. For David Sadler, it really was a blessing and there was no point in disguising it:

I came back after the summer break and went into pre-season training. I was hoping I might get to play in the reserves. There was no sign I might be in line for anything else, because the first-team squad was very large. Then Johnny Giles fell out with Matt and Nobby was also very unhappy about being left out of the final. After the pasting by Everton, Busby made changes. He left out Herd, Gaskell and Quixall, Giles was on his way and he brought in Ian Moir, Phil Chisnall and me. I was astounded.

Leaving out Giles proved to be one of Busby's few major mistakes. Giles was already unhappy at being played out of position on the right wing and didn't see why he should be made the scapegoat for the defeat by Everton. Giles had something of a reputation as a barrack room lawyer, a type Busby always hated, but Giles was so talented his manager had just about tolerated him so far. Now Giles was furious and demanded a transfer and Busby, to everyone's surprise, not only granted it, but sold him at a bargain price to Leeds United. Don Revie didn't even have to offer him a new car. In mitigation, Busby wasn't to know how rapid the rise of Leeds would be, nor the impact Giles would have at Elland Road. Thereafter, Busby was very careful how he handled future requests from talented players, as the disaffected players in the youth team would soon discover. It needed Howard Wilkinson to sell Eric Cantona to United for ten Green Shield stamps to redress the balance. However, at five minutes to three on that first day of the 1963–64 season, at the moment that Alf Wood trotted out at Maine Road behind John Benson, David Sadler was running out at Hillsborough between Denis Law and Bobby Charlton:

> I think I knew I was in a day or two before the match. We didn't see a lot of Matt during training. Jimmy Murphy was the one I saw. He'd taken it on himself to bring through players like me. It was Jimmy who told me. The team went up and there was my name. I was shocked. I suppose I must have rung home and told my father. I was aware when I got into the team that I was replacing David Herd, one of the senior players. He'd scored two goals in the Cup final and he wasn't very happy he was out of the team.

That is a typically modest Sadler understatement. Herd must

119

have been livid, but he was a good professional and fought his way back into the team in October to finish with twenty goals from thirty appearances. David Sadler's debut match against Sheffield Wednesday finished in an exciting 3–3 draw:

> Peter Swan marked me, and he was tough and hard, but I was through and past him and he just hacked me down. It was a very professional foul. That was my best chance in the game, but then we went on an unbeaten run so straightaway I was into training and travelling and playing with the first team. From then on I was part of the first team. It wasn't like Bestie. It wasn't as though once I got in I was never going to be dropped, [which Best was, of course] but I was learning my trade and I was part of things. Physically I was big and strong and George was scrawny. When he was out there he looked as though a puff of wind would blow him over. My physique got me through the reserves and allowed me to compete at first-team level.

David and George started to form a close relationship, nurtured by sharing digs at Mrs Fullaway's house in Chorlton. David had been living on his own, but the Belfast-born goalkeeper, Ronnie Briggs, whose last game for the first team had been in the spring of 1962, was on his way to Swansea Town and Sadler was quick to apply for a transfer to the sought-after Mrs Fullaway. Paying for digs was no problem for a young man who suddenly found he was, in relative terms at least, surprisingly well off:

> When I signed professional forms I was on £20 a week. They had just gone through the abolition of the

maximum wage, but I thought it was incredible to be on £20 a week at the age of seventeen. I mean, that was what Matthews and Finney had been on a couple of years before. Maybe the first contract was for less, but things moved so fast for me at that time.

Jimmy Murphy confirmed that Sadler had indeed signed for £20, but adds that he was puzzled when his first take home pay chit revealed that he had been paid a greater amount, even after deductions: 'His bank training caused him to think there had been some mistake in the accountants, so he handed it back. "What's this for?" he asked. I explained that he had qualified for extra bonuses for first-team appearances and this had boosted his pay far beyond what any teenager could expect, unless he were a pop singer.'

Life was sweet for the two young men, particularly when George made his own first-team debut against West Bromwich, on 14 September, after seven games of the 1963–64 season. David had already scored twice and retained his place in an unbeaten run. George gave the Welsh international full-back Graham Williams a difficult afternoon and David scored the only goal of the game in front of a crowd of over 50,000. Both of them were now earning first-team wages plus win bonuses and, most significantly, crowd bonuses: 'Some weeks we got really healthy wages. It came in cash in brown envelopes on Thursdays after training. Bestie and I by now were good pals and as soon as we had a few quid we'd show up to training in taxis. I didn't drive till I was twenty, so I used a lot of taxis.'

David's run came to an end after twelve matches in which he had managed only two goals. Albert Quixall regained his place, but David played a total of nineteen games in that first season, scoring five goals. It was by no means a spectacular start, but it was very satisfying to know that he was now in the first team and being seriously groomed for future stardom.

Ironically, George's first-team run lasted for just that one match, because he had only been filling in for the injured Ian Moir. Although the other players were polite to him in the dressing room, after the match he knew he hadn't played particularly well. In fact, the other players were being particularly generous, because even in that debut match George was already showing signs of one of the character traits that drove his team-mates crazy. No, not the drinking – it was not passing the ball:

> Once I got it I didn't want to give it to anybody, because I was so used to owning it in the youth team. So while my team-mates were screaming for it, I was trying to beat three or four opponents and doing all the tricks I was used to performing for my B team pals. At half-time Matt told me to move to the other wing, which probably saved me from decapitation [by the increasingly irate Graham Williams], though overall I don't think I played that well.

It wasn't until United suffered two bad defeats over Christmas 1963 that Best's career re-ignited. They lost 4–0 again to Everton and then went to Burnley and were hammered 6–1. For a team that had been challenging Liverpool at the top of the first division, these were two unacceptable results and again Busby was forced to ring the changes. Quixall and Shay Brennan were dropped and the two youth-team wingers, Willie Anderson and George Best, were chosen for the return game at home to Burnley. George had gone back to Belfast for the holidays and it required more than a text message on his mobile to get him back to Manchester. On the morning of Friday 27 December, a telegram arrived at the

Best home on the Cregagh estate, telling George to contact the club urgently. He was to jump on the first available flight back to Manchester where he was due to face John Angus, the Burnley full-back, on the Saturday afternoon.

Willie Anderson was with the first-team squad, but wasn't told that he would be making his debut until 11.30 on the morning of the match, when he was at Davyhulme Golf Club. By that time, it was too late to tell his parents who, like most of the parents of the boys in our story, didn't have a telephone, but someone in the tight Liverpool community where they lived must have heard the news on the radio, because the family immediately flew into action: 'They piled into a car and set off down the East Lancs Road. My sister at the time was nine months pregnant and she was so excited by the prospect of seeing her little brother playing with Best, Law and Charlton that she went into labour just as the car reached the Haydock Park roundabout.' Fortunately, in the midst of this major crisis, the Anderson family got their priorities right:

> Now there's lots of children in our family, but no one else had played for Manchester United, so they dropped her off at a hospital en route and carried on to Old Trafford. After the match they went back to see her daughter, Jane, for the first time. When I went to see them I took George Best with me and all the nurses went potty because, although he was still only seventeen and had played just a few first team games, he just seemed to have that amazing effect on girls – it was like Beatlemania. He was pretty cute.

Willie observed the pre-match routine at the golf club with fascination, feeling, inevitably, a little star-struck in the company of Charlton and Quixall, Foulkes, Setters and Cantwell:

They were playing snooker and drinking Coke. The things they did then, they'd never do now before a game. I was in awe of my team-mates and getting on the bus was wild. That was the biggest crowd I'd ever played in front of and running out on to the pitch with Bobby and Denis was amazing. It made the hair stand up on the back of your neck. Before the match started, in the dressing room, Bobby Charlton came over and said, 'Don't worry, son. Whenever you get the ball I'll be ten yards from you. If you're in trouble just give it to me.' I was up against Alex Elder and they warned me he might kick lumps out of me, but I don't think he did. Mind you, I like to think I was too quick for him to catch me.

United exacted due revenge for their Boxing Day humiliation with a resounding 5–1 win. The crowd got behind the team, cheered lustily for the new young wingers and lifted the whole team. To crown a perfect day, Willie laid on a goal for George. It was proof for the fans that the United youth team production line was back on track, and just the evidence Willie needed that his career at Old Trafford was about to take off. He was still a month short of his seventeenth birthday:

After the game I just couldn't wait to get home. I changed and made a dash to the station to get the train to Liverpool, just as I always did on a Saturday night. Every Sunday I used to go across the local playing field and watch all the games in progress, and on that Sunday after my debut I remember walking across the field and everyone was staring at me. It was a good feeling, but kind of strange. I was only sixteen and a nobody two days before. It made me realise what comes with playing in the Manchester United first team.

Willie stayed in the team for the next match, a 3–2 victory at Southampton in the third round of the FA Cup, but was then dropped until the beginning of March, when he was recalled for the 2–0 win at West Ham, because both Law and Charlton had been injured in the midweek draw at Sunderland in the sixth round of the Cup.

The teamsheets went up on Friday lunchtimes. For most of the youth team it was a question of whether they played in the A team or the reserves. Alan Duff developed a grimly realistic ritual of never looking at the first teamsheet, because he knew he'd never be on it. He always began with the reserve teamsheet, but discovered in the middle of January 1964 that he wasn't on that either: 'I assumed that I'd been dropped. Then I saw Bobby Noble wasn't playing either and then I looked across at the first team and saw that Bob and I were twelfth men for the first-team game at West Brom. That was the middle of the Youth Cup run. We didn't play, but it made us feel good.'

It was particularly appreciated by Duff, because he had just made the same career move that Roger Byrne had made ten years earlier and which David Connor and Glyn Pardoe were eventually to repeat:

In 1963 I was still playing outside-left, but when it got to my seventeenth birthday they never offered me professional forms. I was expecting it, but nothing happened. Nobody said anything to me. Not a word. Bobby had signed. It was during that time I was switched to full-back, when John Aston Sr said to try it out in an A team match, so I did and I went straight into the reserves. I'd played in the reserves as a

125

winger, but I was always in and out, but as soon as I switched to full-back I got into the reserve team and stayed there. I enjoyed it. We got crowd bonuses in the reserves – £1 for every 1,000 over 10,000. I liked playing full-back. I'm not sure I was ever a winger, even though I was in the reserves at sixteen. I wasn't a natural crosser with my left foot. It's just that I would play anywhere. There were a lot of wingers around at that time.

Duff played well at full-back and shortly after the switch was made the club offered him professional forms, to sign in January 1964 when he turned eighteen. Now he thought he had a chance of making it as a United player, for he had felt sure during the first half of the season that he was on the way out as a left-winger. The first game had been something of an eye-opener both literally and metaphorically: 'First game I played for the reserves was away at Wolves and their full-back kicked me into the stands. I picked myself up and said, "What the hell was that for?" I think it was George Showell and he said, "Nobody's heard of you. They've all heard of me." ' It must have been a huge relief to be doing the kicking himself, knowing he was now a full-fledged Manchester United professional, particularly since none of them had a clue about an alternative career: 'I couldn't think about doing anything else. Playing football was all I ever thought about. I always thought I was good enough. It would be someone else's decision to tell me I wasn't.'

That would come soon enough, but as the 1963–64 season progressed, Duff could enjoy himself, because Busby's one great philosophy was to encourage young players to express themselves on the football field. The team talks were exhortations to valour more than anything else:

In the reserves the half-time team talks were given by Johnny Aston or Wilf McGuinness, but Jimmy Murphy was often there as well. There was no tactics. If you'd played well or badly you'd be the first to know it. No blackboards, no worrying about the opposition. You didn't know who you were playing against anyway. A lot of them were first-teamers coming back from injury.

Joining Duff and Noble in that reserve team defence was Wilf Tranter, who played his one first-team game in the 2–0 victory at West Ham at the beginning of March 1964. Tranter was the centre-half who had taken David Sadler under his wing when the Kentish lad arrived in Manchester from Yalding. It was to be the popular Tranter's only appearance in a first-team shirt, a stunning fact that had to be absorbed not only by Tranter, but also by his friends and family, who must have been convinced that it was only a matter of time before he won a regular first-team place. In fact, Bill Foulkes, like Law and Charlton, recovered from injury in time for the Monday night second replay against Sunderland, so Tranter, like Anderson, went straight back into the reserves. That kind of unsentimental demotion also went with playing in the Manchester United first team.

A similar fate befell Glyn Pardoe. After the fifteen-year-old's spectacular debut in April 1962, he had been treading water. He played the first game of the 1962–63 season – the traumatic 8–1 defeat at Wolverhampton – at centre-forward, was dropped for two games and then picked to face Liverpool at Anfield, a game which City lost comfortably by the more respectable score of 4–1. For reasons that made Les McDowall a tactical genius, he was then dropped until after the big freeze, came back in for two games to replace his cousin Alan Oakes at left-half, was dropped again and then played one more match in that relegation season, but at outside-right. If he was looking for consistency, he wasn't finding it at Maine Road.

He must have thought that McDowall's 'resignation' and his replacement by George Poyser, who had been so determined to secure his signature, would presage a new dawn for him, but the 1963–64 season opened with Glyn Pardoe firmly stuck in the reserves with Alan Ogley. By now his versatility was starting to cause problems, because the management seemed unsure as to where to play him. Derek Kevan had arrived from Chelsea to take the place of Alex Harley, who had been transferred at a 250 per cent profit to Birmingham City, and in November Jimmy Murray arrived from Wolves. These two were to tie up the striking positions for the next eighteen months, so clearly doubts were already surfacing as to whether Glyn would be an automatic future choice as a striker. Kevan scored an astonishing fifty-five goals in only seventy-seven appearances. Glyn eventually forced his way into the side in November, but managed only five appearances in three different positions, before finally clinching a place in February and remaining there until the end of the season, making twenty appearances, but disappointingly only scoring two goals. What's more, those came in two of the last, meaningless, three games of a season that started poorly, but then promised much around Christmas, when the Murray-Kevan partnership was responsible for twenty-two of the twenty-seven goals City scored in an inspired spell of just six games.

After Glyn, the youth team graduate with the most performances that season, was Alf with eleven, but he lost his place in mid-February after a 4–3 defeat away to Charlton. Ironically, this was in the middle of the successful Youth Cup run, when Poyser was trying to encourage the youngsters on whom the club's future, and by extension his own, was believed to rest. Indeed, in that match at the Valley, Glyn played centre-forward, Alf centre-half and debuts were given to both Alan Ogley and the right-winger Ronnie Frost, who scored City's first goal that day.

Ogley was in because Harry Dowd had dislocated his shoulder the previous Saturday in a frenetic local derby against Bury, who had given a debut to one of their own youth-team players, a seventeen-year-old lad from the north-east called Colin Bell. It was Bell who opened the scoring with his first goal at Maine Road, and the embarrassment for City could have been even greater just after half-time, when Harry Dowd dived to save a second and probably clinching goal for the visitors, but damaged his shoulder in the process. Since there were no substitutes in those days, Dowd was strapped up and pushed out on to the right wing, while Matt Gray took over in goal.

Seven minutes from the end, and with humiliation beckoning, David Wagstaffe centred from the left, Derek Kevan hammered the ball against the bar and Harry Dowd seized on the loose ball to rifle it home before falling in excruciating agony on to his damaged shoulder. It looked like Alan Ogley might be in the first team for quite a long time, but after just two games in which his defence had leaked eight goals (an embarrassing 0–4 home defeat to Grimsby Town followed the loss at Charlton), Harry Dowd was pronounced sufficiently fit to return. Alan went back to the reserves knowing that time was on his side. He was right, as he was recalled to play in the last five matches of the season, so although he only made seven appearances that year, he felt sure City were pleased with the way he was developing.

It is hard to believe that Ronnie Frost had similar feelings of contentment. He had scored on his debut and kept his place for the 4–0 disaster at home to Grimsby. Although he was dropped, like Alan Ogley, after that humiliation, there was to be no recall for him that season – or indeed ever again. Bobby McAlinden, the youth team inside-left, had experienced something similar. He made his debut on the left wing at home to Preston, as a temporary replacement for David Wagstaffe. His story is a salutary lesson for those who see careers in football the way the Whigs saw history – as a linear narrative inexorably moving towards civilised progress:

> I got into the first team at City early – 19 October 1963, so I was seventeen. It was just about a month after Best made his debut (we were born on the same day) and he was dropped after that one match. I'd play anywhere – when you're a kid you just want to play – and I'd play in goal if I could be in the first team. I was happy to play inside-left or outside-left. Poyser picked me at outside-left, so that was fine. I remember we were 3–0 down at home to Preston and I hadn't touched the ball, but we rallied and scored twice and could have nicked a point, but we didn't. However, I thought I'd done enough and I was quite sure I would be picked to play the next week at Derby, but he brought Glyn Pardoe in and moved Neil Young over to play outside-left, and that was the end of it. Completely the end, as it turned out. It was all downhill from there. I thought I'd get back in, but I never did. Poyser never said a word to me. Nobody said anything to me. I was just back in the reserves.

This is the unforgivable sin with young players. Everyone can understand being dropped, especially if the youngster is temporarily replacing an established first-team player who reclaims his place when he regains his fitness, but to drop the lad after one match, without a word, seems unduly negative and unproductive. It may well be that, taken with everything else the management had learned about McAlinden, one game was enough to confirm that he was too small or simply not talented enough to make the grade, but if that was the case, somebody on the management staff should have had the courage to say that to him directly. Instead, he returned to the reserves and the youth team for another eighteen months before the axe fell.

As the Youth Cup competition progressed, it was clear there was some compensation to be gained in being in the youth team that year. Comfortable 4–1 wins over Oldham and Burnley (despite the acknowledgement of all the players that Burnley had one of the best youth development programmes in the Football League) were followed by a much tougher draw away at Preston, who were led by the redoubtable Howard Kendall. The future Everton half-back was already a star at England youth level and, at the end of this 1963–64 season, as most of our youngsters planned their holidays and wondered what the next season might bring, Kendall became the youngest player ever to appear at Wembley in an FA Cup final.

At Preston, City were handed a slice of luck by the weather. There must be something about the location of Deepdale, because David Connor's experience of the ground is almost entirely connected with fog. First, there was the frantic journey through the fog on Belmont to play for Lancashire Schoolboys, which directly influenced City's decision to sign him. Now, the Youth Cup was similarly affected by the weather: 'We played the first rounds at Maine Road, under floodlights, against Oldham and Burnley, and won easily. After a 0–0 draw at home the fog came down in extra time, when we were 3–2 down in the replay. We waited, but it was called off. In the second replay, Howard Kendall wasn't playing, because he'd been called up by the

Preston first team.' Alan Ogley compares the sudden descent of the fog to the passing of a steam engine leaving the ground blanketed in thick mist. They waited for it to clear, but, fortunately for City, it never did, and in the replay the following week they beat their opponents, who were unluckily, but significantly, weakened by the withdrawal of Howard Kendall, by the comfortable margin of 3–1.

In the next round, City hammered Middlesbrough 6–1, which brought them an extremely difficult quarter-final tie at Elland Road against the emerging Leeds United, which was made even harder when Alan Ogley returned with an injury from an England Youth game and had to be replaced by Mike Dobbs from Macclesfield Schools. In the Leeds goal was the future Scotland international, David Harvey, and he was surrounded by future stalwarts of the great Don Revie side in Peter Lorimer, Paul Madeley, Rod Belfitt, Jimmy Greenhoff and, particularly, Eddie Gray, who tormented the City youth team defence as he later did Chelsea's defence in the 1970 FA Cup final at Wembley.

David Connor recalls Don Revie 'chasing me after the game because he thought I handled it before we scored'. Revie never took kindly to losing at Elland Road, particularly when he had something to feel aggrieved about. John Clay believes Revie offered City £17,500 for him after watching his performance that night, but Poyser rejected it. Leeds went ahead after twenty-four minutes, but Chris Jones equalised before Bobby McAlinden put City into the lead. Leeds closed the gap, but Glyn Pardoe opened it again. The dogged Leeds again drew level, before Glyn headed the winner five minutes from time. It was a famous victory and gave the team great hope as they prepared to face United in the semi-final.

Bobby McAlinden remained friendly with George Graham, whom he had first met when he went down to Villa

Park for a trial at the time when Graham was a young apprentice from Scotland, also far from home. In the late nineties, when Graham was managing Leeds, Bobby returned to Elland Road and ran into Eddie Gray: 'I spoke to Eddie, who's on the coaching staff there, and who played that night. He said, "I remember you. I remember that night when you beat us in the Youth Cup."' Mike Doyle also has memories of Eddie Gray that night: 'Beating Gray and Lorimer was fantastic, and there was a really good crowd there that night. Eddie Gray stuck in my mind. Every time he got the ball we couldn't get it off him.'

Given the result of the semi-final, that thrilling 4–3 victory away at Leeds was the highlight of the season for most of the City youth team and the individuals took considerable pleasure in the performance of the team as a whole. Alan Ogley thinks that, with the exception of Manchester United, that youth team could have beaten any side on its day:

> We were all mates together and we knew we were a good side. We could all play; there were no weaklings in the team; we played as a team. Dave Connor wasn't the greatest footballer alive if you looked at his performances in league games, but he always tried his best and as a team player Dave Connor was a top man. Alf Wood wasn't the biggest centre-half, but he got up there and he won everything.

As you might imagine, Mike Doyle shares the general sentiment, but isn't so generous about certain colleagues:

> We stuck together if we were playing in the B side or the A side – down to earth Manchester lads, all of us. We didn't get involved in the first-team problems. As

groundstaff lads there was Bobby McAlinden from Salford, Bobby Cunliffe and Stan Goddard from Middleton, Alf Wood from Wythenshawe – who was a pain in the arse, a real big head he was – and John Clay and Ronnie Frost, the lads from Stockport.

City's Youth Cup run came to an end on 20 April 1964, when United completed their 8–4 aggregate victory. It was a blow for Johnny Hart and Dave Ewing, who had been with their lads every step of the way, and it was disappointing for them to note that the enthusiasm didn't seem to extend much further within the club. In fact, John Clay recalls that neither George Poyser nor Jimmy Meadows showed much interest in them at all: 'They were only interested in the first team, so their reaction to the youth team was all very low key. Harry Godwin came down to see us because half of that lot were his lads, [but we] didn't see Fred Tilson or Laurie Barnett. Johnny really hated losing.'

Like most of the team, Mike Doyle loved Johnny Hart and the two were re-united when Doyle made it to the first team and Johnny Hart rose to become first team trainer during the golden years of Mercer and Allison and eventually their successor as manager. If he had a fault, it was that he was a little too laid back, never capable of shaking up a dressing room. He was Alex Ferguson's temperamental opposite – a man more likely to pour a cup of tea for a player than hurl it at him.

After the semi-final defeat, there was at least one significant compensation for five of them, as Phil Burrows recalls:

Mike Doyle, Johnny Clay, Ron Frost, Chris Jones and myself all became full-time pros on the same day. Geoff Howard didn't make it. It was always a one-year contract with a one-year option for the club.

Poyser offered me terms with my father and my dad said, 'He wants more than that if he's going to give up his career as a quantity surveyor.' Then my dad got up and said, 'Come on, son. We're going.' I was panic-stricken, but I followed my dad out and as we got to the door Poyser said, 'Come and sit down.' It frightened me to death, but he offered me fifteen quid a week. It was worth it, but the anxiety of that moment terrified me.

At the end of the 1963–64 season, only Alan Ogley and Glyn Pardoe of that successful youth team had made it into the second division as regular first-team players, although it wasn't a major problem for those who were seventeen or eighteen and still with plenty to look forward to. Three out of the four Stockport boys who were signed in the summer of 1962 as apprentices were offered professional terms by George Poyser in the summer of 1964 – Clay, Doyle and Ronnie Frost – but Geoff Howard, who hadn't featured in the youth team, didn't make it and was released. The other three were offered a one-year contract at £12 a week, from which their parents benefited by £3 or £4. However, financial circumstances still forced them all to use public transport. John Clay certainly recalls leaving home at 8a.m. and catching the bus into Stockport, the train from Stockport into Manchester, and then the 76 bus down to Maine Road, to be able to clock on for nine o'clock.

The new professionals looked forward to the close season holiday and the start of their lives as full professionals when they returned for pre-season training in July, but for Alf Wood there was a niggling sensation that after a run of eleven games during the season he hadn't had a sniff of a first-team shirt since February. Although to a lesser extent, the same was true for Ronnie Frost and even Bobby

McAlinden's incessant chirpiness was a little dampened by the memory of that one solitary appearance back in October 1963. The club had finished a respectable sixth in the second division, but Sunderland and Don Revie's emerging Leeds United had taken the two promotion places and were in a different class to Poyser's City side, which looked pedestrian by comparison. Still, they had managed to get to the League Cup semi-final, where they lost 2–1 on aggregate to Stoke City, and at least the outstanding records of Jimmy Murray, who scored twenty-one goals in only nineteen league appearances, and Derek Kevan, who scored thirty goals in forty games, offered as much hope for the future as the best youth team City had ever developed.

Off the field, this was another troubled time in the club's chequered history. Although relegation from the first division did not necessarily trigger the automatic financial meltdown that ejection from the Premiership now appears to do, there is no doubt that relegation still carried serious financial consequences. Ironically, on the surface, it appeared as if City might weather the storm without too much distress. Before the start of the season, Alex Harley was sold to Birmingham City and Peter Dobing to Stoke for a combined fee of around £84,000 and, although crowds dipped, they did so only by an average of less than 7,000.

However, City were still incapable of managing their affairs properly. In March 1964, while United were playing in semi-finals at home and in Europe as well as chasing Liverpool towards the league championship, City were the subject of take-over rumours. Peter Donoghue, a City councillor and the socialist parliamentary candidate for North Fylde, offered to buy the club for £100,000 and to install Danny Blanchflower, who was just about to retire as a player, as the manager on an annual salary of £10,000. City's fixed assets at the time were estimated at £253,952, but their current assets at only £52,645. Meanwhile, a Forward City group was formed, a harbinger of similar movements thirty years later. Its initial meeting in the Lesser Free Trade Hall attracted a crowd of 500, with a further 400 locked outside in Peter Street. Fortunately, despite the fierce passions exhibited, there was no Orator Hunt to provoke a revival of the Peterloo Massacre, which had taken place on the same spot in 1819. City's massacres in 1964 were restricted to heavy home defeats by Sunderland and Grimsby Town.

City fans experienced a small measure of *Schadenfreude* when United lost their FA Cup semi-final 3–1 to West Ham United, in driving rain on a Hillsborough quagmire. Four days later they were knocked out at the quarter-final stage of the European Cup-Winners' Cup, after a catastrophic 5–0 defeat at Sporting Lisbon – on the very same day that the *Manchester Evening News* reported that the car of Les McDowall, the sacked City manager, had been stolen from a garage in Northenden.

Although United continued to chase Liverpool all the way to the finishing post, a 3–0 defeat at Anfield on 4 April effectively sealed Bill Shankly's first league title as manager of Liverpool. Two days later, George Best played in a 1–0 home win over Aston Villa, and two days after that he took the field against City in the first leg of the Youth Cup semi-final. On the Saturday, he was in the United first team which beat Sheffield United 2–1, and four days later he made his international debut for Northern Ireland in a 3–2 victory over Wales in Swansea. If you add in the next league match at Stoke and the second leg of the Youth Cup semi-final at Maine Road, Best played eight vital matches in the space of sixteen days. April 1964 must have been the busiest month in Best's entire footballing career, for the next week was even more pressured with his second international match against Uruguay, another league match against Nottingham Forest and the two legs of the Youth Cup final, making a further sub-total of four matches in six days. Matt Busby, like every other manager in 1964, made no complaints about his players being tired and no attempt to shield what was clearly the most exciting seventeen-year-old footballer in Europe from the trivial distraction of the Home International Championship or the FA Youth Cup.

United clinched the Youth Cup on 30 April 1964 with a 5–2 aggregate victory over Swindon Town. It was a memorable occasion and the United right-back Alan Duff still has fond memories of it:

> We drew 1–1 at Swindon in the final. Albert Kinsey missed an absolute sitter, but we stuffed them in the return leg 4–1. They only had one good player – Don Rogers. We'd had such little success in the past few years in the Youth Cup, we never expected to win it. When we won the cup, I remember being so elated I shook hands with everyone and ran off the field and went back to the dressing room and sat there by myself for a minute, taking it all in, until someone came in and said, 'What are you doing there? The medal presentation ceremony's starting.' I'd forgotten all about it. I wasn't used to it.

All the United players concede that Swindon Town were effectively a one-man team and that Don Rogers, the England Youth international, played United by himself. Dave Farrar thought that if they'd lost that Youth Cup final, considering the extraordinary talent United had at their disposal, they should have all been sacked. David Sadler concurs: 'Don Rogers had carried Swindon through almost on his own. I remember in the final I scored three, and none of them was from outside the six-yard box, but Bestie won it.

He was unstoppable.' Don Rogers had run poor Alan Duff ragged in the first leg, so before the start of the return leg at Old Trafford, Bobby Noble told his full-back partner to do to Rogers pretty much what Jimmy Murphy had told him to do to Ronnie Frost in the first leg of the City semi-final. It obviously worked.

For Busby, Murphy and John Aston Sr, winning the FA Youth Cup trophy was the proof they wanted that the next generation was on its way. After the near relegation of 1963, the FA Cup win, followed by second place in the championship and good runs in Europe and the 1964 FA Cup, suggested that Busby was on the verge of producing a third outstanding team to follow the Busby Babes of the mid-fifties and the Johnny Carey, Jack Rowley side of the immediate post-war years. All of them knew, however, that they needed the traditional production line of the youth team to ensure that the foundations of this third realisation of Busby's dream were properly laid. Best was clearly a prodigious talent and David Sadler had experienced a season in which he had won the junior World Cup with England, the FA Youth Cup with United, played nineteen times for the first team and travelled into Europe, so he was regarded as a near certainty for future success. For the others, there remained the one ingredient without which it would be impossible to contemplate any sort of career in professional football – hope. At the same time, there was already a queue of talented and just as hopeful youngsters forming behind them. How long would they have to force their way into that coveted first-team spot? There was no single, uniform answer for all of them, apart from the general response: 'Not long, lad!'

CHAPTER FIVE

Championship and Disaster
1964–65

At the start of the 1964–65 season, the *Manchester Evening News* replaced Eric Thornton, its long-time Manchester City reporter, with a bright young man who had previously been employed on the *Lancaster Guardian*, the *Sunderland Echo* and latterly the now defunct London evening newspaper, *The Star*. Peter Gardner was to remain on the City beat for nearly thirty years, alongside David Meek, who performed the same role for the newspaper at Manchester United for nearly forty years. These two men were greatly influential in the world of Manchester football. Gardner recalls:

> Eric Thornton had become almost a caricature of the popular conception of a journalist. Eric was losing his memory, if not his mind, and he had an ear complaint which affected his balance. He was a bit of a boozer as well and he'd go out at lunchtime and shout at the enthusiastic sports editor, a very nice man called Vernon Addison, 'Just going for a haircut!' And he'd come back at three o'clock, smashed out of his mind. Vernon wanted a new outlook on City and that's where I came in. He'd asked me twice to go on the paper, and I turned him down both times, and so when he asked a third time I thought I'd better take

it, because I thought I might not get asked a fourth time.

Gardner soon discovered, as City supporters had long suspected, that the *Manchester Evening News* was about as independent of Matt Busby as the *Catholic Herald* was of the Vatican:

> Tom Henry, the editor, was a United fanatic. He went to church with Busby and they were best mates. When he gave me the City job, he said in his gruff voice, because he was a big feller, 'You can say what you like about that lot.' In that first season City were knocked out of the Cup 3–1 at Shrewsbury and I wrote a very sympathetic piece. Vernon took me to one side and told me I'd been too soft on them and I needed to be a bit harsher. Next game, he said, 'Much better – you've got to pull no punches with them!' It was probably because all the focus was on United from Tom Henry. He didn't care about City and I could say what I wanted.

The story that Peter Gardner tells to illustrate the nature of the editor's United bias concerns a game played at St James' Park on 2 January 1960, when Newcastle United beat Manchester United by the overwhelming score of 7–3. The headline in the *Manchester Evening News* that night was: 'Reds in 10 goal thriller'. On the last day of the 1967–68 domestic season, only two teams could win the league championship – City or United, who were level on points, but City had a superior goal average. Peter Gardner reveals that two headlines had been prepared: 'United champs' and 'City champs':

> We had quotes from Matt, Jimmy Murphy and Louis

Edwards, and from Joe, Malcolm and Albert Alexander ready to slip into the paper. At 4.30p.m. City were leading 4–2 at Newcastle and United were 2–1 down at home to Sunderland. Tom was still insisting they use the 'United champs' headline. A compositor called Alan Wild asked Tom what was going on. He must have been a City supporter. Tom refused to concede it was over, so Alan Wild threw the United headline in the bin. Tom Henry screamed, 'No! There's still time for the lads to do it!'

Ah, the sacred freedom of the press!

Peter Gardner had been brought up in Blackpool and had developed his own dislike of Manchester United because they had defeated Blackpool 4–2 in 1948, in one of the best ever Wembley Cup finals. However, Gardner maintains that he was always a journalist at Maine Road and never a fan: 'My philosophy was I had been sent to report a football match, not a football team, because I had always wanted to write for a national paper, but the chance on the *Manchester Evening News* was too good to turn down.'

This was not too dissimilar from David Meek's position. His first job had been writing match reports for the *Yorkshire Post* about York City, where his father was on the board of directors. He had taken the opportunity to move to Manchester from York because in the fifties Manchester was a significant rival to Fleet Street as a centre of national newspaper production. Michael Kennedy, formerly the northern editor of the *Daily Telegraph*, bemoans the way Manchester's status has diminished:

Manchester has changed. It's not the city it used to be. The big change was when the newspapers all moved out of Manchester. When I first went to Withy

143

Grove it was the greatest printing place in Europe. Now it's the Printworks, a coffee shop. It was the *Sporting Chronicle* at first, then it became Hulton Newspapers, then Allied Newspapers, then Kelmsley Newspapers, then Thompson Newspapers, then Maxwell House. And why was the Halle Orchestra the best-known provincial orchestra? Because there were newspapers in Manchester and Neville Cardus wrote about it.

David Meek also managed to maintain a relatively objective attitude to the club on whose affairs it was his job to report:

I was always a journalist. One Saturday afternoon when United had been thrashed, not just beaten, they'd lost their heads and somebody had been sent off and it was mayhem, I just caught it right in my report for the *Pink*. The words had come and it flowed and after the game had finished I walked into one of the lounges with a big smile on my face and one of the United punters growled at me, 'What have you got to fucking smile about?' and I said, 'Well, it's been a great match, hasn't it?' 'What!' he screamed at me. And that's when I realised that what made my weekend was whether I had done well as a journalist and not whether the team had done well.

Meek had assumed his position in the aftermath of the Munich air disaster, when twenty-three lives were lost:

My first manager was Jimmy Murphy. He was under intolerable strain, trying to produce a team and going to funerals. It was impossible to establish a rapport with him at that time because he just had too much on his mind. They were all grieving for Tom Jackson [Meek's predecessor on the *Manchester Evening News* who had died at Munich] and the players. I was twenty-eight years old.

Murphy did an amazing job, holding the fort for Busby, who was fighting for his life in an oxygen tent in a Munich hospital, taking United to a second successive, though losing, Wembley Cup final. David Meek knew, however, that it was the return of Matt Busby that held the key to his future success as the *Evening News'* United reporter:

When Busby came back from hospital, I was introduced to him, because I had never met him before. I felt quite overwhelmed by him and what he had been through. Not only had he lost so many of his players and his staff, but he had also lost his press corps. I think eight journalists had been killed and Henry Rose [the *Daily Express* reporter] was in hospital. That was like another team. There were all these guys wanting to write about his club, and they were all strangers, and I was very conscious how difficult that must have been for him. When he talked to his players he must have seen in his mind's eye Tommy Taylor and Duncan Edwards and Roger Byrne and all those old players who were no longer there. When he talked to the new press he must have seen the likes of Alf Clarke and Tom Jackson and Donny Davies. They were all senior journalists and the number ones on their papers, so I always felt very awkward with Busby, and it took me a long time for me to relax with him. For years I always felt that to be in his presence was rather like being summoned to see the headmaster at school.

The irony of it all is that Peter Gardner always got along famously with Busby and during the sixties he ghosted Busby's weekly column in the paper, while Meek performed the same task for Malcolm Allison.

Busby was surprisingly sensitive to criticism as a manager and Meek had half a dozen summonses to explain why he'd written certain stories. In 1959, their first full year together, the transfer of Colin Webster was to prove the occasion of their first major spat:

> I spoke to Colin, who told me he didn't want to leave the club. He talked about Matt forcing him out from the club he loved, the only club he wanted to play for, and so on. I ran this story and Matt was really unhappy. 'What are you trying to say? What do you think you're playing at? You know I have to get this lad out of here and you're making him into a hero and telling everyone that I'm forcing him out.' Busby was anxious lest it appear that he was being the ruthless manager.

When relegation threatened in 1962–63, Meek could hardly avoid discussing the dreaded topic. Even in those days, many clubs who were relegated parted company with their manager at the end of the season and, astonishingly, despite what he had achieved at Old Trafford, Busby felt himself far from immune. Meek believed he was duty bound to raise the issue with the United chairman, Harold Hardman, but expected to be told the rumours were ridiculous:

> That was what I expected to write, but when Busby heard I'd been to see the chairman he summoned me and said, 'Don't you dare ever to go behind my back and talk to the chairman. I know what you're up to.

You're trying to get the chairman to say, "Busby faces the sack if results don't improve." ' I said, 'How can you even think that? What I was going to write was the exact opposite. I was looking for a genuine vote of confidence.' Busby was so sensitive he thought I was 'making mischief'. The story I eventually wrote was, indeed, that Matt Busby had the full backing of the chairman and the board. Maybe Busby's intervention was to ensure I wrote the story his way.

If Meek thought he would be assimilated into the United family he was in for a big disappointment, and he was constantly frustrated that Busby remained such an emotionally distant man. Once you get past the adulation of Bobby Charlton, you find that such a judgement was common among most of the players who worked for him. Manchester United was Matt Busby's club, his patronage was an essential element for anyone who wanted to succeed anywhere in the club. Yet for all his success, he was still insecure and fearful of the board of directors, as Meek's story illustrates so vividly. As a player, Busby had kept his head down in the dressing room and observed the petty jealousies, the betrayals and the sharp practices, but to promote his belief in the poetry of the beautiful game, it was frequently necessary for Busby to recreate all the comfort and *bonhomie* of the court of the Borgias in Renaissance Italy.

David Meek, who seems on brief acquaintance the most easy-going and courteous of men, was quite deliberately excluded from Busby's inner circle:

I was always disappointed that Matt didn't teach me more. He was always so distant. I'd have liked for him to have taken me into his confidence more and explained what he was aiming at. From his point of view, it would have allowed me to appreciate what he was trying to do. He wasn't what you would call a close man. There was almost a resentment on his part, I always felt, that I would not have been there had it not been for someone getting killed. I found that very difficult to break through. I couldn't talk to Tom Henry about it, because Tom was completely in Matt's pocket. I remember getting a letter from Tom one Christmas time saying, 'We are pleased to raise your salary by one guinea. I have spoken to Matt and he tells me you are doing a good job.' I realised then how important it was not to fall out with the club.

Meek's first years as the United reporter for the *Evening News* were as difficult on the pitch as they were off it. Busby knew perfectly well that great teams are not constructed overnight and, combined with his serious injuries, the prospect of starting all over again from scratch was sufficient to cause him seriously to contemplate the possibility of walking away from football forever. In the event, he did return to Old Trafford and life was indeed just as difficult as he had anticipated. In the 1958–59 season, the first full season after Munich, twenty-nine goals from Bobby Charlton, twenty-one from Dennis Viollet and sixteen from outside-left Albert Scanlon, all three of them survivors of the crash, helped United to second place in the league, which went a long way towards eradicating the memory of a humiliating 3–0 defeat at third division Norwich in the third round of the FA Cup.

However, in 1960 it all started to go wrong. Beaten at home in the Cup by Sheffield Wednesday, United slipped to seventh in the league, a position they could not improve upon the following season when they again went out of the cup in the early rounds at home to Sheffield Wednesday, this time by the memorable score of 7–2. By now, Wednesday must have felt they had exacted sufficient revenge for the 3–0 defeat they experienced at Old Trafford when they were the sacrificial victims of United's first match after Munich, much to the edification of the 60,000 United supporters at the game and the 600 million all over the world who had been supporters for exactly a week and a half. The catalogue of Busby's despair lengthened – a miserable fifteenth in the first division in 1961–62 was followed by the narrow escape from the disaster of relegation in 1962–63.

The players he signed to replace the martyred heroes of Munich were not in awe of him the way his beloved Babes had been. Albert Quixall, the 'Golden Bollocks' of his day, cost £45,000, but never became the subject of crowd adulation as had been anticipated. He also attracted considerable scorn from his team-mates for his performance on the field and justifiable outrage for defecating into other players' boots as a 'practical joke'. The dressing-room atmosphere was poisoned by the personal animosity between Harry Gregg and Bill Foulkes, and between John Giles and David Herd. Law and Charlton were understandably heroes to the United supporters, but there was no great love between the two of them, and when Best joined the holy triumvirate matters scarcely improved.

Busby was unable, or unwilling, to sort out the dressing room and both Maurice Setters and Noel Cantwell were constantly amazed at Busby's tactical naivety. The manager's much-vaunted exhortations of 'Go out there and express yourselves' and 'Make sure you give it to a red shirt' were deeply unimpressive to a graduate of the West Ham academy, where morning training sessions were followed by afternoons at the local cafe arguing with Malcolm Allison about tactical formations with the use of the cruet.

The camaraderie of the Babes era was lost. Bobby Charlton drifted sadly out to the left wing, where his goal tally slipped into single figures, and Denis Law arrived from Torino for £115,000. This was a huge gamble by Busby, for it was a sum the perennially parsimonious Manchester United board felt that the club could not really afford. In fact, they had a case. In Law's first season, despite the twenty-three league goals he scored, the club was nearly relegated and Manchester United could scarcely wait until one of their youth teams produced the fruit ripe for plucking which Jimmy Murphy had always promised to Matt he would provide. That's why the youth team of 1963–64 meant so much to Busby; that's why the seven lean years that had elapsed since their last Youth Cup triumph had hurt so badly; and that's why the youth-team players knew it was so important to Murphy and John Aston Sr that they beat City and went on to win the cup.

If the seven years of famine were not exactly followed by seven years of feast, it remains true that the years 1964–68 saw the final flowering of Busby's genius. In 1964–65, United won the first division title (on goal average from the newly promoted Leeds United) for the first time since 1956–57 and reached the semi-final of the FA Cup, where they lost 0–1 to Leeds after a replay at the City Ground, Nottingham. They also reached the semi-finals of the Inter-Cities Fairs Cup, the precursor of today's UEFA Cup competition. The trouble-makers were moved on. Maurice Setters, after 193 games, was transferred to Stoke City during this season and Noel Cantwell lost his place to his fellow Irishman, Shay Brennan, making only two appearances during the whole season, both of which came in the middle of a run of seven consecutive victories during April 1965. John Connelly was bought from Burnley and was an outstanding success, scoring fifteen goals and playing in every league game of the season. Brennan, Dunne and Foulkes also played in all forty-two matches, while Stiles, Charlton and Best each missed just one match.

On this solid foundation that allowed the youth squad to develop was the championship team built.

The next stage of the youth team's development was the Blue Stars Under-20s tournament in Switzerland, to which United sent a team nearly every summer. While circuit training at Old Trafford in May 1964, Dave Farrar was badly injured:

> One of the circuits involved jumping over the wall into the paddock and running up the steps, in the days when you could do that sort of thing. I jumped, but I landed badly and went over on the ankle. I had to pull out of the tour, and David Sadler moved back to centre-half, and that was the beginning of his second career. I did him a big favour. That was the start of my finish.

Sadler confirms that this was his first experience of life at the back and that he enjoyed it:

> The actual games were all played in a day. Eight teams, eleven-a-side, possibly not ninety minutes. It was physically very hard, but it was youth players, and it was all part of your development. We were all set to go there one summer when Dave Farrar broke his ankle and we didn't have a centre-half. It's funny – and you saw this in training all the time – goalkeepers, for example, when you start playing five-a-sides for twenty minutes at the end of training, one touch or two touch games, the goalies never wanted to play in goal and full-backs wanted to be strikers and strikers were defenders. Some people didn't bother, but others would make something of it. I was now playing defensively, it was just something I did. I enjoyed it,

to be honest. Anyway, on this tour to Switzerland they decided I would play at centre-half. We did OK and I did OK, so when we came back for pre-season training I was starting to play at the back.

The move was not immediately successful. David Sadler made six appearances in the first team during 1964–65, three games at the start and three over Christmas. All were at centre-forward. There was only one goal, which came in a 2–2 draw at Leicester City. First-team action as a regular centre-back didn't arrive for another two years.

Thirty-five years ago there was a concept known as a 'first team', which comprised eleven players. This perfectly adequate concept has recently been subdivided into today's current jargon of the 'first-team squad' and the 'starting eleven'. United had a starting eleven that year comprising Pat Dunne; Brennan, Tony Dunne; Crerand, Foulkes, Stiles; Connelly, Charlton, Herd, Law and Best. Nobody really got into that team unless someone was injured and when they did the crowd wasn't exactly thrilled. David Sadler recalls hearing the groan of disappointment when the team changes were announced: 'At number nine on your programme, instead of D Law, please insert D Sadler.' The crowd felt cheated. It was like paying £37.50 per ticket to sit in the stalls and watching the dreaded appearance, two minutes before curtain-up time, of the stage manager in a rented tuxedo announcing, 'Owing to the indisposition of Dame Judi Dench, the part of Cleopatra at this performance will be played by Gladys Bagshaw.' Sadler says:

All the way up till I hit the first team, I always scored goals at will. Going back to school days, then at county level, and on from there at seventeen or eighteen. I was six feet tall and I'd been big and strong for the past four years, so some of those goals you can account for because of that. I was big and good in the air and I had some ability, so take it all together and that's why I had no difficulty scoring goals at all levels. Even at international amateur level I'd score goals all the time. When I hit the big time, that was the first time the goals dried up. Good players make themselves time. I'd found my level. As a goalscorer. The first division was a step too far for me. I was playing regularly in the reserves and still scoring there but I wasn't playing regularly in the first team, so you'd say to yourself, 'If I had a run of ten to fifteen games I'm sure I could do it,' but that didn't happen till the end of the 1965–66 season when I scored four.

Three of the youth team heroes of 1964 made fleeting appearances during 1964–65. On 3 January, in the third round of the FA Cup, Albert Kinsey, whose hat trick in the home leg had effectively settled that Youth Cup clash with City, made his long-awaited debut in place of the injured Denis Law in a rather nervous 2–1 victory over fourth division Chester. Kinsey was the oldest player in that youth-team clash and in his twentieth year he must have thought the call to first-team action would never come. We can imagine his pleasure as he sat in the first-team dressing room and pulled on the shirt. We can be sure of his delight as he scored the first goal, the other coming from George Best. Even though he was back in the reserves the following week, when Denis Law reclaimed his place, he must have thought that he had done enough to warrant future opportunities. We can therefore be absolutely certain that he was as sick as the proverbial parrot when it slowly dawned on him that he was never going to get another chance. When he left United the following year, it was with the statistic of one goal in a total of one appearance and an understandable sense of injustice.

Centre-half Dave Farrar didn't even get that far, though there were more comprehensible reasons. At first, he seemed to be recovering well from the broken ankle sustained at the close of the 1963–64 season, when David Sadler played in his position in the Under-20s tournament in Switzerland:

> I came back in July for pre-season and the training was good for us and I still had another year to play for the youth team. There was one stage when I knew I was playing well in the reserves and Wilf McGuinness said to me that I'd nearly got a game in the first team the previous Saturday. That was my good spell, when everything was going well. In the reserves, Harry Gregg was in goal and Noel Cantwell was one of the full-backs, Jimmy Nicholson and Nobby Stiles were the wing-halves. You were bound to look good with those guys next to you. There was always someone covering me.

Unfortunately for Dave, this good spell didn't last and one reason for his loss of form was that he simply stopped growing. He had been a massive five foot eight at the age of twelve and didn't gain an inch thereafter. John Aston remembers that Farrar 'was like a giant at fifteen. He was a big lad at school and I used to look up to him – literally – but then he never grew. By the time I was seventeen, I was looking down on him. He didn't grow at all in those two years. He just wasn't tall enough to become a centre-half at United.' The club decided to try him at wing-half, where his lack of height was less of a problem, although the competition for first-team places with Crerand and Stiles in

possession and John Fitzpatrick and Maurice Setters
pushing hard meant that he was effectively another step
back:

> I started to lose it a bit then. That second year of my
> apprenticeship fell a bit flat. I think Fitzy stayed with
> the youth team, and Peter McBride and Jimmy Rim-
> mer, but Duff and Noble couldn't. John Aston could
> because he was the same age as me – born in 1947.
> Willie Anderson was young, so he must have been
> there, but we got knocked out early on by Everton.

For most of the youngsters, playing football for Manchester
United was all that mattered in the world. For all of them,
playing football was certainly the most important feature of
their lives. Except for one. Dave Farrar could simply never
work up any enthusiasm for it. Even at school, his headmaster had to force him to play for England at Wembley
and his memory of the occasion is a trifle jaundiced: 'As a
schoolboy international I played in front of 100,000 people,
and afterwards we were shown round the House of Lords,
and then we went to a banquet, where there were a lot of
long speeches. Every so often someone had to be carried
out with cramp. It was a nightmare.' Dave Farrar never
made it as a footballer because he lacked the two basic
ingredients – height for a centre-half and self-belief for any
position:

> I never had the passion for United that others had. I
> lost all my enthusiasm for the game quite young and
> after I left United I never went to watch a game. It's
> only in the past ten years or so I've bothered to notice
> what's going on. When Busby said to me, 'We're
> going to have to let you go, son,' he asked me what

went wrong. 'I don't understand. You had it all.' I just said, 'I don't know, Boss.'

A further problem was that Farrar never much cared for Matt Busby and was never seduced by his charisma or impressed by his reputation:

I always thought Busby was overrated. He was aloof. He wasn't as good as everyone thought he was. The Eamon Dunphy book [*A Strange Kind of Glory*] is a true portrait. Jimmy Murphy was more down to earth. He was the one who'd make the time to talk to you and encourage you. Busby didn't do that. He just bollocked me after I got sent off.

The dismissal occurred in an A team game against Blackpool at the Cliff:

This forward was winding me up all game, telling me what he was going to do to me, so I let him have it. I got a right bollocking for it from Matt Busby. I was quite shocked. He said, 'You don't do that, son.' He said, 'What you do is kick them, pick them up and say you're sorry. Do it hard, do it properly and then say sorry. Dave Mackay is the best example. You watch him.'

It never seemed to occur to Busby that the fact that the Blackpool centre-forward had also been sent off might have suggested that Dave wasn't the sole culprit in the incident. He says:

My complaint about the United management was that they treated everyone the same. They didn't seem to understand that some players need an arm round the shoulder and some need a slap across the head. They hadn't got a clue. It was bad man-management, but I'm not blaming that for my failure – that was due to my lack of talent and my lack of enthusiasm.

It is clear from talking to all the players that they regarded Jimmy Murphy as the beating heart of Manchester United. Not many of them speak too fondly of Busby. Like many managers of his generation, Busby had sour memories of the way he had been treated as a player and he wasn't about to bring a halt to the tradition of underpaying footballers, despite the abolition of the maximum wage. In 1961, when Johnny Haynes was celebrating his status as the country's first £100 a week footballer, the United players were stunned to be told that, for them, the bright new dawn would mean their wages would be raised from £20 to £25 a week. Dave Farrar believes that United were the worst-paid team in the first division: 'That was all to do with Busby. I used to get lifts from the ground to the Cliff off the likes of Pat Crerand and Nobby Stiles and they'd always be complaining about the lack of money. When Johnny Giles moved to Leeds he was suddenly on megabucks compared to the United lads he'd left.' It is certainly true that Busby and Shankly arranged an unofficial maximum of £35 a week, so that none of their players would be tempted to drive to the other end of the East Lancs Road in search of a better financial deal.

Clearly, Dave Farrar knew that his days at Old Trafford were numbered:

Before I got the chop there was a lot of whispering going on, a lot of rumours. It's like redundancies in any other business. You can sense when something like that's coming on. It never bothered me getting the chop. Busby told me on my own. He pulled me to one side just before the end of the season and said he was letting me go at the end of the season, which was a couple of weeks away. United would circulate my name on the open-to-transfer and unretained list and see what happened.

Ironically, because of his less than fully committed attitude, Dave was released, but he was less than fully committed because he had a greater love than football waiting for him elsewhere. When the other lads were off to the Plaza dancing to Jimmy Savile or playing snooker or on the golf course or chasing girls, Dave Farrar was in blue overalls under a car:

I used to work at the garage in the daytime and then I'd go over to a mate's house and we'd work on cars together till nine or ten o'clock at night. I was dedicated all right, but to cars not football. Taking tracks off bulldozers was fun. I never drank. I had done at fourteen or fifteen, but not when I was working with the cars. I used to go to work with my mate on a Saturday for nothing, just for the pleasure of working with trucks and bulldozers. The boss of the garage said, 'Do you want to come here as a full-time mechanic?' and I said yes. I went part-time professional with Southport, but then I got a kick in the part where I shouldn't and I had to have a hernia operation. The doctor told me I wouldn't play again that season and, by the time I was fit again, Southport had stopped employing all part-time professionals. Then I went to Winsford in the Cheshire League and I stayed there till I was about twenty-two.

Dave Farrar was the first of the United youth team to make

that journey down the divisions and into non-league football, but in his case there wasn't the sadness, the feeling of what might have been, which accompanied the others who didn't make the grade: 'I kept in touch with Jimmy Ryan, but I had no feelings of envy or jealousy or sadness when I saw what was going on with the other lads at Old Trafford, because I just loved what I was doing with the cars.'

The next to attempt the big step up was John Fitz-patrick, who filled the breach at left-half created by an injury to Nobby Stiles in February 1965. Fitzpatrick played well enough in the 1–0 defeat away at Sunderland, but recognised that he was unlikely to displace either Stiles or Paddy Crerand on a permanent basis in the foreseeable future. On the last day of the season he came in for Crerand, for the celebratory match at Aston Villa. It didn't matter if United lost the game because, after a remarkable run of seven consecutive victories, even if they did lose they would still secure the championship on goal average. They duly lost 1–2.

John Fitzpatrick spent the close season in a considerably happier frame of mind than Albert Kinsey, though, because he was sure he still featured, as they say, 'in the manager's plans'. After the deafening silence that had followed his solitary appearance for the first team in the cup match against Ches-ter, Kinsey could harbour no such illusions. Jimmy Rimmer was also a long way from the first team with Pat Dunne, Harry Gregg and David Gaskell all standing between him and first-team glory. However, as a goalkeeper and the baby of the youth team, he had time on his side in a way that the outfield players never did. If he needed encouragement, he got it in full measure from Harry Gregg, who constantly reiterated his belief that young Rimmer was the most natu-rally talented teenage goalkeeper he had ever seen. Gregg was to become the first real specialist goalkeeping coach in the game and was Rimmer's personal mentor for many years.

Two months after John Fitzpatrick made his debut, John Aston also received the call. On 12 April, on the morning of the home match against Leicester City, in the middle of the seven-victory-run which secured the championship, Denis Law was struggling with an injury and Aston was ordered to meet up with the rest of the first-team squad at Davyhulme Golf Club. That in itself was nothing to get worked up about. In the last season before substitutes were used, young players were frequently summoned to undergo the experience of the first team's matchday preparation. Indeed, John Aston had already been through it before:

> Denis Law was in and out with injuries and he didn't know if he was going to play, but then he played, so I didn't know I was going to make my debut until I went in for the pre-match meal and Busby came over and said Denis had failed his fitness test and I was in because I was already in the thirteen. It had happened three or four times before and Denis had always passed the test, so I just sat in the stands and watched the match. They must have had a bit of a shuffle around because George went into Denis's place and I was at outside-left.

He wasn't overcome with nerves, despite the closeness of the scoreline:

> I really enjoyed it. Throughout my career the bigger the match, the more I enjoyed it, and my debut at home to Leicester was a big match for me. You know, playing for a club isn't like supporting it. You get an initial shaking of hands and people saying, 'I hope you

do well,' but it's still a team of individuals and you had to learn the ropes very quickly or you were out. It wasn't a question that people wouldn't pass the ball to you or anything like that, but you'd quickly to make yourself into a competent member of the team to be accepted. It went all right, we won 1–0 and I hit the post. The match just whizzed past.

David Herd scored the only goal of the match in front of 34,114 spectators, a disappointingly modest gate considering the team were playing so well, and United were only two weeks away from their first championship success since before Munich. Like John Fitzpatrick, John Aston was another of the youth team who could spend the summer confident in the knowledge that he could look forward to a bright future at Old Trafford. This confidence was boosted when he started the first game of the following season at outside-left, with Willie Anderson on the opposite wing: 'I think at that time I thought I'd always be at United – it was my club – and we'd always be successful. Subsequent years, of course, proved all those things wrong.'

Aston faced a unique dilemma. His father was the youth-team trainer and unless the talent was as unmistakable as that of George Best, somebody, usually the person who had to make way for him, could always be relied upon to start muttering about nepotism, although the word itself was unlikely to feature too often in the vocabulary of professional footballers. In fact, if anything, John Jr, like Alec Stewart in the England cricket team of the late eighties and early nineties, suffered from the reverse of favouritism. Far from being given the benefit of the doubt, he would have to prove himself over and over. It was, as David Sadler noted, a phenomenon the more intelligent of the players frequently observed:

I thought John Jr handled all that pressure really well. You could sense there was some resentment around the place whenever John got picked for the team – whatever team – youth or first team. If he got picked, then someone was left out to make way for him, and you could always hear that player and his pals muttering about it. 'He's only playing because his dad picks the team' – that sort of thing. John Aston Sr seemed such a straight and honest guy, I couldn't imagine he would even dream of doing anything like that. John Jr was in a difficult position, because it was him or someone else. He wasn't that outstanding a player that he was an automatic pick. There would always have been a choice between him and somebody else.

One way Aston made life easier for himself was by becoming a dedicated trainer. In the runs and the abdominal exercises he was always in the leading pack. Willie Anderson, who was in competition with John for the wing positions, is genuinely complimentary about his rival:

I liked John Aston a lot and respected him, too, even though we were in competition for the winger's place. He was a really great kid. He had that problem with his dad, but he worked his brains out. We'd go training and come back to Old Trafford and then he'd do 400-yard laps round the stadium when we'd all finished. He put in a lot of effort to get where he got.

Nobody could ever complain about his lack of commitment. Unfortunately, the crowd found quite a few other things to complain about, but at the end of the 1964–65 season John

Aston would certainly be included among the group who were likely to succeed.

Success of any description was thin on the ground for Manchester City in 1964–65. A guarded optimism had greeted the new season. The previous year had seen the establishment of seasoned professionals Derek Kevan and Jimmy Murray as a prolific goalscoring partnership. That might not have been great news for Chris Jones and Glyn Pardoe, the youth-team strikers, but if the club could challenge seriously for promotion this it would still be good news for the youth-team graduates as they fought to establish themselves in the first eleven.

The manager, George Poyser, found a place for Glyn at outside-right in the first match of the 1964–65 season. Alf Wood was outraged to have been left out, but Roy Cheetham retained his place at centre-half, where he had played twenty-seven times the previous year. The surprise choice was David Connor, who must have realised that, with the talented Neil Young and David Wagstaffe only two or three years older than himself, he might have to wait a long time for his chance on the left wing. Wagstaffe, however, was becoming increasingly frustrated by the lack of ambition at Maine Road. Unlike the more laconic Neil Young, he was a fiery character, both on and off the field, and he didn't take kindly to the prospect of another wasted year of mind-numbing mediocrity. He was eventually transferred to first division Wolverhampton Wanderers on Boxing Day, after enduring half a season of fitful form, exacerbated by the enforced move to the right wing to allow Neil Young to flourish in his favoured position on the left wing. When the teamsheets went up on Friday 21 August 1964, though, David Connor's name was in the first-team squad:

It was the biggest surprise of my life. They didn't tell

me till I looked at the teamsheet on the Friday lunchtime. I wasn't in the team, I was in the squad, because we had a few injuries. We were playing Charlton at the Valley. It was the last season before you could use a substitute, so they had to be sure the player was fit because they'd be playing with ten men otherwise. Now, Friday night for our family was always chips and fish or chips and pie. Every Friday night, as a lad, I'd rush over to the chip shop. Even when I was a City player I did that. So now I'm on me way to play Charlton and I'm stopping at the Grand Hotel. I'm used to a chip butty and a cup of tea. I come down to dinner in me suit, collar and tie and I'm sitting next to Harry Dowd, a lovely down-to-earth feller, and I'm mesmerised by the different cutlery on each side, and I'm dying for a cup of tea, but some bloke comes round and asks what I want. I don't know what to say. I had to watch Harry Dowd pick up the fish knife. I'd never seen a fish knife. I didn't enjoy it one bit. I was so uncomfortable. Nobody went out of their way to make me feel comfortable, because I was just a young lad of eighteen or nineteen and the senior players didn't know me. I mean, I'd never even trained with the first team. I never trained with Glyn any more, because he was in the first-team squad.

When the City team took the field for that first match of the season, neither Young nor Wagstaffe was fit enough to play and David Connor and Glyn Pardoe formed an unlikely pair of wingers. Playing at inside-right was Barry Stobart, the last piece of the jigsaw newly signed from first division Wolves. He was clearly the missing piece in George Poyser's master plan to take the football world by storm. Together with Matt

Gray at right-half, and presumably the fit-again Neil Young and David Wagstaffe, these four players would provide the ammunition for Jimmy Murray and Derek Kevan to resume their prolific goalscoring partnership. On 13 November 1964, the last piece of the jigsaw was transferred to Aston Villa. Poyser went back to the drawing board, via the snooker table, armed with his constant companions, three ounces of pipe tobacco and an egg butty.

Although never the most self-confident of players, David Connor must have fancied his chances against Charlton's thirty-five-year-old South African-born full-back John Hewie, who was nearing the end of his career, and before he left Manchester, he was given some shrewd words of advice by his old mentor:

> Johnny Hart said only run at three-quarter pace because if you run flat out you'll burn yourself out too soon. In that first half I never got a kick. The bloke's positional sense was outstanding. He just closed me down so nobody could give me the ball. I worked very hard, but I was getting nowhere. In the second half he started to tire and he came at me too slowly and he gave me enough room to get past him. All I needed was five yards and I left him for dead. It was a great feeling.

It was not a feeling shared by the City fans who watched yet another miserable start to what was to become one of the most miserable seasons on record. Derek Kevan scored a consolation goal as Charlton ran out 2–1 winners. Like Frost and Ogley the previous year, David Connor had made his debut in a losing cause at the Valley.

Fortunately, there was to be no second defeat, as Ogley and Frost had experienced. City won their next match, the following Wednesday, thumping Leyton Orient 6–0 at Maine

Road with a hat trick from Jimmy Murray and further goals from Glyn, his cousin Alan Oakes and Kevan. Order had been restored to the universe. We could now envisage George Poyser's blue and white army on the march to the final of the European Cup in two years' time. This fantasy lasted exactly three days. Mighty Northampton Town came to town on Saturday and beat City 2–0. Four days later, Leyton Orient won the return match in east London by 4–3, so the new season had begun with one huge victory and three defeats. It was clearly going to be one of those seasons. Again. Only it wasn't – it was considerably worse than that. Even the youth team was unable to provide any consolation, as it had the previous year. Although Alf Wood and David Connor were too old to be eligible, the rest of the class of 1963–64 were still there, but to everyone's disappointment City lost their first match in the competition 1–2 away at Blackburn Rovers.

David Connor stayed in the side for the first eight matches of the season, three of which were won and five of which were lost. After Christmas and the transfer of David Wagstaffe, he was recalled in time to play in the infamous 1–2 home defeat by Swindon Town, the match which has passed into folklore, having been watched by only 8,015 spectators, huddled together for warmth in a stadium whose capacity was then 64,000. At the time, it was difficult to feel very happy sitting in the Platt Lane stand to watch City surrender to a side led by a fast-raiding centre-forward called Mike Summerbee. It was only later, looking back from the secure heights of the trophy-laden Mercer-Allison years, that you could feel masochistically proud at having been present to witness such an abject humiliation. Certainly, as they trooped off the pitch that day, both David Connor and Glyn Pardoe would have been very surprised to learn what lay in store for them in a relatively short space of time. David played the last thirteen games of the season at outside-right and finished with a highly respectable twenty-four first-team appearances and three goals, one of which came in a genuinely exciting 4–3 home win over Preston North End at Maine Road.

Connor's goal the previous week had come in a 2–2 draw on a Friday night at Ninian Park. This match against Cardiff City marked the debut of the seventh member of the youth team, Mike Doyle replacing the injured Alan Oakes at left-half and doing well enough to be recalled for the final five games of the season in his best position of right-half. The first division championship was only three years away, so it's surprising to be reminded how late in the day Doyle claimed the regular wing-half position as his right, as Joe Mercer took two years to decide whether the number four shirt should be awarded to Doyle, Pardoe, Stan Horne or Roy Cheetham.

The nature of Doyle's selection for the Cardiff match speaks volumes about the stewardship and the atmosphere in the club during this dreadful season, the worst for City supporters until the nadir of 1997–98. At whatever stage Oakes had been ruled out, Poyser suddenly realised he had only ten players for the match to be played on the Friday night. The frantic call went back to Maine Road on the Friday lunchtime. There was only one plane from Manchester airport that would get Doyle to Ninian Park by kick-off time. He grabbed his boots and instinctively raced from his home in Reddish to the nearest bus stop. The bus, of course, as buses do in this situation, failed to arrive. It appeared that Mike Doyle's entire football career was being sabotaged by the South East Lancashire and North East Cheshire public transport company. He thought he had better telephone the club, but realised he didn't know the phone number (or presumably the number of Directory Enquiries, which would have given him the number and that of a reliable taxi firm). Just as it seemed that self-immolation in the manner of a suicidal Buddhist monk was becoming preferable to the continuation of life, he saw the City left-back, Vic Gomersall, driving past. Gomersall was quite happy to drive him to the airport for the plane, which he made with five minutes to spare. Even if the details of this story have become embroidered with the passing of the years (Gomersall was also playing in the match), there is no question that it illustrated the sort of unprofessional incompetence that permeated Manchester City at all levels.

So bleak was the outlook at Maine Road that serious thought had been given to a merger. The *Manchester Evening News* noted bleakly: 'The shadow of Old Trafford will gobble up Manchester City, because there is nobody who is connected to the club who can bring back its greatness.' The proposed merger foundered on the simple obstacle of the benefits that would accrue to each party. From a United perspective, it was very hard to ascertain what the league champions would acquire that would be of the slightest use to them. To City supporters, a merger would simply mean the disappearance of their club. To the young professionals on City's books, a merger would presumably mean they would all be released, as United had enough talented youngsters of their own.

Of the optimistic young men who had taken the field at Old Trafford just about twelve months earlier, only four had not yet been given their chance at first-team level – Dave Wild, Phil Burrows, Chris Jones and John Clay, although Burrows had thought he was close to a full debut in early September:

I only went on one first-team trip, which was when City played at Norwich and David Wagstaffe was sent off for smacking Tommy Bryceland. I was told to go and see if he was all right, but when I got into the dressing room an angry spectator had penetrated the minimum security they had then. I was left trying to shut the door on the Norwich fan while Waggy hid in the bath.

Chris Jones never even got that far:

At the end of the 1964–65 season I broke my leg in a tackle by George Heslop in a reserve team match at Everton. He swiped me, tackled me from behind and broke the fibula. So at the time George Poyser was sacked, my contract was coming to an end, though the club had an option for a further year. Nevertheless, I had to ask what was happening to me as I was still in plaster. It was Johnny Hart who said I'd be OK and they took up the option for the second year. It was a big relief, but they got rid of Dave Wild and Bobby Mac at that point.

For John Clay, the 1964–65 season was particularly harsh and the defeat at home to Swindon Town was memorable in the worst possible way, as it was the day his father died:

He'd been fit as anything, but he'd taken ill in the bakehouse. He used to have to get up at five in the morning and go back at ten at night to keep the fires going. Suddenly, Dad was ill. I couldn't believe it. It started at Christmas in 1963 and his eyes puffed up and for the next twelve months he got worse and worse. Apparently he'd picked up a kidney virus when he was in the Army in Egypt, but they didn't have the technology for diagnosis and treatment then that they do today. He went down to five stone and became progressively more ill. Eventually he had to go into Stockport Infirmary. I was with him when he died, that Saturday afternoon when City were beaten at home by Swindon. I'll never forget that day – 16 January 1965. Never. It was a terrible time all round. I just lost it. I remember Stan Bowles was coming through and he was getting ahead of me in the pecking order and my dad died and it all seemed too much for me. Then I did my ankle ligaments and I was in plaster for weeks, so that just about put the tin lid on things. I was never the same after all that.

John had been the right-half in the youth team side, but now that Mike Doyle had made his debut in that position, it was apparent that Doyle had slipped past him in the pecking order: 'I had more skill than Doyley, but give him his due, he was a big lad and he developed physically to six foot one or six foot two and he made the most of his assets. He did really well.' John was a reserve-team player and, while a year before, that would have been regarded with optimism, now it was a measure of how his embryonic career had stagnated. Of course, he was still only eighteen, far too young to start having significant misgivings about his choice of career, but once the carefree pleasures of the apprentice years had passed and the club had offered professional terms, the lads were judged by the yardstick of other professionals, not by the previous standards of promising kids.

Playing next to John in the reserve team half-back line was Alf Wood, who had failed to establish himself as the regular centre-half. In fact, nobody had established himself as the regular centre-half, despite attempts by Roy Cheetham, Mike Batty and Alf. Then, after a dozen games of the season, George Poyser swooped for the Blackpool number five, a perfectly innocuous man called Roy Gratrix, to whom I took a fierce and instant dislike, bred, I would imagine, only by a crushing sense of disappointment. It was a blow, you must understand, when I realised at 3.03p.m. on that first afternoon that he couldn't jump and that his positional sense left much to be desired. In view of this, it was a little surprising to see that the captaincy was thrust upon him in his second game, but it failed to inspire either his own play or that of his troops, and a 3–0 defeat at Swansea was followed by a humiliating exit from the first round of the League Cup at the hands of the mighty Mansfield, who scored five times to mark one of their infrequent visits to Maine Road. Clearly a defence marshalled by Roy Gratrix could not be compared to the Rock of Gibraltar in any journalistic conceit. In his next starring appearance at home, Gratrix gifted the first two goals to the opposition and then in the delicate, not to say euphemistic, words of Peter Gardner, 'had the misfortune to crown an unhappy match by helping in Les Massie's shot for Huddersfield's winning goal.' Quite.

Although Gratrix lost his place before the leaves were off the trees, there was to be no relief for Alf Wood until the clocks went forward again at Easter. Roy Cheetham replaced Gratrix in November, but the debacle of the 2–1 home defeat by Swindon pretty much finished Roy Gratrix's Maine Road career, although the call then went up for Mike Batty rather than Alf. In fact, during the course of this benighted season, no fewer than five players made an attempt to play at centre-half. On Good Friday 1965, the board of directors of Manchester City FC finally decided on a regime change in the manager's office and George Poyser, his pipe clenched between his famously stained, yellow teeth, and Jimmy Meadows, the first-team trainer whose own promising playing career had effectively been terminated by a bad injury sustained in the 1955 FA Cup final, departed. The directors clearly had no idea where to turn to find their successors and so appointed as caretaker manager Fred Tilson, the centre-forward whose goals had won 1934 Cup final for the club. Tilson was the reserve-team trainer, but the younger players barely recognised him, because whenever they saw him he was always asleep.

Instantly, the mood in the club changed. It got considerably worse. In strict contravention of the Arsene Wenger-approved dietary regime, Mike Doyle was eating chips outside the ground on Easter Saturday, an hour before the home game against Coventry City, when he was tapped on the shoulder by the chairman, Albert Alexander, and told to get changed because he was playing. This unorthodox selection practice was certainly a good way of avoiding the nervousness induced by the United routine of the regular pre-match lunch at Davy-hulme Golf Club, but, coming after the hysteria of his league debut, it left Doyle with an understandably dim view of the club his family had always supported. David Connor scored City's goal in a 1–1 draw in front 10,000 desperate fans with nothing else to do on a bank holiday weekend.

It's possible that Doyle got his second chance because Phil Burrows decided to eat lunch at home, before getting the bus to the ground:

> I turned up to watch a game, I think it was over Easter, and the lads said to me, 'What are you doing here?' This must have been quarter past or half past two, and they said, 'You're supposed to be playing,' and in the lunchtime paper it had said, 'Eighteen-year-old Phil Burrows makes his debut.' Nobody had said a word. I didn't play, of course. I never got near the first team again.

Whoever was picking the team, though (and it could very

well have been the chap outside the ground who used to parade up and down the forecourt in a funereal dark suit and a bowler hat wearing a sandwich board which read, 'The end of the world is nigh'), it was good for our lads. Five of them were now playing together in the first team. Alan Ogley took over from Harry Dowd in goal, Glyn came back at inside-left (and was never dropped again), Mike Doyle played his first game at right-half, David Connor retained his position as outside-right and, most interesting of all, Alf Wood came back, not at centre-half, where such fond hopes had been held for him, but as a big, bustling old-fashioned centre-forward. It didn't change City's fortunes but, ultimately, it certainly changed Alf's.

The last match of the 1964–65 season was a Pyrrhic 2–1 revenge win over Charlton Athletic, in front of a crowd that had grown by leaps and bounds since the gloomy days of the dreaded 8,015 on the fateful 16 January. On 28 April 1965, a massive 8,409 crammed into Maine Road to see goals by Murray and Young take the two points. That was the same day that John Fitzpatrick played his second game in a United shirt at Villa Park, two days after the Reds had won the championship with a 3–1 win over Arsenal in front of 51,000 at Old Trafford.

The end of the season brought a merciful release to the players and the fans alike. Doyle, Clay, Frost and Bobby Cunliffe – who was David Connor's predecessor as the youth team left-winger and had just been transferred to York City – went down to Torquay to work on the beaches, where they met up with Mike Summerbee who, ironically, was doing much the same thing while waiting for a phone call from Joe Mercer to tell him his proposed move from Swindon Town to Manchester City was going ahead. John Clay remembers that both Summerbee and his friend Robin Stubbs, who played for Torquay, were driving MGB sports cars, a proven magnet for young women, then as now.

There were other departures in the summer of 1965 besides that of Bobby Cunliffe, who had played two games at inside-left and one at outside-left in the 1963–64 season, scored in the 1–1 draw at home to Plymouth and then lost his place to Bobby McAlinden, whose City career lasted for exactly ninety minutes. A letter arrived at the latter's Salford home informing him of the club's decision not to renew his contract. He was nineteen years old and his career in English football was at an end, although he didn't yet know that. Instead, he seized on an invitation extended by another player:

> Roy Gratrix said he was going to play in Canada in the summer of 1965 and he said they were looking for an outside-left and did I want to go with him? I'd just had that letter from City saying they weren't going to renew my contract, so I thought that would be a nice way to spend the summer. I'd never been on a plane in my life before then. It was a great experience. I loved America as soon as I saw it – the big buildings, getting paid for playing in the sunshine, everything. Nigel Sims, who used to play for Aston Villa, was out there, and then Alex Harley came out, but he was useless. They quickly sussed him out and got rid of him as soon as they could.

Alas, how the mighty are fallen, but football is an unsentimental business – only fans can afford the luxury of nostalgia. Bobby was regarded by the management as something of a luxury; a talented enough player, but one whose work rate was questionable and whose distaste for the job of tackling back made Neil Young look like Tommy Smith. He was released, along with Ronnie Frost, who had played just the two games in 1963–64, and Dave Wild, who was never offered professional terms. Dave never really made it past the A and B sides, who played in the Lancashire League. He never spoke about the pain his dismissal by City brought, although his neighbour John Buckley, who lived across the road and who wore Dave's cast-off boots and clothes, knew it had affected him greatly. The dismissal could have come as little surprise, though. He managed only one appearance in the Central League that season and already youngsters were coming through, two years younger than he was, and the club needed to create room in the A and B sides for them. Sadly, Dave returned to his work as a wages clerk at Crossley Engineering in Openshaw, before moving on to work in the import/export business at Manchester Airport.

So now there were only eight of the Youth Cup eleven left on City's books and they had no idea who the manager might be when they returned from holiday and whether or not the unknown boss would take to them. Across town, of the remaining ten who had won the Youth Cup, the likes of Bobby Noble, Alan Duff and Peter McBride were getting extremely anxious about their chances of breaking into what seemed like a monolithic Manchester United first team, which Matt Busby would simply never change. There were plenty of changes in store for Manchester City, but for their remaining eight little Indians it was now clear that death would soon be stalking some of them, but no one knew which ones. To contradict Irving Berlin, there is at least one business like show business – it's called professional football.

CHAPTER SIX

They Think it's all Over 1965–66

The sixties didn't swing in Manchester until George Best did. Somehow he embodied Manchester's response to that fashion-conscious decade. At the start of the decade, he had arrived in the city a shy fifteen-year-old from Belfast, but even after his captivating performances in the second half of the 1963–64 season, Denis Law was still the king of Old Trafford. Best's growing social self-confidence, though, developed in the wake of the attention paid to his football by an emerging popular press who had stumbled upon a star who sold newspapers.

On the last day of September 1964, United travelled to play Chelsea in a midweek evening match under floodlights. The team was in high spirits, having won their previous four games. George liked playing just off the Kings Road and he chose that night to demonstrate the first full flowering of his gifts. He scored the first goal in a 2–0 win that took United to the top of the table and gave the Chelsea right-back, Ken Shellito, a truly miserable time, with such a breathtaking display of speed and skill that both teams were seen to applaud him off the field. Among the spectators who rose to acclaim the new star were four apprentices from Manchester City, led by John Clay:

One Wednesday at the end of September 1964, we finished training, had lunch and suddenly decided on the spur of the moment to go and watch United against Chelsea. Someone pointed out it wasn't at Old Trafford, but at Stamford Bridge. We left Manchester at 1p.m. and drove down to Chelsea. The four of us – City apprentices – showed our player passes and they led us out on to the running track and put a special bench out there for us – right next to Jack Crompton [the United first-team trainer and former goalkeeper] and the United bench. They must have thought we were United players. That was the night Bestie had one of his greatest ever games and they hammered Chelsea 2–0. Bestie was just unbelievable that night. I'll never forget that night. Nobody who was there ever forgot it.

As the 1965–66 season started, George was experiencing his first bout of over-exposure to his own celebrity. United made a poor start to the defence of their championship and had won two, lost two and drawn four of their opening eight games. Busby dropped Best with a warning to beware of the dangers into which his social life was leading him. George Best had discovered that potent mixture of alcohol, attractive women and the atmosphere of nightclubs which were to draw him like a moth to the flame for the next thirty-five years.

Manchester's role in the development of music grew apace in the sixties. The Twisted Wheel had been a café in the early sixties, but it was taken over and reopened in 1963, after which it encouraged both soul music and rhythm and blues, with bands like Long John Baldry and Alexis Korner appearing there. Tony Wilson, the founder of Factory Records and a lifetime Manchester United fan, believes that

The Stockport Boys team of 1960, featuring five of those who would go on to play in the 1964 FA Youth Cup semi-final: Mike Doyle (back, left), Dave Wild (back, 4th left), John Clay (back, 2nd right), and Phil Burrows and Bobby Noble (front, centre)

Look, no hands: Bert Trautmann greets Alan Ogley on his first day at Maine Road, July 1963 (*Manchester Evening News*)

Bert Trautmann shakes hands with the 14-year-old schoolboy John Clay (left), captain of Cheshire Boys against a visiting German team

England Youth at a European tournament in Spain, summer 1963, featuring: Bobby Noble (3rd left), Alan Ogley (5th left) and Alf Wood (12th left)

Glyn Pardoe at 17, already a seasoned first-team campaigner (*Manchester Evening News*)

The 18-year-old David Connor, just before his debut (*Colorsport*)

George Best and friend at Mrs Fullaway's digs in Chorlton (*Popperfoto*)

The programme for the first leg of the FA Youth Cup semi-final, at Old Trafford

John Fitzpatrick, John Aston, David Sadler and George Best outside the Votiv Kirche in Vienna on their tour of great European gothic churches

Seventeen-year-old Willie Anderson, from Liverpool, makes his debut for United in December 1963 (*Colorsport*)

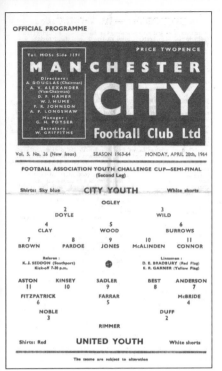

OFFICIAL PROGRAMME

Tel. MOSS Side 1191

PRICE TWOPENCE

MANCHESTER
CITY
Football Club Ltd

Directors:
A. DOUGLAS (Chairman)
A. V. ALEXANDER
(Vice-Chairman)
D. F. HAMER
W. J. HUME
F. R. JOHNSON
A. P. LONGSHAW
Manager:
G. H. POYSER
Secretary:
W. GRIFFITHS

Vol. 5. No. 26 (New Issue)   SEASON 1963-64   MONDAY, APRIL 20th, 1964

FOOTBALL ASSOCIATION YOUTH CHALLENGE CUP—SEMI-FINAL
(Second Leg)

Shirts: Sky blue   **CITY YOUTH**   White shorts

OGLEY

2   3
DOYLE   WILD

4   5   6
CLAY   WOOD   BURROWS

7   8   9   10   11
BROWN   PARDOE   JONES   McALINDEN   CONNOR

Referee :   Linesmen :
K. J. SEDDON (Southport)   D. E. BRADBURY (Red Flag)
Kick-off 7-30 p.m.   E. R. GARNER (Yellow Flag)

ASTON   KINSEY   SADLER   BEST   ANDERSON
11   10   9   8   7

FITZPATRICK   FARRAR   McBRIDE
6   5   4

NOBLE   DUFF
3   2

RIMMER

Shirts: Red   **UNITED YOUTH**   White shorts

The teams are subject to alteration

The programme for the return leg
at Maine Road

Doyle's dazzling debut

By REGINALD PELLING
Cardiff C. 2, Manchester C. 2

IT was a night to remember for 18-year-old Mike Doyle, who made his League debut at wing half for Manchester City because of an eye injury to Alan Oakes.

Doyle was given plenty to think about by the Cardiff attack but he turned in a competent display and helped an enterprising Manchester City to win a point.

Matt Gray swept the Maine road men into an 11th-minute lead with a header, but Ivor Allchurch equalised five minutes later.

Doyle saved City when he cleared off the line from Ellis and a minute before the interval Connor restored the visitors' lead after switching passes with Ogden.

Cardiff came back into the game within three minutes of the restart, Peter King's drive being deflected wide of Dowd by Kennedy.

Mike Doyle's shambolic attempts to get to Cardiff for his debut in February 1965 were obviously worth the hassle

George Best turns away in triumph as Mike Doyle clutches his head and Alf Wood picks the ball out of the City net in the match at Maine Road, April 1964 (*Popperfoto*)

George Poyser, City manager 1963–65, without his trademark pipe and egg butty (*Colorsport*)

Joe Mercer takes his hat off to Malcolm Allison after City win the FA Cup in April 1969 (*PA*)

Johnny Hart (left) and Dave Ewing (right) with Malcolm Allison were key mentors of the City youth teams for many years (*Colorsport*)

Matt Busby with youth team captain Bobby Noble and first team veteran David Herd (*Popperfoto*)

John Aston Sr (left) with Henry Cockburn, two former United stars of the post-war era. Aston played a particularly important role in the youth team's development (*Popperfoto*)

Assistant manager Jimmy Murphy, the beating heart of Manchester United (*Popperfoto*)

Chris Jones at the Hawthorns on one of his sadly few appearances in the City first team (*Colorsport*)

Jimmy Rimmer was unlucky to have waited such a long time in the shadow of Alex Stepney, but was the only one to go on to even greater success elsewhere (*Popperfoto*)

David Sadler at Anfield just before his move into the United defence (*Colorsport*)

the Twisted Wheel was as important in rock and roll history as his own Hacienda: 'Le Phonographe was the one Best went to when he first arrived in Manchester. In those days it was Rowntrees, Mr Smiths and the Twisted Wheel, which was *the* Blues club. It was where Steve Winwood, Jeff Beck and Eric Clapton played when they came here. It was purple hearts, it was speed capital.'

Liverpool was the dominant music city of the time, its legendary status a result of the explosion of new sounds that emanated from there between 1962 and 1965. Wilson believes that Manchester's contribution, however, has been longer-lasting:

> Liverpool is the core music city; it changed music for ever. In 1963 [Manchester's] contribution was Freddie and the Dreamers, then Herman's Hermits. The Beatles stayed pop one album too long and Herman's Hermits were suddenly the biggest band in the world, when the Beatles became briefly unfashionable in late 1964–65. Rock and roll developed in small cities – Memphis, Seattle, Glasgow, Liverpool, San Francisco, Manchester … Normally these cities have three years in the sun – Liverpool's great years were from 1962 to 1965, San Francisco 1966 to 1969, Seattle from 1989 to 1992, and then it's all gone. The bizarre miracle of Manchester is that it went all the way through from the explosion of punk up till today.

Manchester was changing and the music and the football, then as now, were its overseas ambassadors. The Halle Orchestra, which had carried the flag for Manchester's classical music, suffered from the departure of Sir John Barbirolli, for he had cast a shadow over the Free Trade Hall as long as Matt Busby's had cloaked Old Trafford. The

Madchester music explosion of the late eighties had its roots in the environment of the sixties, as coffee bars in town gave way to nightclubs, the bands proliferated and young footballers had somewhere to go in the evening that would give their managers cause for considerable anxiety. Drugs were scarce in those more innocent days, but players' familiarity with alcohol and women was always an indicator for managers and coaches wanting to know which of their charges had the dedication to succeed as athletes and which did not.

It was Best's social life, not his commercial exploits, that bothered Busby, but it was the latter which gave him the financial freedom to begin his flirtation with motor cars, moving effortlessly through the gears of ownership from his initial Austin 1100 to the Sunbeam Alpine, soon to arrive at the Lotus and finally the Jaguar E-type. Players of Best's age group acted differently from the way players had behaved in Busby's day. The generation that went through the Depression, the war and post-war austerity were unfamiliar with and possibly did not even believe in the concept of conspicuous consumption. For a start, they never had anything to consume conspicuously. Matt Busby liked players who went for a game of golf or snooker after training and to the pictures with their wives or steady girlfriends on a Saturday night after the match. Most of his Babes were good lads and, although he tolerated Dennis Viollet's roving eye for a while, in the end he manoeuvred the Munich survivor down the road to Stoke. That was typical of Busby's response. His pre-Munich players understood what the boss wanted, for he was still part of their time.

Pre-Munich there was still room for some of the Corinthian attitudes Busby espoused. He believed that if the eleven players on his team were more skilful than the eleven players in opposition shirts, most of the time his team would win. And, of course, most of the time he was right. His programme notes were always written in the courteous style of the era: 'Tonight we host Real Madrid, the champions of Spain, and may the better team win.' All the players confirm that not only did he write, 'may the better team win,' but that he truly believed in the sentiment.

The boss didn't understand Best at all, because he didn't understand the changing sexual mores of the sixties. The contraceptive pill allowed young women to explore their sexuality without the all-pervasive fear of pregnancy, which had so severely restrained preceding generations. He didn't understand the new financial world that players moved in, either. He and Shankly, and others of their generation, thought football was its own reward and when Denis Law, at the height of his fame, asked for an increase in his wages, Busby had no hesitation in placing him on the transfer list.

To an extent his attitude was hypocritical. John Giles recalls that before the maximum wage was abolished, Busby was frequently to be heard commiserating with his players, telling them they should all be on £100 a week – the magical figure promised to Johnny Haynes at Fulham by his club chairman, Tommy Trinder. However, when the £20 limit was abolished, the United players were offered a rise of £5 and if they didn't like it they could leave the club – but only if Busby agreed to the transfer request. When Ian St John left Liverpool in 1971, his weekly wage was £40. Nobody got rich in those days through playing football.

Best made a new friend as he trawled the fleshpots of Manchester. Mike Summerbee and George became friends in the autumn of 1965, when they met shortly after Mike's transfer from Swindon Town, the day before the start of the season. However, George's pals at United continued to be drawn from the youth side, principally, David Sadler and John Fitzpatrick, neither of whom started the season in the first team, although both the wingers, Willie Anderson and

Johnny Aston, did. Willie lasted just the one game against Sheffield Wednesday before disappearing back into the reserves until April 1966. George moved to inside-forward, to allow Johnny a more regular spot as the left-winger, with John Connelly, the former Burnley player, on the other wing. Aston played twenty-three times that season which, apart from George, was more than any other of the youth-team graduates. However, it was never the joyful experience he so desperately craved:

> I always found playing at United difficult. United were in my blood, but playing for them isn't the same as supporting them. It's like when you meet your heroes and they're not like what you'd thought they'd be. They're just people with maybe a nasty side to them or a silly side to them, but they're nothing like what you think they are when you see them performing on the field.

Aston was a serious, dedicated trainer and when he reached the first team it came as something of a surprise to him to discover that the coaching didn't improve. It was the same complaint that the club captain, Noel Cantwell, voiced: 'I can't remember at United ever being coached. I'm not saying I wasn't, but I've got no memory of it. What I do remember is at Burnley somebody saying, like they were really surprised, "I'm sure they've practised those throw-ins." It was like they were cheating.'

Aston's twenty-three appearances in the first team were a cause of envy to some of the others from the 1964 Youth Cup-winning side, particularly the two full-backs. Bobby Noble growled to his full-back partner, Alan Duff, about the favouritism Busby displayed towards the 'Irish mafia'. They went boozing and to the pictures, to the snooker hall and to the bowling alley near the Old Trafford cricket ground, where they met up with Best and Sadler. Bobby had, by now, abandoned his first car, a baby Austin, in favour of the more glamorous Triumph Herald, but what he really wanted was a first-team place and he couldn't buy that. Alan Duff remembers the frustration they both experienced:

In 1965 I was just a regular reserve team full-back. Neither Bobby nor I could displace Shay Brennan and Tony Dunne. And then there was Noel Cantwell, who was the club captain, waiting to get in. Then one day Busby came up to me and said, 'Jack Rowley is interested in you for Wrexham. Would you be interested in going there? He's coming to the Cliff to see you and Albert Kinsey and I suggest you speak to him.' I knew by then I was just a run-of-the-mill player, so I said, 'Why not?' So Jack Rowley came to the Cliff, talked to Albert and he walked out with him to the car and they drove off. As I saw them go, I was thinking, 'What about me? He never even talked to me!' So I went back to Old Trafford and went to see Matt in his office with this bloody great big desk and before I could open my mouth, Matt said, 'I've changed my mind. You're not going, I want you to stay.' So I was over the moon, because I was convinced he'd wanted to get rid of me. I saw Jack Rowley years later and he confirmed that Matt had told him Albert was still available but I wasn't.

Everyone was stunned at the manner of Kinsey's departure and his rapid fall from grace. Only six months earlier, he had scored on his long-awaited first-team debut. It was rumoured around the club that Busby had turned down decent money from Birmingham City for him during the 1964–65 season, when Birmingham were still in the first division. The deal was done with the unmistakable sign of Busby's ruthlessness. Along with Bobby Noble, Alan Duff had been close to Kinsey and, despite being gratified by his own reprieve, he was sad to see the departure of a close friend: 'I know Busby said to Albert, "You can't come back and bother me now. You can't score a hat trick against us." I know United put a clause in his contract stating that if Wrexham ever sold him United would get half the money, which was original at the time.' Albert Kinsey remained at Wrexham for seven years, scoring eighty goals in 253 appearances for the North Wales club. Alan Duff thought he spent the rest of his career there just to make sure that Busby never got a percentage of his future transfer fee, but at the start of the 1972–73 season Albert Kinsey was transferred to Crewe Alexandra. It is unlikely that Manchester United's percentage of his transfer fee would have made a huge impact on the club's annual accounts.

Although Busby seemed both emotionally and physically distant from the younger players, it is clear that he received regular intelligence reports and he must have known all about their frustration at the limited opportunities available to them. However, he was chasing the holy grail of the European Cup. It dominated his waking hours and, for a brief moment, it appeared that it was within his grasp again. After comfortable aggregate victories over HJK Helsinki and ASK Vorwaerts before Christmas, United were drawn against Benfica in the quarter-final. It was the narrow 3–2 victory at Old Trafford in the first match which caused Busby to issue his famously ignored words of caution before the return leg in the Stadium of Light. It was the night George Best emerged at the centre of the European stage in a virtuoso display of skill and lethal finishing. If he thought he was famous when he woke up in Lisbon on the morning of the game, it was nothing compared to what he would experience when he returned to England the following day, wearing an enormous sombrero he had purchased at the airport in Lisbon. El Beatle, as the Portuguese newspaper *Bola* called him, was on the front pages for the first time and as such he was public property. It was the end of George Best, footballer, and the beginning of Georgie Best, superstar.

He'd gone now. He was still mates with John Fitzpatrick, David Sadler and Mike Summerbee, but his celebrity stretched far beyond the city limits of Manchester and theirs didn't, so slowly but inevitably an indefinable gulf grew between them. Nobody asked David Sadler what music he liked and nobody asked John Fitzpatrick where he got his clothes from and nobody from the *Daily Express* asked Mike Summerbee to ghost a column. As the Beatles were to music, so George Best was to football, and his subsequent meteoric ascent was followed by the inevitable crash and burn in a way that is more familiar to onlookers today than it was to those of us who, mesmerised, could only stand and watch it happen in the early seventies.

Not even Best's sublime skills on the field could win the European Cup for Busby in 1966. In the middle of April, United experienced their now traditional Easter week of passion as their season disintegrated around them. On 13 April, United lost 2–0 in Belgrade to Partizan, the team whom they had all believed were to act as sacrificial lambs on United's triumphant path to the European Cup final. Both Best and Law were suffering from knee injuries. George missed the second leg the following Wednesday, when a solitary goal by Stiles was not enough to overturn the deficit. Willie Anderson came in for his first taste of European football to replace George on the right wing, but it was a deeply disappointing night for United, who had been guilty of underestimating the fighting partisans of Yugoslavia.

Three days later, Willie kept his place but United lost 0–1 to Everton, at Burnden Park in the semi-final of the FA Cup. It was the third successive year they had gone out at this frustratingly late stage. The following Saturday, they were beaten 3–2 at Upton Park by West Ham United and the championship was effectively ceded to Liverpool. There was to be no immediate return to the European Cup for Busby and already he was talking about retirement. He was starting to believe that he was fated never to win the trophy, in the pursuit of which eight young players and fifteen friends had lost their lives. It was a heavy psychological burden to carry.

For the first time in ten years, City finished a campaign on a higher note than United, as they stormed to the championship of the second division. It was an astonishing turnaround in fortunes from the nadir of the previous Easter, when the team was being picked by the chairman looking out of the window of the boardroom. Two years on from the Youth Cup semi-final, it was possible to believe that some of the key players from that side were starting to mature. Admittedly, there was no George Best on the City side to streak across the sky, so the players who were featuring on a regular or semi-regular basis were at the same level as Sadler, Aston, Anderson and Fitzpatrick. Glyn Pardoe played forty games in 1965–66, Connor twenty-nine, Doyle nineteen, Ogley four and Alf Wood just the one, with a final farewell as a substitute in January 1965. By the time the triumphal season had finished it was fairly clear that only Pardoe, Connor, Doyle and Ogley were going to make it from that bunch of hopeful teenagers who had run out to face United at Old Trafford.

Alf Wood and Phil Burrows were early casualties of the Mercer–Allison regime change. It is easy in hindsight to pre-suppose that the replacement of George Poyser with the best manager in City's history was greeted with universal acclaim. In fact, nothing could have been further from the truth. Mercer had been a relatively unsuccessful manager of both Sheffield United and Aston Villa. When things started to go badly wrong for him during the 1963–64 season, his health broke under the strain and he was effectively out of football for a year, during City's season of despair. When he took the job at Maine Road, it was because he was anxious in case he was never to be offered another manager's post, but he was far from being fully recovered. John Clay's first experience of meeting Joe Mercer was deeply troubling: 'When we were first introduced to Joe Mercer we were a bit depressed because it was obvious he was still very ill. For the first few weeks, before Malcolm came, you never saw him. You just heard these stories of how he'd come in for a few hours, but then he'd have to go home and lie down. The bloke clearly wasn't well.' In addition to the worries over Mercer's physical health, Glyn Pardoe had doubts about his mind: 'He was very nervous and he'd get your name wrong. He called me Chris a lot – got me mixed up with Chris Jones. He was a nice feller, but he wasn't well and he got everyone's name wrong.' Phil Burrows felt that the atmosphere changed when Joe and Malcolm came because:

> What they wanted was a first-team squad of sixteen or seventeen players and you soon knew that if you weren't in that squad you were on your way out. I had one or two chats with Joe Mercer, who said he was monitoring my progress and he knew I was doing well, and quite a few times I played in the first team in practice matches, but come the weekend I was always back in the reserves. Whenever Alan Oakes was injured everyone said I'd be in, but I never was.

Alan Oakes missed one match all season, the 2–1 home victory over Carlisle United in September 1965, so Phil's opportunities in the first team were limited and Oakes would play consistently for the next ten years, becoming, in the process, the club's longest serving player, making a record 668 appearances over seventeen years. Phil Burrows was going to have to wait a long time for his big break and he knuckled down to the grind of life in the Central League, but City reserves were surprisingly poor, even when the first team was beginning its impressive U-turn, and he was sucked into the general malaise:

> There was a lot of dead wood in the reserves. Both my seasons in the Central League we finished near the bottom and I think Dave Ewing, who was the reserve team trainer, needed to pick a scapegoat. 'That fifth goal, who were you marking?' he would say to me, and I wanted to say, 'What about the other four?' That sort of thing happened quite a lot. My only ally at that time was Dave Bacuzzi. Nobody ever said to me, 'This is your career here. Set your heights high and really go for it.' Not Johnny Hart, not anyone.

It is odd to hear these stories of those players who fell out with Joe and Malcolm. History, we are told, is written by the winners and certainly all the City history of this era has been written from the point of view of the successful players and the Mercer-Allison years have passed into legend as the time when great players played great football and everyone at the club was motivated by the miraculous partnership of the shrewd, avuncular Mercer and the brash, inspiring Allison. To hear Phil Burrows talk is to read the history of the Russian revolution from the point of view of the Mensheviks.

He makes a valid criticism of the management's failure to offer help where it was needed which echoes the views of Matt Busby expressed by Dave Farrar, Johnny Aston and some of the others. Burrows says:

> Joe and Malcolm were involved with the first team. We did our warm-ups together and training together on the track, then the first-team squad would go on to the pitch and the reserves would be told to get some bibs and some cones and play a game in the car park, but frankly I could have gone into the changing room, got dressed, gone home and nobody would have missed me. That was wrong and dispiriting. Psychology is important in football. Being confident is the most important factor. It's got to come from within, but you need assistance and I didn't get any. Somebody should take you on one side and say, 'How do you think you played? You can do this or that more and it would help your game.' You'd think they'd have been interested in me and wanted me to succeed, but there was none of that.

Alf Wood certainly shares Phil's reservations about the new regime:

> It wasn't the club that didn't want me, it was Malcolm Allison. He felt I wasn't committed enough in training. He'd pick three or four players and work with them, knocking the ball back and forth, sometimes straight at them, sometimes over their heads, and he'd do this with each group for five or ten minutes. First day he whacked it back over my head, so I turned round ran after it, got the ball back and passed it back to him, but he deliberately let the ball go under his

189

legs, so I had to go and get that one as well, and as I passed him I just said, 'Fuckin' hell!' and we never spoke again. Malcolm liked his nightclubs and I wasn't part of his crowd. That would have been in the autumn of 1965.

It had been a kick in the teeth for Alf when Joe Mercer opted to start the season with the old reliable, Roy Cheetham, at centre-half. Alf entertained some hopes that the new manager would want to start with the ex-youth team captain. After three games, Cheetham was dropped to substitute, where he made history by becoming the first ever Manchester City substitute, replacing Mike Summerbee, who had been sent hurtling head first into an iron post in the stand by a Wolverhampton defender. Cheetham's place in the centre of the defence was taken not by Alf, but by the left-half, Alan Oakes. For the next match, Bobby Kennedy wore the number five shirt, then Cheetham returned for one match, after which Joe bought George Heslop from Everton for £25,000. Now the writing was really on the wall for Alf. He played just one full game that season, in November 1965, when he replaced the injured Heslop in the scoreless draw at home to Norwich City.

Chris Jones was possibly the most enthusiastic footballer ever to lace up a pair of boots and even though his career was not to blossom under the new management, he remembers their arrival with his trademark exuberance:

Joe was great. I remember Malcolm Allison making his first appearance in front of us down at Chassen Road in a bright red track suit. He burst on to the scene like a Colossus and he was a great coach, with lots of new ideas on training and diet. Joe was the man who knew who to bring in and they were a great team till Malcolm decided he didn't need Joe.

John Clay remains similarly enthusiastic about Allison:

> Malcolm was tremendous. You could see he liked young players and you could see with the innovative weight training that he was prepared to introduce new ideas. He brought in the athletes Joe Lancaster and Derek Ibbotson for distance running and Danny Herman for the sprints. The training was now really hard but very beneficial.

Alan Ogley was optimistic that the arrival of a new manager would mean a new pair of eyes and therefore a new decision in the battle for the goalkeeping place between Harry Dowd and himself:

> Joe came and he was distant. Malcolm was larger than life. Every player in that dressing room (once it had been sorted out) would have gone through a brick wall for Malcolm Allison. Joe was aloof, away, we only saw him when summat was up or for pre-match talks. Being a young kid I didn't realise till later it was Joe who held everything together. He allowed Malcolm to do what he wanted, but he reined him in when he needed to.

The quiet country cousins, however, had grave doubts. Glyn Pardoe was certainly not impressed by Allison's trademark arrogance:

> Malcolm was very confident, brash and loud – not my cup of tea at all – always shouting. I'd never experienced anything like that before. Big Dave Ewing was

a shouter, certainly during a match, but nothing like Mal. He was the one who was close to the players, but I found him very overpowering. When we got training, we thought he might be a bit of a gobber, he might be a bit fancy, but he was helping us and results started to improve immediately. But I still think he was over the top talking about how easily we'd win matches. I thought that put too much pressure on us.

George Poyser's tactics were restricted entirely to one set play, which only worked if City got a throw-in level with the penalty area. Bobby Kennedy would then throw the ball to Jimmy Murray, standing by the near post, who would back-head it across the face of the goal for Derek Kevan, charging in from the edge of the penalty area, to power home with a fierce header. I certainly remember seeing at least two goals scored this way. That, however, appeared to be the complete sum of City's tactical thinking in 1964–65. In 1965–66 a revolutionary whirlwind hit Maine Road. Malcolm Allison never stopped talking about football and, in particular, about tactics. Peter Gardner recalls that Allison would be making outrageous suggestions to Joe Mercer all the time: 'Let's play with six full-backs and no goalie – that kind of thing. Joe would always say, "Great! We'll try it in the reserves on Saturday" or "We'll try it in training" and then the next day Malcolm would have forgotten, because he'd come up with an even better idea.'

This kind of behaviour soon passed along the footballers' grapevine. John Aston learned about it after talking to Joe Mercer during a reception at the Midland Hotel:

It was a United occasion, but they always invited one or two top nobs from City. Joe saw me and said, 'Hello, Johnny, lad,' and he started talking to me. He was saying, 'Malcolm comes into the office on Monday morning and says, "Boss, I've been thinking all weekend. I've got this most fantastic idea!" And I listen to him and I say "OK, Malcolm, you go off and do that." I never take much notice, because next day he comes in and he says, "Boss, I've got this most fantastic idea …" '

Peter Gardner's story about the six full-backs and no goal-keeper is only stretching the truth by a little. In his later years, when innovation passed well beyond eccentricity, Malcolm Allison was reported to have banned his players from passing with their instep. Then there was the time when he wanted all ten outfield players to adopt a wheel formation so the opposition wouldn't be able to tackle the player in possession, who would break off and shoot when the wheel had wheeled its way into the opposition's penalty area. This idea relied on his team retaining 100 per cent possession of the ball for the entire match, because it was not at all clear how they would ever regain possession once they had lost it, with all ten outfield players locked together in a desperately revolving wheel formation. It might have worked, I suppose, had the opposition broken down in helpless laughter. In the end, Allison seemed to be espousing ideas just because nobody had ever thought about them before, and the reason nobody had thought of them was that, like the endlessly revolving wheel, they would never have worked.

Nevertheless, in the early days of his time at Maine Road, Allison was just glad to have a job after his enforced departure from Plymouth Argyle in the summer. With little change in personnel from the debacle of 1964–65, results started to improve immediately and City lost only one of their first fifteen matches. Alan Ogley failed to displace Harry Dowd from the first team and made only four appearances in goal, but he felt sure his chance would come and, meanwhile, he gave his all in the Central League. David Connor, in his usual quiet way, survived the signing of two new forwards – Mike Summerbee from Swindon and Ralph Brand from Rangers – to keep his place on the left wing, clocking-up twenty-nine first-team appearances. The equally hard-working but unspectacular Glyn Pardoe also secured a regular place, missing only two games all season. However, it seems that, despite claiming nine goals, his highest ever tally, Mercer and Allison decided early on that he was better employed elsewhere on the field, rather than as a striker. As Christmas approached, Allison made Pardoe one of the two key figures in one of his more productive plans.

In 1965, the old-fashioned WM formation was in existence, as it had been for the past forty years, since Herbert Chapman had initiated the fashion of withdrawing the centre-half from the middle of the half-back line to play between the two full-backs. Despite the impact of the Hungarians and their deep-lying centre-forward which had de-railed England so spectacularly in the 1950s, the wing-halves and the inside-forwards still shared most of the midfield duties, with one wing-half more defensively minded and one inside-forward playing as a striker. The two wingers were frequently to be found chewing gum on the touchline as they waited patiently for their own defence to do its job and give the ball to them. There was no suggestion they might care to come back and help out. Number five marked number nine, number two marked number eleven, number three marked number seven, and so on. It was an order as rigid and unchanging as Europe before 1914. Everyone knew their place in this hierarchical society and Malcolm Allison was one of the few English coaches who wondered what would happen if you tossed a bomb into the middle of it. So he did.

The plan revolved around Mike Doyle's prowess in the air. Doyle had played six of the first eight games of the season at right-half, before giving way to Stan Horne and then Roy Cheetham. After City's worst display of the season so far, a 3–1 defeat away at struggling Birmingham, Doyle was given the number four shirt again, but with instructions to swap positions with Glyn Pardoe after twenty minutes or so. Pardoe was wearing the number nine shirt and his disappearance into midfield so confused the Leyton Orient defence that they capitulated completely, as if Hidegkuti and Revie had never existed. Neil Young scored a hat trick, one of them a header, which made it a collector's item. In the next game at Crystal Palace, Mike Doyle scored both goals in a 2–0 victory and, in total, he scored six goals in the next four games, despite his well-publicised distaste for the striking position. Eventually, opposing defences caught on to the move, but it had done its job. City's stuttering autumn came to a halt and what followed was a relatively smooth run-in to the second division championship, with promotion guaranteed four matches before the end of the season.

It was a remarkable turnaround given the disaster of the previous campaign. Promotion miraculously restored the bloom to Joe Mercer's cheeks and it convinced everyone at the club that Malcolm Allison was a tactical genius. Unfortunately, the triumph of the players who had succeeded meant the death knell tolled for those who took little part in it. Six weeks before the end of the season, Mercer called Phil Burrows into his office and informed him that the club had received one or two enquiries about him:

He said he didn't want to let me go, he'd had good reports about me. 'I know what you can do, but we're concentrating on promotion, but if we get back into the first division there'll be a place for you.' So I went away feeling really good, feeling there was something to aim for. Then six weeks later I got the letter. I was called into the office and told that was the end: 'We're not renewing your contract. You'll be hearing from different clubs.' Max Brown and myself were the ones to be released. I never did find out what happened between those two meetings.

Max Brown, who had filled in as outside-right for the second leg of the 1964 Youth Cup semi-final when Ronnie Frost had been injured by Bobby Noble, was not the only other casualty in the summer of 1966. Hopes had not been invested in Max Brown the way they had been in Alf Wood, but Alf's altercation with Malcolm Allison had ensured that he would never be regarded as part of the manager's plans again. In February, he had been included in the first-team squad to play at Bristol City. There was some excitement on the team coach, because this match was to be City's first-ever televised league game on *Match of the Day*, which was demonstrating the BBC's mission to entertain, educate and inform by deigning to cover a match in the second division. If Alf thought he was in with a sniff of the substitute's position because Dave Bacuzzi had been dropped, he was to be disappointed, as Bacuzzi was awarded the number twelve shirt. That was as close as Alf Wood ever got to reclaiming his place in the Manchester City first team:

In the spring of 1966 I received a letter from Australia offering me a position at one of the clubs in Sydney. I went up to see Joe Mercer and he seemed agitated. 'They can't do this,' he said, but he and Malcolm had obviously arranged it. A few weeks later he called me in to see him and said he'd had an offer for me from Shrewsbury and did I want to go? I said, 'If you don't want me, there's no point me staying here.' 'That's right,' he said. I was very disappointed. We'd just bought a house the week before in Poynton and we had to sell it again, because we were getting married in July.

After just thirty-two first-team appearances in three years, Alf Wood signed for Shrewsbury Town at the end of June 1966. Nearly forty years later, he states quietly, but passionately, 'Leaving City upset me for a long, long time.'

Leaving the club having 'failed' hurt all of them, no matter how the 'failure' was measured. They had to explain to their families and friends, who had watched their triumphant upward progress with such pride. From their team-mates there came mixed reactions. There was sorrow and sympathy from friends; a sense of, 'There but for the grace of God, go I' from the reprieved; and a critical approval of the termination from rivals who had noted the same faults that had caused the management to lose patience. Glyn Pardoe remembers the fate of Stan Goddard, his contemporary on the groundstaff for two years. Goddard had been his closest friend, but when he left Maine Road, he was so dispirited that Glyn believes he simply gave up the game. It was not an atypical reaction.

So then there were six. Only Ogley, Doyle, Clay, Pardoe, Jones and Connor now remained on the staff as Manchester City regained their place in the top division in May 1966, with Summerbee and Bell of the holy trinity now safely and profitably installed. Chris Jones was scoring prolifically in the reserves, but the call to first-team action never came. Mercer had bought Ralph Brand and Mike Summerbee as his first two acquisitions, so he had new and significant competition in his attempt to win either a winger's or a striker's position. When Brand scored only twice and was dropped before the end of October 1965, it was David Connor who benefited, not Chris Jones, as Neil Young was moved inside to vacate the position of outside-left. When Jimmy Murray was dropped from the centre-forward position it created an opportunity for Allison to experiment with Glyn Pardoe and Mike Doyle, which understandably upset him even more. Unlike Alf, with the encouragement of Johnny Hart and Dave Ewing, Chris couldn't have tried harder, but when City opened their campaign in the first division in August it was Murray and Young who took the striking roles. Chris Jones was left to fret in the reserves, perfectly aware that there were other youth-team graduates coming up behind him, who were also being encouraged by Ewing and Hart. That, after all, was their job.

At least Jones stayed fit. John Clay's life was blighted by injury. He, too, was aware that Mike Doyle's inspired spell of goals in December 1965 and January 1966 had now firmly established him in the new manager's good books. Doyle had also grown and filled out, while Clay still lacked the physique to make a strong physical impact on the pitch. To make his position even more difficult, he broke his leg in a reserve team game at Everton and his recovery was both painful and short-lived: 'Malcolm made me run up and down the stands in the short plaster I was wearing, but it set me back, there was no doubt about it. I might have got an opportunity in that promotion season if I hadn't broken my leg just then and it all could have been so different. And then I broke it again within a few months of coming back.'

Clay's agonies in Manchester were matched by those of Bobby McAlinden in the Potteries, when he returned from his first summer in North America:

I think I could have gone to Mansfield, but I'd got an offer from Stan Matthews, who'd been a guest player in Canada. He'd just retired and he was going to manage Port Vale and he wanted me to come there, so I did, but he never put me in the first team. I was playing all right – banging in the goals in the reserves right, left and centre, but I never even got a game for the first team. I was now getting very disillusioned. You're very naïve as a kid – you don't understand the dark side of the game.

That omission was soon rectified. During his time in the reserves at Port Vale he received a phone call from Glentoran, one of the top sides in Northern Ireland, who said they needed an outside-left and a centre-forward. It's illuminating to realise that receiving a call in the McAlinden household was no straightforward matter of picking up the receiver since 'their' telephone was situated inside a telephone box at the top of the road. Having managed to get Bobby to the phone, the club manager admitted to his prospective new player that the club had no chance of winning the league, but they were desperate for a good cup run because they hadn't won the trophy for a long time. Jimmy Meadows was now the manager of Stockport County and he allowed Bobby to train during the week at Edgeley Park, while Glentoran guaranteed to fly him over to Belfast every Friday to play in the match the following day. After most games, he would get the plane back to Manchester on the Saturday night, unless Glentoran were playing way out on the coast somewhere:

I was getting maybe twenty quid a week for this, which was not a lot because soon after I went there results picked up. We got beaten on goal average for the league, but we won the cup, beating Linfield in the final 2–0. Terry Conroy, who was about to go to Stoke, scored both. They wanted me to come back next season, so I asked for a retainer during the summer, but they said they couldn't or wouldn't do that. So I said, 'Stuff it!' and I went off to South Africa, because I'd been invited there by Billy Haydock, who I'd played with at City. Glentoran didn't want to let me go, but at that time, because of apartheid, South Africa weren't in FIFA.

It was a far from inspired move. Owing to their new status as cup winners of Northern Ireland, Glentoran were drawn to play Benfica in the European Cup-Winners' Cup. Benfica were a great side, despite their capitulation to George in March. Glentoran drew the home leg at the Oval 1–1 at the start of the 1966–67 season and, contrary to all expectations, they also drew 0–0 in Portugal, Benfica scraping a win by the narrowest of margins on the away goals rule. Everyone who had assumed Glentoran were going to be thrashed took notice of that result and made the reasonable assumption that the team had some useful players. Bobby, of course, was not among them and he still bitterly regrets having left Ulster in a huff at the end of the previous season: 'Six or eight of that team, plus a couple of reserves who were older than me and couldn't get into the team when I was playing, they got transferred to English clubs. Meanwhile, I was in South Africa and missed it all.'

Not all of those who failed to make the grade at the two Manchester clubs disappeared into obscurity, but it is a sobering thought that very few of those who were abandoned while still teenagers went on to greater glory on the football field elsewhere. Many are called: heart-breakingly few are chosen.

CHAPTER SEVEN

Triumph and Tragedy
1966–67

Bobby Noble and Alan Duff had been fulminating about Matt Busby and the world from their positions as full-back partners in the Manchester United reserves for two long years before Bobby made his first-team debut in April 1966. He was only in for that one game, but he reappeared in the last match of the season, a meaningless 1–1 draw at home to Leeds, and began pre-season training with considerable hopes, and not a few misgivings. He would be twenty-one in December and, for all the encouraging words he had heard over the past two years, the fact was that unless he soon broke the stranglehold on the first-team full-back positions exercised by Shay Brennan, Tony Dunne and the club captain, Noel Cantwell, whom he and Duff called the Irish mafia, it would be a clear sign that his future lay elsewhere. When the teamsheets went up for the first match of the season, at home to West Brom, Brennan was at right-back and Dunne was at left-back. Bobby was furious:

I told Jack Crompton, the first-team trainer, that I wanted to see the Boss. So I went into his office to see him. 'Come in, son,' he said (he always called you son). 'What can I do for you?' Now I'd played for England Youth and won the Youth World Cup with

John Hollins, Harry Redknapp, Johnny Sissons, Don Rogers, David Sadler ... Anyway, I told him, 'Boss, I don't think there's any future for me here.' 'Oh, why's that, son?' 'If one of the full-backs has a bad game you put Cantwell in. If he has a bad game you bring Tony or Shay back.' He said nothing for what seemed like hours. Then he just said, 'You're not leaving while I'm here' and that was it. What do I say? Thanks, Boss? No thanks, Boss? I wanted a transfer. My mate Johnny Hollins asked if I fancied going down to Chelsea and I did.

Busby knew time was running out if he was to achieve his great ambition of winning the European Cup. It meant United had to win the league again in 1966–67 and then mount a fresh assault on Europe the following year. Although George was likely to be around for a good many years yet, Bobby Charlton had already had ten years at the top and Denis Law was clearly at the peak of his career with ninety-six goals in the four seasons since his transfer from Torino. As Best got greedier, Law got less prolific, but in 1966 the celebrated trio were irresistible. Bobby Noble was a more than useful reserve. He was going nowhere.

Unfortunately for Bobby and Alan, the season began well for United. They hammered West Brom 5–3, but the defence was creaking and, despite scoring twenty-one goals in the first ten games (nine of them by Law), United had conceded nineteen. On 1 October they crashed 4–1 at Nottingham Forest. Changes in the defence were now unavoidable. Pat Dunne, a £4,000 buy from Shamrock Rovers in the summer of 1964, had won a championship medal, but not the good-will of the crowd. Busby ruthlessly discarded him and spent £55,000 on Alex Stepney from Millwall. It was an inspired choice for all but Jimmy Rimmer, whose future progress at first-team level was to be permanently blocked by Stepney.

Rimmer was still only eighteen when Stepney arrived at Old Trafford. However worried he might have been by the new man's appearance, Jimmy Murphy assured him that he had many years left in the game and there was no reason to be unduly despondent. Rimmer nodded and accepted the logic of the argument. Bobby Noble had never shared the goalkeeper's phlegmatic approach, but this time he didn't need to. Busby didn't look to the transfer market to strengthen the full-back position. At long last, it was Bobby's time: 'Next Friday, Jack Crompton tells me I'm in the first team. I wondered if he was having me on, but I looked at the teamsheet and I was in there against Blackpool and we won 2–1. We were flying to Italy that week to play Fiorentina in the Anglo-Italian Cup and I think we won there, too, and then I was never dropped.'

Bobby Noble is the great forgotten talent of Manchester United in the sixties. After he came into the team in October, United lost only two more games the rest of the season, one of them being the Boxing Day match away at Sheffield United in which Bobby was sent off, although since he played twenty-nine consecutive league games that season it appears that he escaped a ban by the FA disciplinary committee:

I went in full monty against Alan Woodward and I must have missed him by an inch. It looked worse than it was, but I was sent off. I told Alan Duff in that Youth Cup final to give Don Rogers one early on and he wouldn't want to know after that, because he was the star man down there. You've got to do that with star players – let them know you're there early on. I remember Eddie McCreadie at Chelsea – I went over the ball at him, before he could do it to me. I fouled him, but I didn't say sorry, though I saw him rolling over. They were a hard side, that Chelsea.

Bobby's uncompromising attitude on the field won respect from the player generally regarded as the toughest right-winger in the land during the late sixties. Mike Summerbee only played against Bobby once, in a derby match at Maine Road on a foul day in January 1967, but it was a confrontation he has never forgotten: 'Bobby Noble was one of the best left-backs I've ever played against. I don't think I got a kick that day. He just put me out of the game. He was so strong and aggressive.' The only winger whose physical aggression gave Bobby any trouble was Johnny Morrissey, who, like Summerbee, could dish it out as well as take it.

Bobby's uncompromising attitude off the field was equally in evidence. He gives a qualified 'he was all right' to Denis Law, but regards Bobby Charlton as 'a miserable bugger', in particular censuring the son–father relationship he observed which existed between Charlton and Busby. Bobby Noble never bought into the Busby myth, that he was some kind of gentle paternal figure, who looked out for his family of young men, encouraged and protected them. In Bobby Noble's experience, Busby was an emotionally distant man who ruthlessly exploited the youthful dreams of his young players and was the prisoner of a clique of senior players – in particular, Charlton, Crerand and the Irish mafia. It was John Aston Sr and Jimmy Murphy who made Bobby the player he was, not Matt Busby.

And what a player he was. All the Stockport Boys who played with him were grateful he was on their side. It was no coincidence he put Ron Frost out of the game in the Youth Cup semi-final. He knew all about Ron from their days at Stockport together and John Clay knew all about Bobby: 'I played against Bobby Noble in that very first trial that

Tuesday night in 1960. Bob was smaller than me, but he was the strongest, quickest, meanest, nastiest tackler you ever saw in your life. He was a wing-half then, but United pushed him back to full-back. He was a tremendous player.' David Meek concurs, believing that Bobby Noble was possibly the best tackler he ever saw. In fact, all the football journalists thought Noble was a certainty to be Ray Wilson's long-term replacement. He was bound to be the England left-back in Mexico in 1970 and West Germany in 1974.

On 22 April 1967, United drew 0–0 at Sunderland to extend their unbeaten run to seventeen matches. Only three matches remained – home games against Aston Villa and Stoke City and an away match at Upton Park. United were coasting serenely towards their second championship in three years, pursued, to no avail, by Nottingham Forest, Spurs and Leeds United. Bobby was twenty-one years old and on top of the world. A championship medal would be his if United won their next two games (which they did). An England career and football immortality were beckoning. On St Valentine's Day two months earlier he had married his girlfriend, the glamorous blonde Irene, and settled down into a club house in Sale. The Nobles were in a group of players who had all got married and lived down in that area of Manchester. Life could scarcely have been more perfect.

The players used to drive to Old Trafford, leave their cars at the ground and take the coach to the away ground from there. Just before midnight, the coach bearing the tired but happy United party arrived under the Munich memorial. It will come as no surprise that players drank in those days. They drank frequently and deeply, particularly on a Saturday night after a match. Nobody was likely to ring up the tabloids and 'inform'. Why would it matter anyway? As long as they won and entertained on a Saturday afternoon they would be allowed to walk naked down Deansgate carrying two pints in each hand and smoking a fag – though this philosophy was never actually put to the test.

Alex Stepney asked Bobby if he wanted to join the goalkeeper, George and the others who were making their way into the centre of town. Bobby shook his head. Irene had invited friends up for the weekend and was expecting him to come straight home. Instead, out of habit, he drove over to the Greatstone Hotel, which was less than a mile from Old Trafford. It was a favourite haunt of the United players, because it was close to the ground and they could relax there without the hassle they got in more public places. Bobby just wanted a couple of pints to wind down.

He didn't stay much more than half an hour and as Saturday night turned into Sunday morning he was in the Triumph Herald and speeding along the road back to Sale, through the late-night drizzle. There was almost no traffic on the main road and through the mist he could see the familiar lights of the Blue Arrow garage on Washway Road. He would be home in a couple of minutes. Those lights were the last thing Bobby remembered. A Mini, driven by a man called Thomas Lovell from Runcorn, turned across his path into the garage. Bobby crashed head-on into the car and was bounced like a toy against the garage wall. He lost consciousness immediately. A passing off-duty nurse forced open the buckled door to find Bobby slumped over the steering wheel. He was not wearing a seat belt.

In their home, Irene could hear the sound of the ambulance racing to the scene of the accident. Initially, she didn't equate it with the fact that her husband wasn't home by 1a.m. but when the clock ticked by to 2a.m. and then, agonisingly, to 3a.m. she knew something terrible must have happened. She rang the ground, she rang the other players, but the only answer she received was that they had arrived back safely after 11p.m. and Bobby had driven off by himself. At 4a.m came the dreaded arrival of the policeman who delivered the news that her husband of two months was in a coma in Altrincham General Hospital.

When she arrived at the hospital she was told that after ascertaining the extent of his injuries, the doctors estimated Bobby's chances of survival at no more than fifty-fifty. Bobby had severe chest, leg and, most frightening of all, head injuries. He remained on the danger list for three days and it was a week before he could even recognise Irene. The broken leg and cracked ribs healed, but there was nothing anyone could do about the head injuries. It was deemed too dangerous to operate so close to the brain. The following Saturday, as Bobby Noble was coming out of his coma, United beat Aston Villa at home 3–1. The following week, on 6 May 1967, as Bobby was contemplating the wreck of his life, United won 6–1 at West Ham to clinch the title in the most scintillating, entertaining manner. Tony Dunne moved across to left-back and Shay Brennan was recalled to right-back. The season for Bobby ended as it had begun, in bitter frustration, but this time the frustration was not going to be eased by the inclusion of his name on a teamsheet.

Bobby and Alan Duff had been friends and partners both on and off the field for five years, but 1967 turned out to be their nemesis. Alan didn't have quite the rage that Bobby had at being left out of the side, but then he didn't have quite the talent either. After the scare of 1966, when it looked like he was on his way with Albert Kinsey out of the club, he was almost relieved to be back in the reserves. After all, he was playing a decent standard of football for the team he loved with Bobby, Noel Cantwell, David Sadler, Brian Kidd, Carlo Sartori, Francis Burns, Jimmy Ryan and Willie Anderson. It wasn't a bad reserve team and once Alex Stepney joined the club in September 1966, the goalkeepers varied between Pat Dunne, Harry Gregg and Jimmy Rimmer. He enjoyed the lifestyle as well as the football and Wilf McGuinness, who was the second team coach, was still encouraging him.

Yet still there were too many little signs which caused him to doubt his eventual success. In 1964, United received a letter from the FA which Wilf showed to Alan because he was involved with the England Youth setup. They wanted Bobby Noble, Albert Kinsey and Eddie Harrop to go for England Youth trials, but the club decided that, rather than Eddie, another Manchester-born youngster whose promise outstripped his ability to deliver, they would send Alan:

> We played a trial game at Villa Park and coming back in the car afterwards Wilf said, 'You'll get picked Bobby, you'll get picked Alan, but you won't, Albert.' He'd had a mediocre game and my hopes got built up – and then knocked down because I didn't get picked. Len Badger got picked instead, but I thought if I was having a trial for England Youth my career must be going forward; I must be a decent player. Anyway, Bobby went off to the Canary Isles and I think they won the tournament there.

It hurt, of course, that Bobby got picked for the first team ahead of him when Shay Brennan was dropped in October 1966, but even that decision left Alan puzzled by the manager's sixties version of what later came to be known as 'mind games':

> I'd got injured in the reserve team the previous Saturday and I thought it strange that on the following Friday Matt Busby came into the treatment room and asked how I was. That had never happened before. He asked Ted Dalton, the physio, will he be fit for tomorrow and Ted told him I had no chance. Matt

said, 'That's a shame. If he'd been fit he'd have been in the first team tomorrow.' Bobby played instead.

A week later, Alan was fit again, but now it was obvious that Tony Dunne, Bobby, Shay and probably Noel Cantwell lay between him and a first-team place. He cornered the manager in the referee's changing room:

> I knew there was no chance of Tony Dunne ever being dropped, because he was such a class player, so I asked Matt, 'What are my prospects?' But there was no real answer and he said, effectively, 'Take it or leave it.' He wouldn't even tell me if I was still in his plans or not. Now I started getting very disillusioned. I was nearly twenty-one and Bobby was in and Shay was out and I was going nowhere. So, nervously, I asked Matt for a transfer. I said I thought I might be better off elsewhere and what did he think my prospects were, but he just said, 'Right, I'll put you on the transfer list. You'll be open to offers.'

Even at a distance of forty years, all the players talk with a shudder about how difficult it was to steel themselves for a confrontation with Busby and how they dreaded just such an outcome. A shocked Alan asked Noel Cantwell, the club's PFA representative, to find out how much money Matt wanted for him. Cantwell came back a couple of weeks later and told him that Derby County, who were in the second division at the time, had offered £5,000, which was a large sum for a player without a first-team appearance to his name, but Busby had turned it down, informing them that he wanted £7,500. Derby couldn't afford to pay it and interest cooled, as it did at Bury when the scenario repeated itself:

So I just plodded on and nothing happened. Then, towards the end of that season, April 1967 it must have been, Matt called me into his office and told me he'd had a letter from Walley Barnes in South Africa, who was looking for a full-back, and Matt told me that if I wanted to go to South Africa I could go for nothing, but if I wanted to stay in this country I had to stay on the transfer list and they would want money for me. If I was in South Africa I was out of danger for him, but I could ask for a nice signing-on fee. I was so disillusioned, I just said, 'OK, I'll go,' so I went to South Africa. I felt just terrible leaving United. I felt I should still have been there.

For Alan, the bitter irony of this conversation was that it took place just ten days before Bobby Noble suffered his terrible injury. Alan long maintained the feeling that if he hadn't asked for the transfer he might have got the chance to step up instead of watching Shay Brennan return to the side:

Maybe I should have gone back then and said, 'I'm staying and I'll fight for my place,' but then if Matt had really wanted me he'd have scuppered the free transfer, wouldn't he? It really upset me that I could have gone to Bury or Derby, played regular second division first-team football and got back in that way, but Matt wasn't having any of it.

As the club celebrated another championship triumph and the knowledge that they were back in the European Cup, Alan was packing his bags. His sister, who was working in a local hospital, had been sharing a flat in Manchester with another nurse, called Beryl. The Welsh nurse and the Yorkshire footballer fell in love and married on the first Saturday after the end of the season. The following day they boarded the plane that would take them to a future life in South Africa. It was a long way from home and, like Bobby McAlinden and the other players who wound up in South Africa, it turned out not to be quite the land of sunshine and fresh fruit on every tree that they had anticipated.

For the youngsters who weren't going to make it, being at a successful club could be worse than being at a failing club. It was clear to Busby in 1967 that he had found the perfect blend for his next, and possibly final, attempt on the European Cup. There were some talented kids coming through the junior ranks, in particular Brian Kidd from Collyhurst, so the lads who had been around for four years or so were now considered disposable. Willie Anderson was just as much a victim of this thinking as Alan Duff. After five first-team appearances in 1965–66, Willie made only one in 1966–67 and that was as a substitute in the 2–2 draw at home to Liverpool. Both United goals were scored by George Best. Somehow it was fitting that a match against Liverpool should be his final appearance. Anderson was a Liverpool lad and had always wanted to play for the Anfield club. His family still lived in the city and his accent has survived forty years' absence and a transatlantic transplantation:

There was constant pressure on the kids at Old Trafford. I got a couple of runs at it, but I soon realised I was never going to make it there. The competition was so intense. I was nineteen when I was transferred to Villa. They always moved you on when you got to nineteen or twenty, because there were so many talented young kids coming up behind you. The transfer itself came out of the blue, but I was ready to go. Indeed, I might have told them I'd like to go.

Unlike with Alan Duff and Albert Kinsey, and later John Aston, United didn't force Anderson to leave, so his memories of his departure from Old Trafford are free of rancour:

> Busby and Murphy didn't force me out. They kept asking if I was sure I wanted to go, and I didn't have to leave, but I knew that I did if I wanted regular first-team football, so I didn't feel, like so many others say they do, that leaving Old Trafford meant the only place after that was down. When I went to Villa, they were still in the first division, but they got relegated that year, so I suppose it was down in a way. Playing for the reserves, even at Old Trafford, isn't like playing regular first division football.

So now it was clear who was going to make it at Old Trafford and who wasn't. Anderson, Duff, Farrar, McBride and Kinsey were gone and Bobby Noble was lying in hospital with serious head injuries, his career in ruins. Jimmy Rimmer had yet to make his first-team debut, but he was still young, and John Fitzpatrick had made just three league appearances at half-back, because Stiles and Crerand were irreplaceable as the first-team half-backs, but both the lads were considered strong future prospects. From that amazingly talented Youth Cup-winning side of 1964, only three players had really made it by the end of the 1966–67 season – George Best, David Sadler and John Aston.

Winger John Connelly's United career came to an abrupt end. He had played in one of the England games in the World Cup during the summer of 1966, scored twice for United in the first six games of the new season, been dropped and then swiftly transferred to Blackburn Rovers. Busby was no sentimentalist when he considered a player's time was done and his attention now switched to John Aston, who played twenty-six games in this championship year, with four substitute appearances, scoring four goals. His place was nearly secure, as he played in every game from mid-November as the regular outside-left, missing only three games with injury in February. However, although Busby might have wanted Aston in the team, the United supporters were considerably more dubious and their lack of conviction soon transmitted itself to the player:

> I'm not sure that I ever felt, 'I'm a first-team player now and I've made it,' but obviously I was playing regularly in the first team in the three seasons leading up to the European Cup. Life was always daunting at Old Trafford. It wasn't difficult to play as such and it wasn't that I didn't play to the best of my ability, but it was always a very nervous experience beforehand. I was much happier when the game started but the build-up, going to Davyhulme Golf Course and playing a game of putting, seeing familiar things in Trafford Park on the coach on the way in, seeing the crowd building up, I'd always think, 'I'd better perform today or else ...' so I found it more daunting than the Denis Laws and the George Bests and the Bobby Charltons. I had to overcome that atmosphere.

He didn't always succeed. Sometimes the hostility he experienced from his own supporters shredded his confidence: 'I went through a period, like Ian Bowyer at City, when the crowd didn't like me. That's what I found so difficult. I mean, I love the club, I still do, and I was a big fan, but the fans turned against me. It brought out a side of my character that stood me in good stead, because I had to grow up.'

Although it was exciting to be playing in the

championship-winning sides of Busby's third successful team, and to be playing alongside the great players of the day, Aston was aware that the experience was always going to be a double-edged sword:

> I was playing in that team with Best, Law and Charlton and, if you put decent players in a team with them, then, by comparison, they're going to look a lot worse. I know I looked more mundane than those stars. When the ball came to me I could feel the crowd willing me just to give it to another red shirt. They didn't want me to have it at all. We played in front of between 40,000 and 50,000 people and that, ironically, made it slightly easier, because it was just an anonymous roar, whereas 1,500 in a reserve match can be worse, because you can hear everything they say. I always think goalkeepers must have a thick skin, because they're stood still and they must hear things all the time.

Aston was by no means the only player to suffer in this debilitating way, though, and he remembers with grim irony the story of one of the young players who was on the way up at Old Trafford behind him:

> I remember I was playing at Luton and I was driving home after the game and Tommy Docherty, whom I've never met actually, was on the radio. United had just been given a going over by QPR, and Don Givens had scored two, and I had a chuckle to myself because Docherty said, 'This player should never have been allowed to leave Old Trafford.' But Don would never ever have made a player at Old Trafford. He was driven out by the crowd. They

derided him and he only played a handful of games. His personality was that of a decent Irish lad and a bit of a waif. He had to leave so he could blossom elsewhere, but that was what it was like as a player. Old Trafford was a cauldron. You sank or you swam and Don was a sinker.

There is something deliciously ironic in the foreknowledge that 'Young John', as he was always known to distinguish him from his father, was saving up his greatest ever performance in a red shirt for the greatest night in Manchester United's history.

David Sadler played in thirty-six of the forty-two games in that successful league campaign of 1966–67. It was the season that saw the gradual transformation of the goalscoring youth team prospect to the seasoned first-team defender. Ever since he had filled in for the injured Dave Farrar in the youth team tournament in Switzerland, David had been playing more and more at the back and enjoying it. He, too, knew all about the abuse of the crowd and somehow, if he didn't have to appear in the forward line instead of one of the hallowed trinity or the free-scoring David Herd, it came as much a relief to him as it was to the crowd. Bill Foulkes was coming to the end of a long career and David was obviously a candidate to take over, but he was also being used in midfield, frequently alternating with Nobby Stiles. His job description could not have been simpler. He was to win the ball and give it to Charlton or Crerand, whoever was the nearer. You didn't need a blackboard or one of Don Revie's dossiers for that. It was a task David was getting to enjoy far more than coping with the pressure of kicking or heading the ball into that ridiculously small net. The transition, however, was gradual rather than abrupt:

I can't ever remember anyone saying, 'Right, from now on you're going to be a centre half.' There was never anything like I went in one day and I was a centre-forward and I came home and I was a centre-half. I enjoyed playing at centre-half, even in the reserves. It was totally different obviously, but it really suited me and I felt comfortable doing it. For a while I had nothing to lose, because mentally I'm still thinking that I'm a centre-forward, so if I went out and played crap as a centre-half it didn't matter. But the longer it went on, I started to think, 'I like this. I like facing the game. Instead of having people whacking at the back of my legs because I have my back to the game but now everything is in front of me.' It just suited me and it became fairly apparent that was what was going to happen.

David began to establish himself in the first team as a defender or midfielder at exactly the same time as John Aston and Bobby Noble, in the autumn of 1966:

I can't remember the first game as such, but by this time substitutes were allowed and I remember being sub and coming on for most of the game. I think it was against Sheffield United, because I had to mark Mick Jones before he went to Leeds. In those days, Bill Foulkes almost never got injured, but this day he did. He was injured early on and I was on the bench, so they said, 'Right, on you go.' I went on and I played well.

David and George were still good friends, even though their off-the-field lifestyles were starting to diverge dramatically. The days of the snooker hall and the bowling alley were effectively over by now, even though George and David were still both officially registered at Mrs Fullaway's. George and Mike Summerbee rented a one-bedroom flat in an old Victorian house in the Crumpsall district of Manchester on the reasonable grounds that sex orgies were not encouraged by the club's landladies, although I have always wondered how they decided who got the bedroom and who got the couch in the living room. In 1967, David met Christine in the Greatstone Hotel, where Bobby Noble had drunk his last pint on that fateful night. Christine had been to art college in Salford, studying graphic design, moved to Paris for six months and only trailed home to Manchester after the money ran out. Her parents also went to the Greatstone Hotel and it was there that she met David Sadler after a night game at Old Trafford. They were married after the European Cup final the following year.

David had long since ceased to worry about money. His basic wage had risen steadily over the four years since he had signed professional forms, from £20 a week to £30 a week. Even deducting £5 for Mrs Fullaway and about the same for the Chancellor of the Exchequer, it still left a healthy surplus, because as his first-team appearances became more regular, he started to benefit from the large crowds United's winning brand of football was attracting. The players would receive £1 for every 1,000 over 40,000 and £2 for every 1,000 over 50,000. Well, it doesn't compare favourably with the £92,000 Manchester United are currently depositing in the bank account of one of their midfield players on a weekly basis, but then a day return to London by train cost £2.85 and the likelihood was that it ran on time and didn't come to an unexplained stop outside Stoke for an hour and a half.

After Bill Foulkes was injured against Sheffield Wednesday, David was handed the number five shirt on a regular basis. When he returned after six games out in time to play against Sheffield United over Christmas, David was restored to the number nine shirt, but he was no longer automatically being asked to perform as an old-fashioned centre-forward:

> 1966 was the World Cup and most sides were playing 4–3-3, which meant two centre-halves. Nobby was the defensive midfielder for England, but at United he played more as the other central defender, a quick little player to feed off the big centre-half, and that's how it went even the following year. Nobby started with his knee problem, so I would play together with Bill for that reason, and I'd play around Bill. Nobby and I would work as a team. Sometimes I'd be the deepest defender, playing with Bill, but as in the European Cup final, I would play as the defensive midfielder. It worked for us that Benfica pushed Eusebio right up front, so Nobby could take him out of the game, but if he went deep I'd look after him and we didn't want Nobby coming in front of me.

David had been part of United's sixties European experience from the start, because they had won the FA Cup in his first season in 1963. Busby's aim, however, had always been the European Cup and therefore neither of the other two European competitions merited serious attention. He echoed Bill Shankly's reaction to the UEFA Cup, the successor to the Inter-Cities Fairs Cup. When the Liverpool manager was asked about it, he affected ignorance. 'I wouldn't know, son,' he shrugged. 'We've never finished low enough to qualify.' It was the European Cup that made winning the first division so important, as David Sadler confirms:

> I think the players rated the league because of the forty-two games, but the club saw it as the only way

into the European Cup. I remember very clearly losing to Partizan Belgrade, because there was a feeling it had to be that year – that was when the team was ready. Going on after that the team would have to be broken up. Teams have a four- or five-year cycle, so having started in 1963, after 1966 there was a concern that we wouldn't be able to hang on for a minimum of two years.

In view of their extensive European travel in the sixties, when going to Europe was neither as relatively cheap nor as commonplace as it is today, during the Cold War, Sadler and the United team in general could have been affected politically by journeys to countries behind the Iron Curtain:

I remember being quite worried about the prospect of a nuclear bomb, but then I'd been to East Berlin to play football. I'd been through Checkpoint Charlie. We got stopped there for ages and ages, because we had to fill in all those forms. Some clown had filled in his name as 'James Bond' and the purpose of his visit as 'spying', which is so childish and ludicrous, but we ended up being stuck there for hours. We always suspected that the idiot was Crerand.

It's comforting to know that the infantile behaviour exhibited by some professional footballers has a long and proud history and is not simply a product of Sky television money or the invention of the premier league.

European competition was still a pipe dream for Manchester City in 1966–67. Despite the useful team that Mercer and Allison were building, it was only their second season together and they found it hard going in the first division. After three matches they had taken five points out

219

of six and were, for one breath-taking weekend at the end of August, top of the league, but they then promptly lost four out of the next five games and seven out of the next nine, so that by the end of October they were twenty-first and facing an immediate return to the second division. After a particularly embarrassing 4–1 defeat to Fulham at Craven Cottage at the end of November, Mercer dropped Harry Dowd and gave Alan Ogley his longest-ever run in the first team.

This was Alan's big chance. He'd waited a long time for it and he wasn't going to let it go to waste. Initially, things were far from promising. Three defeats and a draw from the four league matches between mid-December and mid-January kept City hovering around the relegation zone, but at least the scale of the defeats had been reduced, because they were all by a single goal. In fact, Ogley conceded just fifteen goals in seventeen league games and, during January and February 1967, the club was embarking on a grimly determined Cup run to follow the previous season's march to the sixth round. A disappointing 1–1 draw at home to Ipswich in the fifth round was followed by a 3–0 victory in the replay at Portman Road. It was City's best result of the season and it came the day after the winners had been drawn away at Leeds United in the next round. For Alan Ogley this was the chance to demonstrate to Don Revie that he was the number one goalkeeper at Manchester City, after the upsetting business with the car and Revie's unscrupulous attempts to entice him on to the Elland Road staff. In addition, it would be wonderful to demonstrate the fact to his parents, who would make the short trip up the road from Barnsley.

The Saturday following the victory at Ipswich saw City fulfil their league fixture at Elland Road. The match ended in a scoreless draw – a frustrating result for many spectators, but always a satisfactory scoreline for goalkeepers. Alan Ogley was twenty-one years old and his future prospects were highly attractive. In March 1966 he had married Diane, his childhood sweetheart from Barnsley, who then gave up her job in Barnsley when they moved into a small house in Bury, around the corner from Les Dawson. Within three months she was pregnant. Alan was ambitious only in the best professional sense of the word and there seemed no reason why he shouldn't realise all the dreams he had nurtured when he came to Maine Road to work with Bert Trautmann. However, on 1 April 1967, three weeks before Bobby Noble's crash and with almost the same suddenness, Alan Ogley's career disintegrated.

In the match at Bramall Lane, City went in at the interval trailing by a Mick Jones goal, headed past Ogley six minutes before the break:

> I'd had a really good game up to that point, but when we got back to the dressing room Joe Mercer really started on me, saying I should have done this and I should have done that. I thought it was out of order and I just blew my top. I took my shirt off, threw it on the floor and went into the showers. At that time, of course, there were no goalkeeping subs, but the red mist had descended. At the end of the day I was ashamed of what I did, but Malcolm took me to one side – and Malcolm's a big bloke. He addressed me in no uncertain terms and told me I shouldn't have done what I did. He built me up and told me to get my gear back on and go out there and prove myself. I went out there and I had a blinder. We finished up losing to that one Mick Jones goal.

It was entirely out of character for Alan to have behaved in that manner. He was a model professional, always calling the manager 'Boss' and the chairman 'Sir' ('It's the way I was brought up'). All the stories about 'Mister Magoo', as told by other players, are gently humorous, almost invariably concentrating on Alan's legendary status as the only blind goalkeeper in the Football League. Paul Hince and Stan Bowles were by no means the only culprits to play tricks on him, but they used to delight in waiting in the corridor outside the reserve team dressing room until Alan had taken off his enormous spectacles and then shouting, 'Morning, Magoo!' and giggling as poor Alan screwed up his eyes, trying to identify the origin of the greeting. In reserve matches it was rumoured that one of his defenders would shout as the corner kick was being taken, 'Jump now, Alan!'

Even in that first youth team year, the United lads knew all about the alleged blindness of the City goalkeeper. John Aston recalls: 'What I remember is being told he had shocking eyesight and if someone shot from thirty yards he had to make a great save, because he never saw it till it was six foot away. I think he may even have been the England keeper, but that was probably the reason he never made it.' Ogley was indeed a brilliant shot-stopper. During his long spells in the reserves, Alan's dedication never faltered, even if his eyesight did. Everyone seems to have a story about Alan's contact lenses, which were not the small designer objects many people wear today, but enormous things that looked like they would poke your eye out, which he carried about in a snuff box. Most stories revolve around the game stopping while twenty-two players and three match officials crawled around the City penalty area on their hands and knees, looking for the contact lens that had fallen out of Ogley's eye in a goalmouth skirmish. By far the most interesting story, however, concerns a reserve team match at Wolves, in which Paul Hince was playing at outside right:

It was an awful night in the middle of January, cold,

misty and rainy, and when they opened the skip they discovered that they'd left Magoo's contact lenses behind at Maine Road. So Dave Ewing said, 'What are you going to do, Magoo?' and he said, I'll play in me bins. Everyone laughed and so he said, 'All right then, I'll play without them.' I seem to recall that he was found facing the wrong way when we kicked off. I think he might have been talking to the goalpost. The full-back had to turn him the right way, but it's true that we only lost 2–1. One of the lads had told the ref about Magoo's disability, because he came into the dressing room at half-time and asked if we wanted him to put a pea in the ball, so Magoo could hear it coming.

Hince concludes this after-dinner anecdote with the information that all the City players were in the bath before someone realised that Ogley was still out on the pitch, guarding an empty goalmouth, in a deserted Molineux and wondering why the crowd had fallen so silent. This, unfortunately, is pure fabrication. However, it is clear from all the stories that no one had an unkind word to say about Alan, whose only desires in life were to play in goal for Manchester City and England and look after his wife and children. This is what makes it so hard to understand what happened in the dressing room at Bramall Lane that April Fool's Day. Alan might not have been remembered as a potential full international, especially since Gordon Banks was at the height of his glory in the late sixties, but he was certainly in the manager's plans:

Alf Ramsey took me to a tournament in Gibraltar on a four- or five-day trip to play against the Gibraltarians and the Army out there. I was taken along with Tony Macedo [the Gibraltar-born, long-serving Fulham goalkeeper] and I know for a fact that I was being educated in the right way to play for England. I reckoned I was number four in the country at the time. Ron Springett was probably above me, but he was falling out of favour with Alf and he was getting older, so I could have become deputy to Gordon Banks. I was in front of Stepney. It was Banks, Bonetti, Ron Springett and me. To be honest with you, I just blew it.

It was a spectacular explosion. Mercer and Allison said nothing to him after the Sheffield United match, despite his inspired display in the second half. That in itself was nothing unusual. City were still facing the very real prospect of relegation and the management would hardly have been in ebullient mood as the coach returned across the Pennines. Joe had spoken to Peter Gardner immediately after the game and told him that Harry Dowd would return to the side for the sixth round cup tie at Leeds the following Saturday. This report appeared in the first edition of the *Manchester Evening News* on the Monday morning. Alan picked up the paper and was incensed. Joe never announced Saturday's team on the Monday before the match, unless someone was injured and unavailable for selection. Again, completely against his nature, Alan stormed into the manager's office. As a rule he hated going up the stairs, because it usually meant he was being summoned to the headmaster's office for a ticking off. This time, though, it was Alan who was on the attack:

Joe said I needed to have a rest. I said I didn't need a rest. It was the sixth round of the FA Cup. It was a game I needed to play. He said Harry was in and I was in the reserves. I said, 'I'm not having this' and I walked out. I went back downstairs and I went to see

Malcolm in the trainers' room. I said if I can't play in the sixth round of the FA Cup I'm not playing in the reserves. Malcolm said, 'You won't be playing in the reserves. You're coming with us.' He understood that I wasn't in a fit state to play reserve-team football. Malcolm was brilliant – by far the best coach I ever worked under. Absolutely superb.

Mike Doyle recalls Ogley coming back into the changing room, stripping off his kit, getting dressed, storming out of the ground and driving away without saying a word to anyone. Ogley remembers that he and Allison went out on to the training field and for three days the coach spent precious time working with him, even though City had a vital match on the Saturday and he wasn't playing in it. He just wanted Alan to get everything out of his system – which he did. Ogley didn't play in the reserves, but travelled back across the Pennines to watch his team-mates lose unluckily to a Jack Charlton goal scored by the big centre-half standing on the goal line in front of Harry Dowd and obscuring the flight of the ball from the corner kick. Had the taller Ogley played ... The atmosphere calmed down thereafter, but Harry Dowd played the last eight games of the season, three of which were won and only one lost, so that City finished in the relatively respectable position of fifteenth in the first division. Alan Ogley and Joe Mercer never spoke again. Today, in his home in Barnsley, Alan Ogley will accept most of the blame for what happened:

It was me. I blew it. If I'd been the manager and my goalkeeper had done that to me, he'd never have played for me again. But I don't know why on the Monday the manager didn't get me in and say what I'd done was unacceptable and if I ever did that again

I'd be on the list. OK, I might not have played against Leeds, but it would have been different and my whole career would have been different.

Even Mike Summerbee, who usually has nothing but kind words to say about Joe Mercer, concedes that the manager made a mistake in the way he handled the Ogley situation:

He read it wrong. Sometimes, Malcolm or the boss would have a go at me. They knew if they told me I was crap that I could raise my game another 25 per cent, but I think in that incident the boss picked on the wrong player. I think what really upset him was the shirt being thrown down and the walking out. That's not what you do. What you do is to say, 'Right, I'll fucking show you. He's picked on the wrong person.' Alan Ogley was the sort of person who needed a pat on the back, not a bollocking. Alan was a lovely lad, a very sensitive person, and he just took it the wrong way. I wish he had said 'sorry' to the boss, even if he was right.

Alan Ogley wishes much the same thing: 'I thought that Malcolm would always see me right, but Malcolm was working for Joe. It was Joe's club. And quite rightly so. So nothing was said.'

Glyn Pardoe's initial suspicions of Mercer's ill health and Allison's braggadocio were eventually ameliorated by promotion in 1966 and the manager's increasingly successful ability to distinguish Glyn from Chris Jones. He was aware, too, of the *esprit de corps* which was considerably more boisterous and encouraging than the downbeat atmosphere he had experienced in the first-team changing room when he had made his debut: 'The first time Colin Bell joined us we were down at

Lilleshall. We were in dormitories and he came in and we'd done his bed up a treat. All the sheets were tied round the headboard and he couldn't get at any of them, and no sooner had he untied them than golf balls were being chucked into the room and went flying over his head. He must have wondered what he'd done, joining us.' This kind of nonsense is now greatly encouraged by psychologists specialising in 'team bonding'. Mercer's Marvels managed to do it all by themselves: 'We just gelled and we were so confident – there wasn't a team in the world we didn't think we couldn't beat. It seemed to come out of nothing. It was a wonderful team spirit. It was tough that first year back, but you could see progress.'

That progress began when Glyn Pardoe was told to change to the position in which he finally became the top-class player he had always threatened to be. It came early in October 1966, the week after a humiliating 1–4 home defeat to Tommy Docherty's bright young Chelsea side. Terry Venables had left to join Jimmy Greaves at Spurs, but the west London side, with an inside-forward trio of George Graham, Peter Osgood and Charlie Cooke, was far too good for City's fragile defence. Glyn had started the season at right-half, but had been moved back to centre-forward as Mercer and Allison sought desperately for a goal from somewhere. Summerbee, Bell, Crossan, Young and, initially, Jimmy Murray could scarcely find a goal between them and the consequent pressure that exerted on the defence was too much for that brittle unit. The week after Chelsea had inflicted that sound thrashing, Tottenham Hotspur arrived at Maine Road on the identical mission.

Bobby Kennedy had started the season at left-back, but he had been injured and replaced by David Connor, who was also injured in that Chelsea match. Pardoe's move to left-back, then, was born out of necessity as much as tactical genius. Glyn was due to mark the Spurs right-winger John Robertson, who had a devastating turn of speed:

> I thought he might give me a bit of a chasing, but he just knocked it past you and ran, and that was what I wanted. Then two weeks later I was up against Willie Morgan at Burnley and he was supposed to be tricky, but I found I could handle him. I was confident about playing at full-back, because I'd played at the back at school and I just felt I could play anywhere. I was a natural right-footer, but I could use my left OK and I think it helped being right-footed at left-back, because when the ball is coming from that side it's more natural to get the ball away with your good foot. I think it was an advantage really, as long as you could use your left foot. I thought of myself as two-footed – it was part of the job.

Would that that were the case today. Glyn's performances over the next three years were a professional delight. In Glyn Pardoe and Bobby Noble, Manchester contained the obvious successors to Ray Wilson as the regular England left-back. It was a mystery to everyone in Manchester how Terry Cooper got the job, particularly if Alf Ramsey had seen how Mike Summerbee gave Cooper such a hard time every time they faced each other. At the beginning of December 1966, two months after Glyn found his true position, Chris Jones was finally given his chance in the first team. Phil Burrows and Dave Wild had left the club, so he and John Clay were the only two left from the youth team of three years before who had yet to be awarded a first-team call-up. According to Paul Hince:

> Chris was infuriatingly keen and eager, a real head-banger. When the teamsheets went up on the Friday

he used to go apeshit if he wasn't in the first team —
'How long can they keep me out?!' he would scream.
Once we played a very physical encounter at West
Brom and I can remember crossing a ball from the
right wing. It was two yards from their goalie and
fifty-two yards away from Chris Jones and he just
put his head down and charged for the ball. The
goalkeeper could see Jonesy was coming towards him
like a rhino — and he headed the goalkeeper's head.
He was out cold and Dave Ewing had to charge on
with the smelling salts.

Despite the humiliation of seeing former right-back, Mike
Doyle, played at centre-forward instead of him the previous
year, Chris managed to retain his enthusiasm, a key element
which clearly Allison had not detected in Alf Wood and Phil
Burrows. Hince has great respect for Chris Jones' physical
courage: 'Chris was a great lad to have on your team — brave
as a lion or stupid. We played a Senior Lancashire Cup
match at Oldham and Chris Jones dislocated his kneecap,
which came right round. He didn't want to come off. He just
wanted it twisted round the right way again.' It was his
unquenchable enthusiasm, as well as his prolific scoring for
the reserves, which so impressed Dave Ewing and Johnny
Hart. They made a point of constantly encouraging Chris, as
did the scout, Harry Godwin, who had rescued the young lad
when he was leaning dejectedly on the fence at the end of
that very first trial day, six years earlier.

Chris Jones' debut came in the home match against
Nottingham Forest. The opportunity arose because Summerbee, who had filled in at centre-forward when Jimmy
Murray was dropped, was serving a suspension for having
been sent off against Newcastle and Alan Oakes had been
injured in training. Chris was being marked by the Scottish

veteran centre-half, Billy McKinlay. He was desperate to
score, but it was the other stand-in, Bobby Kennedy, who got
City's goal in a dull 1–1 draw. The following week, Chris
kept his place for the visit to the Hawthorns while, to his
satisfaction, Mike Doyle continued to ply his trade in the
reserves. City, who had won only four matches since August,
took both points in a fine 3–0 victory against the side that
had recently dumped them out of that season's League Cup
competition. Glyn scored the first goal and Chris notched the
second: 'Johnny Crossan was screaming for it, but I pulled it
away from the dead-ball line and smashed it into the net.
Afterwards, Johnny Crossan still thought I should have
passed to him.' The following week Summerbee returned,
but Neil Young was now injured, so Chris kept his place for
the third consecutive match. The following Saturday, however, Neil Young was fit again: 'I was dropped back down
into the reserves. Joe was very nice about it, but Youngy was
one of the stars of the first team. I understood that, but the
press was saying I should have been kept in the first team. I
enjoyed playing for the first team. It's where I thought I
belonged.'

Mercer and Allison weren't so sure. At the end of March
1967, the Liverpool-born left-winger, Tony Coleman, arrived
from Doncaster Rovers for the princely sum of £12,000 and
Neil Young was moved into the inside-left position, thereby
pushing Chris further down the list of possible first-team
strikers. If Chris Jones was a headbanger, Tony Coleman
was a psychotic lunatic. A talented, self-destructive player,
with an irrepressible liking for everything in the world that
managers hate – particularly gambling, drinking and practical jokes – Coleman spent two and a half whirlwind years at
Maine Road. He arrived, according to legend, with his boots
wrapped in a brown paper parcel, a legend that was possibly
created in order to invest Coleman with the properties of a

homeless waif who was looking for a kindly foster family. The only Fosters Coleman wanted came out of cans, and if the boots were indeed wrapped in brown paper, it was probably because he'd given the bag they were previously in to a bookie in payment for some long-standing debt.

Nevertheless, at the age of twenty, Chris Jones could spend the summer break of 1967 knowing he had had his initial run of games in the first team, he was clearly in the plans of the manager and coach, and therefore he could look forward to a decent season in 1967–68. It was to be hoped that City wouldn't have to face yet another battle with relegation. Not even Malcolm Allison in one of his wilder prophecies could have dreamt what fate held in store for the players, staff and supporters of Manchester City in the season that began in turmoil in August 1967.

CHAPTER EIGHT

Annus Mirabilis
1967–68

There are some years which are destined to linger long in the memory for both private and public reasons. In 1759, General Wolfe in Canada and Robert Clive in India added so greatly to the lustre of the burgeoning British Empire that a song was written to commemorate their achievements. Two hundred years later, innocent schoolboys in Bury, Lancashire, were forced to gather round the piano in music lessons and warble the jingoistic hymn, 'Hearts of Oak': 'Cheer up, my lads/'Tis to glory we steer/To add something more/To this wonderful year.' No doubt in 1759, lyricists were already congratulating themselves that the expanding power of the British Navy was enabling them to rhyme 'slaves' and 'waves' so appropriately.

The year 1963 wasn't immortalised in song in quite the same way, although the Beatles' first number one hit, 'Please Please Me', certainly evokes something of that time for those of us who spent six shillings and eightpence (thirty-three pence in new money) on its purchase. Despite the absence of jingoistic songs, 1963 was a truly memorable year, including as it did the revelation of the Profumo Affair, the Great Train Robbery, the assassination of President Kennedy and Manchester City's relegation from the first division after Denis Law's disputed penalty – and 1968 was another. Momentous circumstances at home and abroad gave those of us who lived through them the feeling that we were witnessing the making of history at first hand. Events at Wembley Stadium and St James' Park jostled for attention with the imminent collapse of Western governments and bourgeois values before successive onslaughts of European students, radicals and intellectuals.

In the United States, in April 1968, Martin Luther King was shot dead outside a motel in Memphis, Tennessee. Two months later, Robert F Kennedy was assassinated in the Ambassador Hotel in Los Angeles at the moment of his victory in the Democratic party's primary election in California. In August, Mayor Daley's cops attacked anti-Vietnam war demonstrators on the streets of Chicago as the delegates voted Vice President Hubert Humphrey their candidate to face Richard Nixon in the November presidential election. In France, *Les evenements* of May 1968 within twelve months brought down the ten-year administration of Charles de Gaulle, sending the old man into pouting exile in Colombey les deux Eglises. In Czechoslovakia, the Prague spring of Alexander Dubcek was followed by the arrival of Russian tanks in the streets of the capital and brutal reprisals by a Communist regime determined to reimpose its rule over a sullen, but cowed, people.

In Manchester, the destiny of that year's league championship and the European Cup were understandably regarded as considerably more important than the impending disintegration of Western civilisation. Defeat for either team in those competitions might have brought forth into Albert Square a Mancunian version of Jan Palach, the brave martyr of Wenceslas Square. Fortunately, in neither case was it necessary and May 1968 in Manchester was the greatest month in the city's footballing history.

The boys of 1964 were all men now, twenty-two years old and hardened by six or seven years of exposure to the bump

and grind of professional football. For three of the United
players, 1968 brought immortality at Wembley. In the semi-
final of the European Cup, at the stage where United had
already fallen in 1957 (against Real Madrid), 1958 (against
AC Milan) and 1966 (against Partizan Belgrade), they were
drawn against traditional rivals Real Madrid who, if not as
good as the redoubtable Puskas, Di Stefano team of the late
fifties, were nevertheless still formidable opponents. In the
first leg at Old Trafford, Aston made the solitary goal for
Best to score, but it was a slender lead to take to the
Bernabeu fortress.

The return leg wasn't played for another three weeks,
during which time United let the league championship slip
from their grasp after an extraordinary Monday night 6–3
defeat at the Hawthorns and a surprising 1–2 capitulation at
home to Sunderland in the last game of the season. It seemed
as though the manager and the players were concentrating
on what might happen in Spain the following Wednesday.
What followed was a first-half pasting by a rampant Madrid,
before a distinctly unlucky own goal by Zoco restricted the
home side to a 3–1 lead at half-time.

David Sadler had long since settled into his role in
defence or as a defensive midfielder, but this was the night
that David Sadler, the teenage goalscoring prodigy, was to
make a triumphant return:

It was a fantastic atmosphere and we were getting
slaughtered when we went off at half-time. Matt said,
'I don't mind losing, but let's go out with some pride,'
and in that ten minutes, between him and Jimmy
Murphy, we managed to get our heads up. I had been
playing very deep, but Matt told me to push forward
as much as I could. Midway through the second half a
cross came in, the keeper came out, missed it and it hit

my foot and deflected into the goal. We hadn't been out of it, it just felt like we were, but at 3–3 on aggregate the whole tie changed – it was like someone had turned the radio off, the crowd went so quiet. And then a few minutes later, it was Bill [Foulkes]'s turn, which was strange because he scored so rarely, though he went up for corners like they all did. It was a classic striker's goal and it was 4–3 and we were through.

Celebrations were not restricted to the Red portion of Manchester. The entire country was seemingly *en fête*. Of all the players, it probably meant more to John Aston than to any of the others, because he had been a boyhood fan:

The best night I ever had as a supporter was at Maine Road [in February 1957] when United beat Bilbao 3–0 and Johnny Berry scored the winner. I saw all those European games – Borussia Dortmund and beating Anderlecht 10–0 – and at the time the thing that used to fascinate me was the map of Europe on the back of the programme. They used to have little flags in every country and for the teams that were left in the competition the flags were black with white lettering and it would say 'Real Madrid' in Spain and the teams that were knocked out were the reverse. I used to study that map as a kid and wonder who United would play in the next round if they beat this lot. I wondered what it must be like to travel to Poland and places like that. At Wembley in 1968, all those special feelings from those European nights of ten years back came together. It was kismet, destiny. That's the only way I can describe why I just felt that everything was going to go right that night.

Of course it did, particularly for John, who did to the Portuguese full-back exactly what he had done to Mike Doyle at Old Trafford in the Youth Cup just over four years earlier: 'Busby always said to go out and enjoy the occasion, so I did, because I could see the full-back was one of those heavy-set guys I like playing against. I remember the first time I got the ball I knocked it too far ahead, and I knew I'd given myself too much to do, but I scooted past the full-back and I knew I was on a winner then.' Aston was arguably the best player on the field that night, causing thousands of United supporters to claim that they always knew he was brilliant, they'd known it all along, and they could never understand why the rest of the crowd had taunted him so mercilessly. David created the opening goal for Charlton and George scored the vital second goal in the first minute of extra time. The combination of Wembley as the venue and the tenth anniversary of the Munich air crash mixed with national feelings about Busby and Charlton, in particular, to raise this ordinary game of football to one of mythic status. George, John and David knew that:

> The European Cup night was the greatest of nights and will remain so for all our lives. We never spoke about Munich, but we were constantly aware of it. Matt, Bobby and Bill were survivors and we just knew how important it was to them, but at that time it was never on the agenda. In later years, you talk to Bobby about Duncan Edwards, you understand the depth of the emotion. For people like Jimmy Murphy, who was the heart and soul of Manchester United, the European Cup is mixed up with that and with Munich. Matt was never a well man again after Munich. He had this one terrible need inside him to win the Cup for the boys who had died. I think

sometimes he felt he had personally killed them in his
pursuit of this romantic, glorious dream.

John Aston makes a valid and very healthy comparison
between Busby and Ferguson, and between United and
football then and now:

> When I talk about Busby or my father or Jimmy
> Murphy, or the coaching or the training, you've got to
> look at it historically. To Matt Busby it was a great
> sporting occasion, I'm sure. His desire to win it was
> no less than that of Alex Ferguson, but he viewed life
> in a different way. Those men went through a war.
> My father was getting shot at. Now football takes on
> a different perspective, when things like that have
> happened. Football was a sport and the European
> Cup final was a tremendous sporting occasion, but
> that's all it was, no matter how important. If we'd lost,
> we'd have survived it.

It's not a popular view in the commercially dominated,
shallow world that football inhabits in 2004, but it is likely to
stand the judgement of history better than most of what
currently passes for analysis.

David, George and John were still the youngsters of that
European Cup-winning side, apart from the precocious
Brian Kidd, who celebrated his nineteenth birthday by scoring the third goal that night. John Aston's friends were
David, George, Jimmy Ryan and John Fitzpatrick. They
formed their own card school on the coach travelling to
matches. Bobby Charlton, Bill Foulkes and Shay Brennan
sat apart, because they were of a different generation. For
them, as for Busby, somehow the triumph of Wembley 1968
laid so many ghosts to rest that it became the end of the

fifties' dream, not the start of something greater to take the club into the seventies.

Best, Sadler and Aston were particularly conscious of this feeling. The soul seemed to pass from the body of Busby's Manchester United, even as Bobby Charlton lifted the trophy. Next season, despite reaching the semi-final of the European Cup again, where they were somewhat unluckily knocked out by a potent combination of AC Milan and the referee (1–2 on aggregate), they began their long slow decline. It took replays to get past both Birmingham City and Watford in the FA Cup, before they lost to Everton in the sixth round, and in the first division, the sole gateway to the European Cup outside of winning it, they could only finish a disappointing eleventh. Busby retired and handed over to Wilf McGuinness, setting in train the years of torment. The lads might have been only twenty-three or twenty-four, but their great days in the game were effectively over. What remained were six or seven years of professional football of an increasingly poor standard and, in Best's case, a lifetime of notoriety. And these were the guys who had 'made it'.

Alan Duff listened to the commentary from Wembley on the radio, because there was no such thing as television in the South Africa of apartheid, presumably because in monochrome they couldn't separate the black pictures from the white ones: 'To get a decent reception we had to sit on the roof of a building. I'm a big United supporter, so I was delighted they won. It had been a great time for me at Old Trafford. It was just the last year when I grew so disillusioned and disheartened.' Alan was finding it hard going in South Africa, despite the fact that the team he was playing for, Highland Park, won their league both years he was there. However, he was constantly thinking about the mistake he felt he had made in leaving England:

I remember telling David Herd I was going to South Africa and he said, 'Don't go, don't do it!' I said, 'I'm on my way out here if I stay in England,' but he just repeated, 'Don't go! Even if you have to drop down into the fourth division, stay over here.' But I wouldn't listen. He warned me that once I left this country I was out of circulation and it would be almost impossible to get back in. And it was true – that's what happened.

At least Alan was still playing football. Bobby Noble hadn't even that comfort, as he sat and watched the European Cup final on television. Halfway through the 1967–68 season Bobby had attempted a comeback in the Lancashire League, where he had played as a sixteen-year-old apprentice: 'I played some B team games, but I always knew it was impossible from day one. I'd fractured my skull. I was in a coma for weeks. They thought there was pressure inside the head, but they didn't operate because they wanted to see what it was like when the swelling went down.' He was markedly slower than he had been. The old rapier-swift, hard-tackling full-back had gone forever. The crash had produced brain damage, which destroyed his balance and his co-ordination and gave him permanent double vision and the humiliating side-effect of incontinence. The United physiotherapist, who had arranged for John Aston Sr to be operated on by a surgeon in a dinner jacket and an alcoholic haze, was not impressed: 'Ted Dalton came down and said it was all in my mind and I should run it off, but I had permanent double vision. I finished up in Harley Street and then I was operated on in Manchester Royal to try and level the eyesight.'

Busby kept him in the first-team squad, so that he was regarded as an injured player and paid accordingly. It preserved his basic wage (which was about £40 a week less tax and national insurance), but there were none of the financial perks he had come to expect – the crowd and win bonuses and appearance money. The rent on the club house was only thirty shillings a week, but what was crippling was the depression that consumed him entirely. His remarkable wife, Irene, recalls that for the first few weeks of married life she thought she was the luckiest woman in the world, because while all her friends had to manage on £5 a week, Bobby gave her £10 for the housekeeping. This feeling of luxury was to be brief. Thirteen months after the crash outside the garage in Sale, Bobby's former team-mates were running round Wembley Stadium with the European Cup, but his career was in ruins. He was now twenty-two years old.

For different reasons, Alan Ogley watched City's triumph in the early part of the month with similarly mixed emotions. He started off the season in the first team and played resolutely in the opening game, a scoreless draw at home to Liverpool, but after the next match, which was lost 3–2 away at Southampton, he was dropped (he admits that at least one of the goals was his fault) and Harry Dowd was recalled. This time the exclusion was to be permanent. Mercer and Allison had been looking at the promising young Stockport County goalkeeper, Ken Mulhearn. When Harry Dowd broke a finger in a 1–0 defeat at Arsenal on 23 September, and with the derby match at home to United coming up the following Saturday, the City management team moved into action. At least Malcolm Allison did:

Joe said he had nothing to do with my transfer from City. Malcolm had conducted that. All my dealings were done through Malcolm. And Malcolm was always part of us – downstairs with us, a player's man. Joe wasn't there. It was Malcolm who told me that Stockport were interested – they'd been promoted to the third division the previous year – and Jimmy Meadows was the manager. I said I didn't want to go, but Malcolm asked me to go down there and listen to Jimmy, so I went. I worked out that City were trying to get shot of me – that was a big surprise. I could have said no, because I was still under contract, but I knew they wanted Ken Mulhearn and he would go into the first team, and Harry would be the reserve keeper, so where did that leave me? It didn't take a genius to work out the answer.

There were some compensations. City players were not earning big money and the £60 a week he thinks he was earning at City was matched by third division Stockport. Additionally, a transfer to County meant he wouldn't have to move house and uproot the family, and the road from Bury where he lived to Stockport's training ground was relatively easy to negotiate. So he moved from a side on the verge of the first division championship to one that had recently been in the fourth division. He was to become a folk hero at Edgeley Park over the next nine years, but the days of possible top club honours and England caps were gone forever.

In 1972, after Joe Mercer, too, had been manoeuvred out of Maine Road by the ambitions of Malcolm Allison and his supporters, Alan Ogley and Joe Mercer met again after a friendly match against Coventry City, Mercer's new club. They talked for the first time since Alan had thrown his goalkeeping jersey on the floor of the Sheffield United dressing room in April 1967: 'That was the first time we'd even talked about it, because I'd blown my top originally and he'd put his foot down and said he was the manager of the club. He dropped me and I never spoke to Joe again till that day at Stockport, all those years later. We didn't swear at each other, we just never spoke. It was a friendly, quiet talk.' Joe Mercer had reached the heights with five trophies in five years, but Alan was around for only one of them. The incident in question had taken place five years earlier and was a source of deep regret for Alan, but Joe had too many other regrets and he never really recovered from the inexplicable manner in which the most successful manager in the history of Manchester City suddenly lost his job, even as his side was challenging for the league championship again.

The triumph of 1968 was not a particularly satisfying experience for Chris Jones. After three successive years as the leading goalscorer in the reserves, he too played in that opening match, the disappointing 0–0 draw against Liverpool, even though he wasn't fit:

> I didn't do myself justice. We got away with 0–0. I had one chance. Youngy ducked and I caught it on the volley, but I didn't take it. Then I played against Sunderland in February on the day that Mike Summerbee made his full international debut against Scotland at Hampden. We won 1–0 with a goal by Francis Lee, but the next week Mike was back and I never played in the first team again.

Since he played only those two games, he didn't collect a championship medal.

After the memorable 4–3 win at Newcastle in the last game of the season, City arranged a friendly against Bury to exhibit the trophy to their fans. It was a festive evening and included a much-appreciated appearance by Malcolm Allison. Playing for Bury that night was a curly-haired young forward called Bobby Owen, who scored two skilful goals. Mercer and Allison sat up and took notice. Chris Jones saw them, read what Peter Gardner was reporting in the *Manchester Evening News* and decided to confront the manager to clarify the situation:

> After we won the league and had been to America, I went in to see Joe at the start of pre-season training, in July 1968. Malcolm Allison blew hot and cold with players. I wanted to know what my future was, because I'd played six games and I'd scored so many goals for reserves, and Joe said, 'I want you to stay,' and I said, 'I've got a sneaky feeling Malcolm doesn't.' He said, 'I don't care what Malcolm thinks. I'm the boss here and I want you to stay. You're the centre-forward and you can do a job for me.'

It was exactly what Chris wanted to hear, but this supposed clearing of the air simply clouded the issue, because now there were two kings sitting on the Maine Road throne. It was the unfortunate consequence of success and it perpetuated the long-standing and impeccably observed Manchester City tradition that, if things are going particularly well on the field, this must be the perfect moment to destroy everything off the field. Mercer had been ill when he had arrived in the summer of 1965 and, in an unguarded moment, had said to Allison that he would be happy to hand the club over to him in two years. In two years, however, they had won the second division championship and were setting off on a glorious campaign that would bring them the first division title in spectacular style. Suddenly, Joe wasn't ill any more and any thought of retirement had been banished. This convenient amnesia did not afflict Malcolm Allison, though, and over the next two years he and his supporters mounted a relentless campaign to destabilise the boardroom, even as the players on the field were giving the club its most sustained spell of success for over thirty years. Chris Jones was not entirely comforted by Mercer's expression of support:

> I went outside and Malcolm asked me if I was going down to training in Wythenshawe Park. I said yes and Malcolm came with me. He got in the car and he said, 'What's the boss been saying?' I said, 'He thinks I should stay and fight for my place.' He said, 'I'm going to sign Bobby Owen and I don't think you should. If Swindon come for you, take it. I'm going to play Bobby Owen.' I just said, 'Well, that's your opinion. Joe thinks I'm good enough to stay here and fight.' But it was a veiled threat. I knew it and I left and I've always regretted it. I should have gone and talked to my mentor, Johnny Hart, but I didn't.

Chris Jones signed for Swindon Town two weeks later on 25 July 1968. It broke his heart to leave Maine Road:

> I loved playing for Manchester City – local lad in a light blue shirt, number nine on his back, top team in Manchester, that's what it was all about. Just to train at Maine Road was wonderful and then to play in a Central League game there and score goals! I scored for the reserves before I did for the youth team. I should never have left, because the great days were still to come and I wasn't part of it. Manchester United were there to be beaten.

I can't prove it, but I strongly doubt whether the legion of players who have pulled on the light blue shirt since then can look back at their time at Manchester City and talk as passionately as this about the club, the ground and the supporters, even though they have been poorly served by the management. Today's players are motivated by different forces.

The opening match of what turned out to be the triumphant 1967–68 season included four members of the youth side of 1964 – Jones, Ogley, Pardoe and Connor. At right-half, the left-footed David Connor replaced Mike Doyle, who was suspended for having been sent off at Nottingham Forest in a 2–0 defeat at the end of the previous season. He kept his place after the defeat at Southampton for the trip to Stoke, where City were crushed 3–0. Mike Summerbee spent the entire ninety minutes fighting with the left-back, the violence transmitting itself to the unsegregated supporters, among whom I was standing. It was a distinctly unpleasant afternoon. It was 26 August and it seemed we were in for another season of struggling against relegation and hoping Manchester United didn't win the European Cup. In the event, neither prognostication came true.

David Connor had played at centre-forward in the defeat at Stoke, with Roy Cheetham at right-half and Mike Doyle at inside-left. It was the match that convinced the crowd, as well as Mercer and Allison, that the club was going to have to break its transfer record to sign Francis Lee. A side with David Connor at centre-forward was not going to win the cl ampionship. It took another six weeks before Lee arrived, s 't was probably desperation that caused the management to make the crucial changes that eventually brought its reward on the last day of the season. For the return match against Southampton, in front of the regular attendance of 22,000, Summerbee moved to centre-forward, Paul Hince was given his second start on the right wing, Mike Doyle substituted for Roy Chetham at right-half and Neil Young moved to inside-left to accommodate the return of Tony Coleman on the wing. Miraculously, with the exception of Francis Lee, who was transferred from Bolton Wanderers in early October, the team that was to transform the fortunes of the club suddenly took shape.

It wasn't great news for David Connor. He played in ten out of the forty-two league games that year – in seven different positions. It was the start of his years of wandering, unable to find a regular position in the team because he was so useful in so many different areas of the pitch. It was as if the role of substitute had been specially designed for him. It did not please him, but his temperament was such that he was incapable of complaining to the management. David Connor, nicknamed Tadger by Johnny Hart, was the perfect team player, always willing to subordinate his own desires to the demands of the club.

At the end of the season, Paul Hince discovered that they were on the same wages, despite Connor having made nearly a hundred first-team appearances, as opposed to Hince's eight. The winger persuaded him to join the growing list of players waiting outside Mercer's office to demand a pay rise to a wage level consistent with the club's newly acquired status as champions of the Football League:

> I'm about number sixteen in line. I knock on the door and before I got in Joe shouted, 'Oh, not you as well, Tadger! You're not asking for a pay rise too, are you?' By this time I'd already given up hope. 'Tadger, let me put it like this to you, son. See that barrel?' I looked, but I couldn't see a barrel anywhere. 'It was full of money, but Summerbee's been in here, then Lee, then Bell ...' and he went right through the team. 'They've all had a dip and there's nothing in it. Look!' I looked where he was pointing, but I still couldn't see anything. He said, 'There's nothing left, so bugger off!' So I did. As I went out I passed two young apprentices and I was asking myself why I didn't say anything when I heard Joe

Mercer call out, 'Next!' So I said to the apprentices, 'If he asks you to look in a barrel, don't look 'cause it's not there.' I go down the corridor and I can hear Joe shouting out, 'I hope you're not coming for a pay rise ...' in exactly the same tone of voice he used with me.

He returned to find the curious Paul Hince waiting for him downstairs. When asked eagerly if he had got the much-needed pay rise, Connor shook his head, then added, 'But he said I was a great player and his door was always open.' Mercer knew his man. To David Connor, such praise was more valuable than the extra £5 a week the manager might have been forced to concede to a more voluble player.

Joe Mercer had been a top-class international wing-half in his day and he knew one when he saw one. For the first two years of his managerial term at Maine Road, he had looked for a right-half to complement Alan Oakes' reliability at left-half. He tried any number of players – Stan Horne, Glyn Pardoe, Roy Cheetham and Matt Gray, as well as Mike Doyle, who had played nineteen games in the second division championship but only fourteen in the first year back in the first division. It was his emergence, in the autumn of 1967, that settled the defence and the midfield. From a player unsure of his place in a struggling team in 1966–67, he grew in stature so rapidly that in 1968 he was picked for four England Under-23 matches. Mike Doyle had always been a combative individual. To this day, Alf Wood and Chris Jones will remark on the fact as soon as his name crops up in discussion, but nobody could fault his commitment. Of that Youth Cup side he was one of the two unalloyed successes.

The other one was Glyn Pardoe. Just as the name of Mike Doyle will arouse memories of confrontation with other players, that of Glyn Pardoe will evoke nothing but respect and affection. That is not to suggest that Pardoe was a soft touch. Glyn could be immensely tough in his own way but, like his cousin 'our Alan', he was always quiet, modest and unassuming. In some clubs, such players become victims. Glyn was too steely a competitor to arouse that response. However, his and Alan Oakes' noted abstemiousness did occasionally lead to their being exploited by the coach, for whom abstemiousness was no virtue, as Peter Gardner recalls:

> In September 1970, City were playing Bologna in the Anglo-Italian Cup and we were staying in a luxury hotel in Rimini and Malcolm was buying champagne for everyone, putting the charge down to Alan Oakes and Glyn Pardoe's room. They neither of them drank, they wouldn't care. They shared a car, they were inseparable, till Colin Bell joined them and then Mike Doyle – they were big mates. Lovely modest man, Glyn Pardoe. It was a master stroke to switch him to left-back. He was a natural athlete – a sprinter as a kid and a great golfer, too.

Like Doyle, Pardoe had found his natural home in a team in which his gifts could flourish. They were both twenty-one years old when the championship was won. There seemed no reason why they should not play together for Manchester City for another ten years.

The championship season saw both the rise and fall of John Clay. After five years on the staff, he finally made his long-awaited debut. It had been a long wait and, as others from that youth side were given the chance to take the stage before him, he could have been forgiven for bemoaning his fate:

> I was desperately frustrated at not getting in, but I

249

wasn't the type of person who went knocking on the manager's door, demanding to know why he wasn't playing. And I was playing quite well in the reserves. Dave Ewing said I scored the best goal he'd ever seen at Maine Road, picking the ball up from the corner, wriggling along the by-line, beating about eight men and scoring. I scored at Everton from about thirty-five yards, which was unusual for me. I'm sure Malcolm heard about it, but I never got stuck into the first team.

There was usually a reason. By and large Malcolm liked young players, he liked how open they were to new ideas. You couldn't tell Roy Hartle and Tommy Banks to play with six full-backs and no goalkeeper. He must have suspected something about John Clay, who was of course known as Cassius:

> I just didn't progress, plus I didn't look after myself the way I should have done. I didn't put any weight on and I can remember being with Stan Bowles in the Bus Stop Club at six o'clock one Saturday morning. That wasn't like me at all. I'd just lost it. Plus I went to Bredbury Hall, when that was the local place to be, and I was there till late. If my dad had been alive I wouldn't have done all that.

The grammar school boy was turning into a manager's nightmare, which was puzzling, because he was a bright lad who could see the consequences of his actions and who had always applied himself diligently to the world of work outside the game: 'I always worked. I was always thrifty. I sometimes worked at the big bread place in Stockport called Birkett & Bostock. Once I worked at Birkett's for seven twelve-hour night shifts, but I came out of the place, walked down the road and I bought a Mini, brand new, for 600 quid in cash.' Unfortunately, a new John Clay was beginning to emerge, one who frequented nightclubs rather than workplaces. Malcolm Allison was such a frequenter of nightclubs and a consumer of both champagne and publicity that he positively encouraged his first-team players to celebrate their success. For outgoing individuals like Francis Lee and Mike Summerbee, it came naturally. For introverts like Bell, Pardoe and Oakes, it was contrary to their characters, but team spirit was high and the dressing room was united. For young players it was a different matter. The combination of Tony Coleman, Stan Bowles and John Clay was one the management regarded with deep suspicion:

> Stan was an amateur, then an apprentice, then a pro, before TC came and joined City. Me and Stan were inside-forward partners in the reserves for about a year, so we went into town together and went into the bookies together. I'd had a job before, when I worked for Parkinson's, who were big bookmakers in those days, and I was going out with the boss's daughter – Pauline Parkinson. But now I didn't have a job and I hung out with Stan at the bookies, at the dog track and in clubs. I didn't go completely off the rails, but I certainly wasn't as disciplined as I should have been just at the time when I was trying to break into the first team. I was a fixture in the reserves by now and I was getting depressed and disillusioned, because I felt I should have had a run in the first team. If they'd stuck me in when I was seventeen or eighteen I'm sure I would have done the business.

One reason for his lack of promotion were the bad injuries

that blighted his first two years as a professional. Another was his unfortunate encounter with Joe Mercer on one of the rare days when Joe turned up to a Central League game. As a rule, John played inside-right, with Paul Hince on the wing outside him. The two of them became very close and, with the mischief-making Stan Bowles at inside-left, this was a combination of talented scallywags that the manager knew had to be sorted out, as Hince recalls:

> We had a system, so when Cassius got knackered, which he did after twenty-five minutes, I'd go inside and he could go and have a rest on the wing and get his breath back. We did this week in, week out. Nobody minded, because Dave Ewing was the reserve-team coach and he liked us. Anyway, one day Joe Mercer came to watch us and at half-time he summons us and he's puce with rage. 'You two – in the treatment room now!' and we knew that's where you always got a bollocking. He started off shouting that we were two of the youngest players on the staff, and he picked the team, and we were supposed to stick to our positions, not have a rest. Then suddenly John Clay started laughing and I noticed, too, that Joe Mercer had got two ties on, one on top of the other. He had a brown tie and a green tie on top of that, and he stopped, not realising what we were laughing at, and he just stormed out.

Great fun, but not the best way to persuade the manager to play you instead of Colin Bell. There must have been a good chance that John Clay would have been released at the end of either the 1965–66 season or the 1966–67 season, because his injuries had restricted the appearances he made and it seems unlikely that Joe Mercer appreciated being laughed at, even if he was wearing two ties. The fact is that John Clay was a greatly gifted footballer and it seems clear that both Mercer and Allison accepted the fact and decided to give him one more season. John had been a travelling reserve, as part of a thirteen-man squad, a number of times already:

> I remember one match at Southampton when everyone had said I was going to make my debut and I didn't, and then I went to Fulham the following week when everyone said I'd be playing, but again Stan Horne was picked instead. I was knocking in goals every third game in the reserves, but never got the chance to step up.

He sat on the bench with a number twelve on his back three times before finally coming on at Maine Road, as the substitute when Tony Coleman was injured in the match against Wolves in October 1967. That day also marked Francis Lee's first appearance and ended in a comfortable 2–0 victory. After a three-game losing streak, it set the team off on an eleven-match unbeaten run which lasted until Boxing Day, when they lost, slightly unfortunately, 2–3 away at West Bromwich. That was another disappointment for Clay:

> Colin Bell and Mike Doyle had been injured in the 4–2 win at home to Stoke on the Saturday. The West Brom Boxing Day match was three days later on the Tuesday and I was sure I was going to play, but Stan Bowles replaced Colin at inside-right and Stan Horne took Mike's place at right-half. I wasn't even sub – Roy Cheetham came on when Tony Coleman was injured. Anyway, we lost that one and sure enough for the return match on the Saturday I was in at number eight, instead of Stan Bowles. Now I knew that Stan

Bowles had been out all night over Christmas Day and he was in no condition to play at the Hawthorns, which he proved because he had an absolutely horrendous game. I remember Malcolm coming into the bath afterwards and absolutely blasting Bowles. Stan, of course, didn't give a toss.

He also didn't get another game for a year. John took the field in Colin Bell's shirt for the match against West Brom at Maine Road, where City had scored eighteen goals in their previous four matches. By now the crowd was expecting not just victories, but victories by thumping margins. They tried hard enough against West Brom, but nothing went right for them that day and they went down to an entirely unexpected defeat, the first at home since United had beaten them in the derby match at the end of September. It had been a miserable Christmas and John was not in a position to celebrate his first team debut: 'I just never got into the game. I didn't get much of the ball off the lads, but having said that, we battered them and on any other day it could have been 6–0 to us, but they got a goal early on, and another one just before the end.'

For the next game, away at Nottingham Forest, Clay was dropped and the ever-reliable David Connor took over the number eight shirt. City won 3–0 and John Clay never played for Manchester City again.

Glyn Pardoe and Mike Doyle were young twenty-one-year-old regular first-team performers in a side that was destined for more success. John Clay was an old twenty-one-year-old reserve team player who would have to dislodge Colin Bell or Mike Doyle to claim a first-team spot, while Stan Bowles and Tony Towers were coming through the junior ranks and were younger than he was. As the first team began its charge to glory, John Clay was preparing himself to face the fact that his dream of success at Manchester City was never going to happen:

> I suppose I had vibes that the chop was coming. I remember coming back from Newcastle, where we'd just won the championship, and reserves like Stan Horne and Chris Jones and me wound up at Bredbury Hall. We ended up on the stage and everyone was buying us champagne. It was the most wonderful night – everyone knew me because I was the local lad. I felt slightly removed from the celebrations, because I was just a reserve. I'd played no real part in the championship victory, but that reception was just incredible. A couple of weeks later I got the letter saying they weren't going to renew my contract. I was twenty-one. That summer I went back to Bredbury Hall – this time, serving behind the bar.

Opinion about John Clay is mixed. Paul Hince, who played with him a long time, is convinced that, but for the succession of injuries, he would have made a first-team player: 'The outstanding player in that 1964 youth team was John Clay. John Clay was the ideas man and he had wonderful control – and he was great at head tennis. Clay could have done anything, but for those broken legs.' Clay feels, similarly, that it was the injuries which destroyed him. Even today he is still suffering: 'I'd had so much frustration with injury. This lad backed on to me just as I was jumping for a corner and the ankle just went. I must have been to twenty physios and it's never really gone away. Eventually I had to give up squash because of it.'

Glyn Pardoe accepts that Clay was skilful, but feels he shirked tackles and some of the hard work in training and on the field that midfielders have to accept. He was the author of his own downfall. He had the talent, but he lacked the drive to transform it into a durable professional technique. Chris Jones thinks that, for all his ability, Clay's game needed opening up, that he didn't attempt enough defence-splitting passes, but what nobody denies is that he was as talented as anyone in either of those 1964 youth sides, except, of course, for George. John Aston certainly appreciated his skill: 'I always had great respect for John Clay. I thought he was a very, very good footballer.'

On 13 July 1968, as the Manchester City players returned for pre-season training in a year that would see them follow their league championship with the capture of the FA Cup, that very, very good footballer signed for non-league Macclesfield Town. Of the twelve City players from the class of 1964, it was now clear that only Doyle, Pardoe and Connor had graduated with honours.

CHAPTER NINE

These We Have Loved

There was never any love lost between George Best and Mike Doyle. The mutual antipathy probably started in their apprentice days in the Lancashire League games they played against each other, but it was confirmed over those two legs of the Youth Cup semi-final. Even today, Mike Doyle makes it very plain that George Best was never much of a threat to City, certainly he never posed anything like the danger that Bobby Charlton did. George scored only three goals in all the derby matches he played and two of them came in the Maine Road encounter in May 1971. United's 4–3 victory in front of a relatively poor crowd of 43,636 was an almost entirely meaningless last match of a mutually disappointing season. It was a night in which the biggest impact was made by the presence of Eamon Andrews and his big red book, as Matt Busby's last match in charge was marked by his appearance on *This Is Your Life*. David Meek called it 'the friendliest derby for years' – an oxymoron if ever there were one. Tony Towers wore the number four shirt for City that night. Mike Doyle was not playing.

The earlier derby of that season was as memorable as this one was forgettable. The balance of power had swung dramatically in Manchester since the spring of 1968. City had stormed to the first division title after a thrilling 3–1 victory at Old Trafford had ended over ten years of inferiority and had, in the following two years, inflicted a number of significant defeats on the traditional enemy, including a League Cup semi-final and three successive league wins at Old Trafford. The last of them came in December 1970 and it was the culmination of the lingering dislike Doyle and Best had always felt for each other.

George had been having a bad time in 1970. It was no fun being a superstar if your life was lived in a goldfish bowl, particularly if you were playing in a poor team whose form was deteriorating. He used to enjoy training each morning. The match on Saturday was the icing on the cake, but since the match was now ninety minutes of purgatory, there seemed little point in bothering with mixing eggs, flour, sugar and water and setting the oven at gas mark five. In December 1969, City had beaten United in the first leg of the League Cup semi-final, thanks to a dubious Francis Lee penalty, awarded by the referee, Jack Taylor, from a position somewhere just outside the centre circle, five minutes from the end of a pulsating match. Best had already been booked and when they left the field he childishly knocked the ball out of Taylor's hands. The referee reported it and, in the sort of idiotic over-reaction in which football disciplinary committees have long specialised, the FA banned him for four weeks. Shortly before an FA Cup semi-final replay against Leeds United at Villa Park, George was engaged in what *Private Eye* always calls 'Ugandan discussions' with a married woman in a Birmingham hotel bedroom, to the consternation of his infuriated manager. On the pitch later on, Johnny Giles let him know exactly what he thought of such unprofessional behaviour. It was Leeds who went on to meet Chelsea in the final.

Thus it continued. Everything was going wrong for George. Busby had moved upstairs and the heart and soul seemed to disappear from the team with him. The new manager, thirty-two-year-old Wilf McGuinness, was locked in battle with the senior players, who were the same age as he was. The youth system had dried up. Brian Kidd was a worthy successor to the lads of 1964, but George was contemptuous of such players as Steve James and Carlo Sartori who, in his opinion, diminished the lustre of Manchester United. James was being groomed to take over the mantle of Bill Foulkes, but it was soon apparent that it was not a good fit and the club signed a ready-made replacement when they bought Ian Ure from Arsenal for £80,000. The playwright, Jack Rosenthal, planned to tax each of United's 40,000 regular supporters the sum of £2. When the full £80,000 sum had been collected, he intended to send the money to the United board with a note asking that Ian Ure be returned to Arsenal by the first available train. George was twenty-four years old and should have been approaching the height of his career. Instead, he felt it all slipping away.

Yet another defeat by City at Old Trafford seemed likely. Derby match defeats hurt like no other, which is why so many of them are frenetic affairs, full of desperation and anxiety, players and fans frantic with worry lest the opposition make their daily lives a misery for the next six months. In the last few years, United had suffered more than their fair share of such crippling defeats and the December match duly went the same way. Francis Lee, a player United could never control, scored a hat trick as City inflicted a 4–1 drubbing. To make matters worse, if that were possible, the other goal was headed home decisively by Mike Doyle. Scoring at the Stretford End against the hated red devils was Mike Doyle's most publicly shared fantasy. City supporters, especially those who had seen him tormented by John Aston on his first appearance on that ground six and a half years before, knew exactly what that goal meant to Mike Doyle. So did George.

Considering the punishment that was constantly inflicted on him, George had an excellent temperament. He knew he was better than his opponent and that the best way of getting his own back was to make them look stupid, and in return they knew that George could never be kicked out of the game. He was too brave to be intimidated in that obvious way. On the other hand, he was no saint and, in professional footballing parlance, he knew how to look after himself. George confesses that in the despair that was enveloping him in 1970 he was spinning out of control on the pitch, collecting regular bookings and lashing out at other players and the officials.

In the derby match of December 1970, goaded by City taking the lead and the ineptitude of the players around him, George Best chased a lost cause as Glyn Pardoe easily cleared the ball upfield. Instead of pulling out of the pointless tackle, Best kept going and slid into him, long after the ball had left Pardoe's foot. George calls it a sliding tackle on a wet slippery pitch that looked worse than it was. Glyn disagrees:

> He jumped at me. Don't get me wrong. I'm not saying he meant to break my leg. That was a different matter, but he went for me. All my weight was on the foot he landed on and I felt it go. I knew it was gone and as I was dropping I was waving to the bench. Before I hit the deck, I knew it was completely smashed. I dropped to the floor and they carried me off. Then the St John ambulance man pushed on the leg as I was lying on the trolley. I can't remember much after that because they put me under a general anaesthetic.

George also knew that the leg was badly broken, because

there was a terrible cracking noise and instantly, 'my old adversary Mike Doyle was screaming in my face, calling me this and that and threatening to do me.'

To understand what happened next it is important to recall not only the long-standing enmity between the two, but also the nature of the friendship between Mike Doyle and Glyn Pardoe and the temperaments of the two men. Glyn is one of those people who induces in others nothing but feelings of respect for his abilities on the field and warmth as an individual against whom it would be impossible to harbour any ill will. What Mike Doyle saw was not just a badly timed sliding tackle, as George claimed:

> He launched himself at Glyn and there was no part of Bestie's body on the ground when he hit Glyn's shin. It was a thudding sound and I went over and I could see Glyn holding his leg, but his toes were pointing the wrong way. Bobby Charlton got hold of his foot and held it together. I said to Glyn, 'Are you all right, pal?' and he said, 'I'll be all right when it stops hurting.' I just completely and utterly snapped. Glyn and me, we'd been together since we were apprentices. I got my hands round Bestie's neck and Brian Kidd had hold of me and I think Tony Book got hold of Brian Kidd, who was trying to get my hands off George's throat. I still think, to this day, that Bestie was after me for some of the things I'd said. But that still rates, even now, as one of the worst tackles I ever saw.

Glyn was carried off on a stretcher, clearly in agony. As well as the players on the pitch, everyone in the crowd knew it was a badly broken leg. In 1970, in the wastelands of medical pre-history, broken legs ended players' careers. The history

of the game is littered with famous broken legs – Dave
Mackay, Dave Whelan (who went on to start JJB Sports) in
the 1960 Wembley Cup final, Allan Brown scoring the winning goal in the 1953 sixth-round tie even as his leg snapped
and, of course, the tragic Derek Dooley, the prolific Sheffield
goalscorer who underwent an amputation after gangrene set
in. That had been nearly twenty years before. Surely Glyn
Pardoe wouldn't suffer anything like that sort of fate?

When I talked about the incident to both Glyn and
Mike Doyle, thirty-two years after it happened, the years
seemed to roll away and the pain and the trauma were
experienced afresh. Both men became emotional. Mike
Doyle is still incensed about the tackle: 'As long as I live, I
will never ever forget or forgive George Best for that.
Never ever. I can't ever remember Glyn even getting
booked – he was so quick and strong he didn't need to foul
anybody. They couldn't get past him anyway.' Glyn and
Mike were always close friends. They roomed together,
played a lot of golf together (both excellent players) and
Mike's eldest son recently married Glyn's daughter. Mike
understands exactly what motivated Roy Keane to revenge
himself on Alf Inge Haaland, but the difference is that
Mike was not interested in breaking George's leg and
trotting off after the inevitable red card:

> When play resumed, the whole team was really, really
> fired up. I hit Bestie with four tackles within the next
> ten minutes – but not one foul. Every single time I got
> the ball, but every single time I made sure that soon as
> I got the ball I hit him with my shoulder or he got an
> arm somewhere. What I wanted to do to Bestie was
> what Roy Keane was talking about. I did it when play
> started, but I did it fairly. I didn't go over the top, just
> making sure my foot made contact with the ball.

If Mike had known was happening to Glyn in hospital he might not have been so restrained. The medical team discovered that there was an artery trapped and it was slowly strangling the blood supply. If Glyn had been conscious, it would have been even more traumatic, but fortunately he was under a general anaesthetic and had no idea how close he was to losing the leg. Paul Hince later talked to Freddie Griffiths, one of the City medical team who accompanied Glyn to the hospital:

> Freddie Griffiths said that the aftermath was like something out of an Alfred Hitchcock film. The leg had turned black because of the trapped artery. They arranged for him to be operated on immediately at the Manchester Royal Infirmary. At one stage some-one said, 'If we don't get this artery free in the next ten minutes the leg's going to have to come off because of the danger of gangrene.' There was absolute silence in the room as they worked to release it. Freddie Griffiths was looking at the clock on the wall and three minutes ticked by, then four, then five, then six, and Freddie knew Glyn was going to lose the leg, then suddenly he heard a sound and the surgeon said, very nonchalantly, 'OK, that's all right now.' Still that finished him, though. He played forty-four more times over a six-year period, but he was never the same.

Glyn came round about four or five hours later and was solemnly told that if he hadn't been so fit it was quite likely he would have had to have the leg amputated. Meanwhile, his wife Pat was shopping in the centre of Manchester with their six-month-old baby girl, when she was stopped by somebody who had been listening to the commentary on the radio. This was how news was passed in the days before mobile phones.

After the game was over, Mike Doyle told Peter Gardner that he was glad that Brian Kidd had grabbed him, because if he hadn't he would certainly have choked George Best to death. An ashen-faced George was relieved to hear Joe Mercer sympathise and tell him he knew it was an accident. The general feeling was that George had made a wild and dangerous tackle, but there had been no intention to hurt him. Glyn and Mike aren't so sure. It seems likely there was intent to hurt, but it seems doubtful that, with the exception of Roy Keane, any player would deliberately set out to injure a fellow professional. Mike claims that George's foot was two feet off the ground when it crashed into Glyn's shin. What seems utterly incredible is that, after Glyn was carried off, George was merely booked and City were awarded a free kick. Simple justice cried out for the 4–1 win, which City collected in a one-sided match.

George then compounded his error by refusing to go and see the shattered Glyn as he lay in hospital. Mike Doyle became incandescent with rage at the slight. He spoke to Peter Gardner, who ran the story in the *Manchester Evening News* saying that George hadn't even made so much as a phone call to the hospital, let alone been to see Glyn. Mike says: 'I think that report in the paper was the only thing that made the United players go and see Glyn, and if that's the case it's a poor, poor shame.' Glyn is a little more understanding about Best's breach of professional respect: 'Bestie came eventually, but it was way after, maybe eight or nine days after. He didn't want to come. I think that must have been out of embarrassment, but I think they made him come.'

Mike Summerbee was caught in the middle of this heated argument. He, like everyone else who ever played with him, has nothing but the greatest respect and liking for his colleague:

> My game improved just by playing against Glyn in practice matches, because on a Saturday I rarely came up against anyone as good as he was. Glyn could play anywhere on the park, any position, up front, midfield, anywhere, and that made him invaluable for us, but it might have discouraged Alf Ramsey from thinking of him as a specialist left-back, and that's why he kept picking Terry Cooper.

However, Mike and George had also been extremely close friends, almost since the day Mike was transferred to City in August 1965, and their friendship had survived the fierce rivalry on the field and the banter of life in Manchester. Mike Summerbee ran over to Glyn as he lay writhing on the ground and saw Glyn's foot pointing the wrong way. It was a horrific sight, akin to that of the Coventry City defender David Busst, who broke his leg so badly at Old Trafford that Peter Schmeichel vomited in the goalmouth when he saw the result. Best admits he wanted to walk off the field when he saw what had happened and Summerbee confirms that it was the sort of injury that made all the players question whether it was worth carrying on. In the event, it fired up City and finished off United. From his uniquely privileged position, Mike Summerbee observed the growth of the bad feeling between Best and Doyle:

> Mike Doyle is an emotional man, he's a Manchester lad and sometimes situations crop up like that and he'll get carried away. That's what made him into the player he was – aggressive and emotional. There was never any love lost between Mike Doyle and George

Best. They never really respected each other. It probably started with that youth-team game. George would try to take the piss out of players like that and Doyley, being the aggressive man he is, would fight back. In those derby matches there was so much emotion. The supporters and players alike would read in the papers the build-up to the match from the Monday onwards. It was much bigger then than it is now and it affected the supporters.

Meanwhile, back at the hospital, Glyn's recovery process turned out to be more complicated than anyone had at first realised:

Norman Shaw was the specialist and he was fantastic. He put me in plaster from my toes to my hips for nine months. After four months he took it off and looked at it with an X-ray and he said, 'Well, I'll give it another four or five weeks and if it isn't healing the way I'd like I'll give you a bone graft.' Before I went home I said to him, 'Can I have it done now?' and he said he was thinking the same thing. 'I'll have you in on Tuesday morning,' he said. He took fifteen inches of bone from my hip and packed it into the bottom of the leg. That same night I found I could actually move up and down the bed with just a bit of pain. He did a great job, because the bone simply wasn't knitting together properly.

Seven months after Glyn's leg was broken, I joined Manchester City to take part in pre-season training. It was, to say the least, an odd feeling for a supporter to be changing in the dressing room alongside players I had spent years of my life watching and discussing. On the first day, I looked for a free spot in the way anyone does in a changing room, being careful not to upset anyone by inadvertently sitting in the wrong place. I took off my jacket and hung it on the nearest peg. Instantly, Mike Doyle was on to me. 'You can't use that peg. It's Glyn Pardoe's,' he said sharply. Immediately I removed the jacket, fearful lest the intrusion had somehow set Glyn's recovery back a few more weeks.

In the event, it was two years before Glyn pulled on the pale blue shirt and trotted out alongside his colleagues again. By then, Willie Donachie had made the left-back position his own, so Glyn only managed six appearances in the 1972–73 season. Both Joe Mercer and Malcolm Allison had left the club by then, but in the 1973–74 season, under Johnny Hart and then the unpopular Ron Saunders, Glyn took over the right-back position from Tony Book, who had finally retired at the age of eighty-three. It was Glyn's last hurrah. Although he managed thirty-one appearances and even a farewell Wembley appearance in the losing League Cup final against Wolverhampton Wanderers, it was obvious to everyone that he was no longer the brilliant left-back he had been before George's flying leap. In 1974–75, as Lee and Summerbee also bowed out, Glyn failed to displace Colin Barrett and Geoff Hammond from the right-back berth and made only six appearances as substitute for the injured Donachie. It was over. It had been over since that horrible day at Old Trafford. There was a melancholy symmetry about it. His career came to an end on the Old Trafford pitch, just short of seven years since he had been City's star player in the Youth Cup team and had encountered George Best, United's star player. Now, one had brought the other's career to an effective close:

I was never the same after that, never had full movement again. I lost my sharpness. I thought I'd be OK, but I wasn't. I never got back to where I was before, because though the right leg eventually healed, the left knee started to go, because of the strain I'd put on it carrying that plaster around for nine months. A specialist looked at it, the damage was basically under the knee cap, and he said that it was buggered, so I packed it in. I was very unlucky to break the leg, but I consider myself very fortunate to be still walking about and playing golf and so on. I've got the cassettes, but they're for the kids, the grandkids – I've got a grandson and granddaughter now – but I don't look at them myself.

There were two compensations for Glyn. His wife, Pat, enjoyed having him around the house for a year. They'd been together since they were fourteen years old, but had never spent quite that amount of time in each other's company. They enjoyed it. When the specialist gave Glyn the worst possible news, his old full-back partner, Tony Book, was now the manager and the club offered Glyn a position on the staff, effectively doing what Johnny Hart (who had been promoted up the managerial ladder until he had fallen off the top of it) had done all those years before with Dave Ewing (who was still there) and Steve Fleet:

I was lucky in that when I finished playing I went straight on to the coaching side, so I still had going in to work each day; I still had the dressing room camaraderie and the banter. That's why I didn't miss playing too much – I was still in the game, still involved. I liked training, because it meant I stayed fit, and I liked training with the kids, because it kept me young. I played charity games till I was fifty.

Glyn's record with the youth team was outstanding. In his

first season they reached the FA Youth Cup quarter-final. In his third and fourth they were beaten in the final by Millwall and Aston Villa. Eventually, in 1986, Glyn secured his greatest triumph when his team, which included Paul Lake, Dave White, Paul Moulden, Andy Hinchcliffe and Steve Redmond, beat Manchester United to win the FA Youth Cup at last. In the late seventies and throughout the eighties, he produced as talented a crop of youngsters as ever came off the conveyor belt of a first division club. He was happy and he was successful, the perfect combination for the gods of football, who cannot resist the temptation to urinate in the gardens of the blameless. What undid Glyn in the end was the chairman's inability to choose a decent manager. With every turn of the revolving door in the manager's office at Maine Road, there came a new administration and the fear that each one would bring his own cronies on to the backroom staff. Glyn had been in football long enough to appreciate the constant danger:

> The end was going to come sooner or later. We had so many managers at City I was lucky to stay on the coaching staff as long as I did, really. It was Peter Reid who wanted to bring his own mates in. As soon as he fetched Sam Ellis in, I knew it was all over. I remember talking to Ray Pointer, who'd been at Bury, and he said as soon as Sam Ellis went there he cleared all the old staff out. I could see it coming then.

The fact that he could see it coming with grim inevitability did not greatly soften the blow when it landed. He had been there since the late fifties and he was removed in the early nineties and, despite the fact that he was in his mid-forties, he had no idea what he might do once he was finally out of the game. He felt initially that there might still have been a place for him somewhere. His track record as a youth-team coach was second to none. It was obvious he had been fired for classic football political reasons, which cast no doubt on his innate abilities. The phone would surely ring soon, but it didn't and he steeled himself to apply for a job. Glyn is a shy, retiring man and the prospect of selling himself on the employment market was anathema to him:

> I applied for one job – the youth-team post at Villa when Ron Atkinson was the manager. I never even got an interview. He gave it to one of his mates and I'd never even heard his name before. I thought, if that's the only way I can get back into football, by being up somebody's arse, then it's not worth it. I didn't bother after that. I just cut it dead. I was hurt.

Even sadder was the breach with Manchester City. Peter Swales, the chairman whose professed love for the club was proclaimed in all the media interviews he so eagerly sought, never lifted a finger to help the man who had given his physical health for the team. If you look at Glyn's leg today it looks like a road map of Great Britain. This is the result of the tackle made by George Best over thirty years ago. Glyn Pardoe's veins ran with pale blue blood. From the day he was fired to the day Manchester City left Maine Road, he only once returned to the ground where he had spent over thirty years. In December 2001 his cousin Alan Oakes' son, Michael, played in goal for Wolverhampton as they fought a close battle with Manchester City for promotion into the Premiership. A friend had a spare ticket for the game and Glyn went along with him: 'I was sitting in the Kippax and after the game I just went home. I didn't want to feel anything. The game was crap and the whole experience did nothing for me.'

Eventually, he took a security job in the reception at Barclays Bank. It's easy work and it's busy, so the days of his later life pass by comfortingly quickly. Occasionally, people recognise him, which pleases him, but though he looks at City's results and hopes they do well, he is no longer emotionally engaged with the club or the game. He lives a few miles from Winsford, where he grew up, and he remains stoic in the face of his hurtful and disappointing exit from football. Unprompted, he counts aloud his blessings in life – his wife and children, his career, however abbreviated, the affection of the fans who remember him. His daughters, one of whom is a hairdresser and the other a bank manager, have blessed him with grandchildren. One of the daughters married the son of Mike Doyle, a fitting testimony to the battles the team-mates fought together, not least over the tackle that ended Glyn's career: 'I'd like my kids and grandkids to have a better life than mine, but it'll be difficult, because I've had a great life.' Typical Pardoe sentiments.

One game above all will unite Glyn and his daughter's father-in-law in the affection of all City fans of a certain age. In the League Cup final of 1970, City were due to face West Bromwich Albion at Wembley on Saturday afternoon, having played the first leg of a European Cup-Winners' Cup quarter-final against Academica Coimbra on the previous Wednesday night. This first match was a fractious affair, played out in the warmth of a Portuguese spring, which ended in a scoreless draw. Returning to a snow-bound Britain, their flight was diverted to Birmingham. A long and laborious coach journey followed and the players crawled into bed in their London hotel at 2.30a.m. on the Friday morning.

The Wembley final kicked off thirty-seven hours later and within five minutes City were a goal down to a Jeff Astle header from a centre which Corrigan should have caught. It wasn't until the middle of the second half that City drew level, when Glyn's corner kick eventually ran free to Mike Doyle, who thumped it home. City were desperate to avoid extra time on a Wembley pitch that looked like a cabbage patch and took its toll on City's tiring legs. In the end, it was Glyn Pardoe, wearing number eleven on his shirt but playing in midfield, who neatly hooked the ball past Osborne, the West Brom goalkeeper, and the lunge of a despairing defender. It was the last goal he ever scored for City and it won a Wembley final. There are worse ways to go.

On the basis of what we saw in April 1964, nobody would have chosen Mike Doyle over Glyn Pardoe as the player most likely to go on and play for England, but the former's career was dramatically prolonged by the decision, in 1973, to convert him from a right-half, in which position he had won eight England Under-23 caps, to a central defender in a back four, initially alongside Tommy Booth and eventually his international colleague, Dave Watson. It was Johnny Hart who made the change.

It was almost his first decision after taking over as manager in March 1973, when Malcolm Allison fled to Crystal Palace. During the 1971–72 season, Allison and his supporters had staged a boardroom coup, which had isolated the old chairman Albert Alexander and his preferred manager, Joe Mercer. At the end of the season in which City had been six points clear at the top of the league at Easter and managed to lose the championship by a single point to Derby County, Joe Mercer was forced out of the club he had built and his job was given to the voracious Malcolm Allison. Alexander retired, bemused that the success Mercer had brought had been so wilfully cast aside, and his place was taken, disastrously, by Peter Swales. It was the start of a long night in the boardroom, into which light only fell twenty-five years later when David Bernstein took over, by which time

City were about to be relegated to the third tier of English football. Johnny Hart, who had been at the club for twenty-one years as a player and a further ten on the coaching side, was seen as the perfect choice to calm the troubled waters. When Malcolm Allison left the club, they had taken one point from their previous six games and were due to play the fearsome Leeds United, with a sixth defeat in seven games looking certain. Mike Doyle recalls:

> I came in through the players' entrance and I was heading towards the changing room when I heard John's voice shouting from the trainers' room, 'Doyley, come here! I'm going to do something today that you might not like.' I said, 'Who to?' He said, 'You, you daft bugger. I want you to play in the back four and put Allan Clarke out of the game.' I said, 'What system are we playing?' and he said, '4–4-2, but I can change it to 4–3-3 or 4–2-4.' I said, 'Do the rest of the lads know?' And he said yes, so I said, 'How come you told me last?' We were having a bad time at that point, but we won 1–0 against that great Leeds side. That was the making of me, that switch. On the Tuesday I went in to see John and asked him if he wanted me to stick in that position and he said, 'If you play any more games like that you'll end up playing for England.'

Mike Doyle had the career every one of those City youth players of 1964 wanted. He was a regular in the first team for ten years, captaining the club in his final days and lifting the League Cup at Wembley, the last City captain to raise a trophy, if we discount the legendary second division play-off final prize of 1999. Doyle played five times for England in 1976 and 1977, under Don Revie, but his last appearance was in an embarrassing 2–0 defeat by Holland on a night when no collection of eleven players could have lived with the men in orange. A few weeks later he collided with Joe Corrigan in the goalmouth at West Ham and his top-class career was almost finished:

> I knew straight away it was going to be a long one. I was out for eight months. Roy Bailey helped me a lot, because when they took me out of plaster the injured leg was an inch thinner than the other one. He came out with me and pushed me and pushed me and bollocked me. I went into the physio's room one day and Freddie Griffiths gave me a wrapped present for having worked so hard to get fit, and I unwrapped it and it was the biggest pair of hiking boots you'd ever seen. They weighed a ton and I had to put them on. I could barely walk out of the tunnel. He said, 'I've got a treat for you.' We went round the ground and out through the exit between the Platt Lane stand and the Kippax and into the car park. We're stood at the bottom of the steps to the Kippax. There were ninety-one of them to the top so Roy says to me, 'Get in front of me, Doyley,' so I do and next thing he jumps on my back. I said 'What the **** are you doing?' 'Get your arms under me legs. You're giving me a piggy back to the top.' I got back to fitness and the injured leg ended up being a quarter of an inch bigger than the good leg.

Sheer bloodymindedness got Mike Doyle back on to the pitch, but it was obvious he wasn't the same player. He made thirteen sporadic appearances the following season, but like Glyn and Colin Bell, who also limped back into first division football, the ageing, battered body eventually claimed its victim. At the beginning of June 1978, fifteen months after the injury sustained at West Ham and sixteen years after cheeking Bert Trautmann in his first weeks on the ground-staff, Mike Doyle was transferred to Stoke City:

> I went to Stoke and then to Bolton. My knee was always a problem. I had a cartilage out when I was at Bolton and I decided to call it quits when my contract finished there, but then Jimmy Greenhoff rang me up when he was manager of Rochdale and said he could do with some help. That was the worst thing I ever did. Jimmy said there was potential at Rochdale, so I went down and had a chat with him and I said, 'OK I'll give it a go.' Then I got a growth under the heel – it was like walking round with a drawing pin stuck in there – and I had to go for cortisone injections. The medical facilities at Rochdale were, shall we say, not up to what I was used to at my previous clubs. Jimmy signed his brother Brian and what a pain in the arse he was. Jimmy was very quiet, though he spoke his mind, but when Brian came ... As soon as Brian and Jimmy got together for Rochdale, the spirit disappeared and I couldn't wait for the season to finish. I was sensible enough to realise that was it. I had to make a decision. I was enjoying my golf and all I had to look forward to was more injuries.

It was an agonising way to end a career that had touched the heights. Mike was by no means the most gifted of that City youth team, but he had other qualities which allowed him to succeed when others failed:

> The ones who didn't make it didn't have the mental toughness. I wasn't afraid of anything. I had no

brothers or sisters, so I had no one to look after me, but in football you're on your own when you're on the pitch and it's just down to you. The ones who dropped out didn't have that mental toughness. Bobby McAlinden was a bit of a Jack the lad. He was patting the first teamers on the back, ''ow are you, mate?' that kind of thing. At the end of the day he had no bottle, couldn't stand a tackle. He had a great left foot but no strength, either physical or mental. And the best way to sum up Alf Wood in those days was he was a bully. He came to City with a big reputation from Manchester Boys and England Youth. He was either a centre-forward or a centre-half and in my opinion he couldn't play either – simple as that. It was an ego trip for Alf. 'I'm the captain of the Man City youth team.' Waste of space!

The passing years have clearly not entirely mellowed Mike Doyle. If you think he was vituperative about his own team-mates, I leave it to the imagination of the reader to evoke the words that were used to describe George Best and the tackle that ended Glyn Pardoe's career.

The door that shut on Glyn Pardoe in December 1970 should have opened for David Connor. Like Glyn, he had gradually retreated over the years from the forward position he took up as a youth to the more defensive positions which became available when Lee, Bell, Summerbee, Young and Coleman made that forward line an automatic choice. In the championship season, David made ten appearances, with a further three as substitute when the purchase of Francis Lee in October turned out to be the fabled missing piece of the jigsaw. Those ten appearances were as replacement for the injured or suspended Doyle, Lee, Pardoe, Young and Coleman. His success was, he feels, his undoing:

Eventually I played in nine positions. That was my biggest problem. Malcolm Allison knew that I could fill in so I played when someone was injured and as soon as he was fit again I was dropped. I never obtained a regular position. It was Malcolm who saw how fit I was, and he decided to use me in those man-marking positions, and I think my skill factor deteriorated because I was just chasing after someone else. I had this great concentration, you couldn't ruffle me in any way, and I've been spat at and kicked and everything. There's no way I would react and in the whole of my career I was never booked.

The highlight of this specialist job came at Villa Park in March 1969, in the semi-final of the FA Cup. Tony Book had ruptured his Achilles tendon during pre-season training and David, of course, filled in at right-back. As soon as Tony Book recovered full fitness after Christmas, David was dropped, but returned spasmodically until City found themselves facing Everton in the semi-final and needed to nullify the impact of Ball, Harvey and Kendall in midfield. Connor was never more than six feet from Alan Ball for the entire ninety minutes. City supporters joked about Connor following Ball on to the Everton coach at the end of the match or even into the toilet. It was an outstanding job and typical of the way David was always asked to subordinate his personal ambitions for the good of the team:

Alan Ball wasn't quick enough to get away from me. Even if he caught me on the turn I'd catch him up within five yards. Best was different, because he was brilliant going left and right. I'd been taught by Johnny Hart to always point a man a certain way. Best could get right up to me and I hadn't got a clue which way he was going to go. He was the only player I ever faced who could do that to me. That was when he was in his heyday. I played against him again maybe a year and a half later, when he was going through some of his personal problems, and then he would disappear from the game for twenty minutes.

As Mike Doyle delights in pointing out, George was never the threat to City that Bobby Charlton posed. Nine months after he had snuffed out Alan Ball in the FA Cup semi-final, Connor performed the same job on Bobby Charlton in the semi-final of the League Cup:

In that match at Old Trafford everybody expected me to mark George Best, but he wasn't in the game for ninety minutes and the man who was making United tick was Bobby Charlton. He never stopped. One minute he was helping the full-backs, the next he had a shot up the other end. It was decided I would mark Charlton and stop him playing [like Beckenbauer did in 1966]. I went to shake hands with him at the end of the game and it was odd, because he was such a nice guy. Anyway, he said, really ungraciously, 'You'll win nothing playing like that,' or something like that. I suppose he was just disappointed at losing and knowing City were at Wembley again, because on that night he must have run miles. With Alan Ball, I remember thinking I had another gear left, but with Charlton that night I had to concentrate for the full ninety minutes, because he worked so hard trying to help players and always wanting the ball. He got very frustrated, because he couldn't get the ball as much as he wanted and because we were a quality team. I was never more than five yards from Charlton that whole night and he didn't like it at all. Charlton wasn't like Ball, who got so frustrated he hit me. Charlton wouldn't hit anyone, but he never stopped grumbling the whole game. I have to say, though, I thought that night he was absolutely outstanding.

Always the bridesmaid, never the blushing bride. Even after those two magnificent, selfless performances, David Connor was not selected to play in either of the Wembley finals that followed. In the League Cup final, Mercer and Allison packed the midfield with Bell, Doyle, Oakes, Heslop and Pardoe, leaving Francis Lee to run all match up front by himself. In the FA Cup final, Tony Coleman returned to face Leicester City and David Connor resumed his regular place on the substitute's bench:

My disappointment was not that TC came back for the final, but I thought he might have given me ten minutes on the Wembley pitch. At one point they started to warm me up, because TC wasn't playing very well and their right-back was Peter Rodrigues, who had him in his pocket, and Joe said, 'Right, you're coming on.' They really weren't pleased with TC, because at one point he told Malcolm Allison where to go. Then we went and scored. Malcolm apologised to me, but it took him about three weeks. He wanted to keep the format once we'd scored and 1–0 was too narrow a lead to start improvising. I got a medal, went up the steps and all that. Don't forget I was a local lad, so to go to Wembley for the Cup final with your local team was pretty thrilling.

Connor was also part of what was then seen as a unique Wembley experience. The excitement of getting through the last league game (usually lost) without injury, the arrival of the new Cup final suits, the constant build-up in the papers and the inevitable badgering for tickets by long-lost relatives and friends were all part of what made the FA Cup final so special. It's gone now. It's just another match on Sky Sports, a minor key adjunct to the destination of the Premiership title and the Champions League (which never seems to me to have the cachet of the European Cup). In 1969, football supporters cared passionately about the FA Cup. In those far-off times, before the Leyland Daf or the Sherpa Van Trophy, just to get to Wembley was, for most players, the summit of their ambitions. On the coach taking the team down Empire Way, passing those happy fans in their club colours, David Connor recalled just how far he had come in the past six or seven years:

> I never forgot those trials down at Chassen Road, Urmston. All those young hopefuls, and some of them were really good players, or so I thought, but their names would be called at the end of the session and I'd never see them again. Johnny Hart used to say it wasn't because these players were no good with the ball, it meant that they might not have the right attitude to become a professional player. There's things you have to give up if you want to be a professional.

Connor never solved the problem of being every manager's dream utility player. He felt that Mercer and Allison saw him as someone who would save them a transfer fee in four different positions. The only reason they would let him go was if they needed the money:

> Twice I went to see Harry Catterick at Everton. He

wanted me, because he said he saw me go for a fifty-fifty ball with Colin Harvey and Harvey pulled out at the last minute and he got hurt. He wanted me to play on the left with Kendall, Ball and Harvey, playing four in midfield. At the time [1969] City were looking for money and I'd just got married and bought my house in Heald Green. At first Everton agreed to me staying here, but then they changed their mind and said I had to go and live halfway between Manchester and Liverpool. At the time I was on £60 a week and Everton would have raised it to £70. It wasn't much of a rise, considering I was going to a club didn't know a lot about. Also, Catterick liked the fact that I could play in all these different positions and I thought I could end up in the same position again. So it collapsed and then Joe Mercer sent for me and told me they'd sold Stan Horne and Bobby Kennedy and someone else, so they didn't need the money and they'd like me to stay.

Anyway, the next minute he tried to transfer me to Tottenham. I went down there and again they offered me £10 more, but the cost of living in London was so much higher it wasn't that attractive. I should have negotiated, but I just wasn't that type of player. I really wish I'd had an agent when I was a young man. There was no way I could go upstairs to Joe Mercer and demand more money. I was very shy. Bill Nicholson looked sixteen foot high to me sitting behind the boardroom table.

So David Connor returned to Manchester and continued to do everything that was asked of him. Meanwhile, other youngsters were coming up on the blindside and passing him – Stan Bowles and Tony Towers in midfield, Ian Bowyer and

Ian Mellor, who each took over the number eleven shirt after Tony Coleman had pulled one prank too many and found himself transferred to Sheffield Wednesday in October 1969. Connor was slipping inexorably down the rankings. In 1968–69 he made twenty league appearances, the following year just eight. After Glyn was injured, the left-back role went to the specialist Arthur Mann and, though he began the 1971–72 season in that position, he was injured in the 1–0 win at home to Liverpool at the start of September 1971 and Willie Donachie claimed the role he was to fill with such unassuming success for the next nine years. In January 1972, a few months short of ten years since he had signed full professional forms, David Connor eventually left City for the murky waters of second division Preston North End.

This season was to be Mercer and Allison's swan song. The purchase of Wyn Davies just before the season started seemed to do for the team what the purchase of Francis Lee had done four years earlier. The goals flowed, the victories piled up and the team was settled in a comfortable 4-2-4 formation, with Summerbee and Mellor providing the crosses for Lee and Davies. On 2 October, David Connor filled in for the injured Mellor and scored his last goal on his last appearance for his boyhood club in a 2–0 victory at West Brom. Davies' arrival was bad news, too, for Neil Young, who had been Lee's principal companion up front throughout the glory years. Preston decided to buy both Young and Connor in a special January sale 'two for the price of one' offer.

The decisive reason for the purchase was that Malcolm Allison was becoming obsessed by the tantalising (for him) prospect of signing Rodney Marsh from Queens Park Rangers for £200,000. City were never a rich club and, in addition to the capital investment, the board had to consider where Marsh's weekly wages were coming from. Selling Young and

Connor would mean a crucial saving of their two salaries and allow the club to indulge Allison's fantasy. In the 1–0 win over Liverpool in which David had replaced the injured Colin Bell, Connor had suffered ruptured ankle ligaments in a clash with the Liverpool centre-forward David Johnson:

> Today they'd have scans and proper treatment, but in those days at City it was, 'Let's strap you up and hope you'll be all right.' But after that injury I couldn't even train without my ankle swelling up. I needed surgery and looking after, but I never got it. The Preston manager, Alan Ball Sr, came in for me because his son had always gone on at him about what a great player I was, after what I'd done to him. Youngy was in dispute with the club and he'd been dropped for Wyn Davies. If they sold us, Malcolm could afford Rodney Marsh.

It seemed like a reasonable move to Connor, who was only twenty-seven years old and had another two years on his contract still to go. Preston made attractive offers to both players and City sweetened the deal by promising each of them a testimonial game, but they never materialised and, when the former City players arrived at Deepdale, the experience turned into a nightmare:

> We didn't go for the money Preston offered – it was the guarantee of the testimonial that was so important to us. I'd done ten years at City and I had so much trouble at Preston it was unbelievable. Even the guaranteed 5 per cent of the transfer fee [about £2,000] didn't come. Your money was never there when it was supposed to be. Nowadays, you'd go to the PFA, but in those days it was different because the PFA wasn't as strong. Now

the players are financially strong; they're as big as the club. In my day no player was like that.

Connor threatened Preston that if they didn't pay him the long-delayed signing-on fee that was his of right, he wanted a free transfer, to which they didn't take kindly. Preston were in dire financial straits and the players soon discovered that cheques were bouncing: 'Facility-wise it was poor, plus Alan Ball wasn't a great manager and results were poor, so he was under pressure. I wasn't being grand, just because I'd come from a top first division club, but everything that had been promised never materialised. It really got to me.' The agreement with City was for a testimonial match for each player within two years of the transfer date of 21 January 1972. Neither Young nor Connor has ever been granted the game, although Neil Young's case has since evoked a certain amount of local feeling. David Connor remains the forgotten man of the Mercer–Allison years and the failure to deliver the promised testimonial is in many ways a perfect symbol of how his time at Maine Road, however exciting periodically, was never the satisfying experience his selfless dedication to the cause warranted:

I left City with Neil Young and I've still got a grievance with City, because I never got a testimonial. I've had a letter from Mr Bernstein [City chairman, 1998–2003] apologising, saying he didn't know anything about it and he would pass my letter on to the Old Players' Association. I feel annoyed, because my old mate Neil has made about £35,000 from three or four dinners and he's still complaining that he never had a testimonial, and there's me and I've never had anything. Both of us were promised and City know that.

The story of the missing testimonials reflects Manchester City in a very poor light. David Connor recounts it all with mounting emotion:

> When the board changed and Swales came in and the managers all changed, it was obvious City weren't going to do anything. They didn't care. So eventually Preston gave me a free transfer and I ended up going back to City for two more seasons under Tony Book. Unfortunately, I had a bad ankle and I did my cartilage as well, so I never played in the first team. Everyone I knew at the club, from Book to Ken Barnes, they all got testimonials and I never did. Tony Book had been a great player and when he got sacked as manager he got a £25,000 pay-off and a second testimonial.

You can see how badly it still rankles. He, like Neil Young, eventually received a cheque for the five per cent of his signing-on fee from Preston, which arrived just before he left Deepdale in 1974. It had taken nearly two years and was paid up reluctantly, with the specific intention of stopping Connor causing trouble for the club with the PFA. He was looking forward to the return to Maine Road, although he knew he was carrying the long-term cartilage injury. He quickly discovered that Tony Book's chief coach, Ian McFarlane, didn't rate him; but he could live with that, so desperate was he to get back to the source of his complaint about the testimonial. Sadly, he also soon realised that his enquiries were leading him into a cul-de-sac. The more he asked, the more he was blocked. The more the club refused to listen to him, the crosser he got. The crosser he got, the less likely the club was to do anything for him. Quiet, shy Tadger, who had been bamboozled out of a pay rise by Joe Mercer's story of a mythical barrel out of which Lee, Bell and Summerbee had scooped all the money, changed character and when he left City for the second time, after nearly three years without a first-team appearance, he was considerably more aggressive. He had to be. It was a question of survival. He went into management at non-league Macclesfield Town and then Bury, but to this day what bothers him more than anything is the way he was treated by Manchester City, who refused to honour their promise of a testimonial: 'I was a good guy. I never gave anyone any trouble and I earned very poor money, didn't get any bonuses or signing-on fees. I did nearly thirteen years at City and I thought testimonials were for people like me.'

Unfortunately, the agreement with Young and Connor was made verbally. It had to be, because of the tax-free nature of the practice. Now players who never have to work again after the money they've made out of football, are routinely awarded testimonials. That was never the purpose of the testimonial match. At least Gary Kelly at Leeds and Niall Quinn at Sunderland had the good grace to realise that there are other people in the world who need to be helped more than the average long-serving Premiership footballer. In Connor's case, there is an additional personal note to be struck:

My dad died about five years ago and he died a broken man, because it was his big idea that I'd get a testimonial and walk on the pitch and maybe there'd be about 15,000 people there and I'd wave to my dad. But it never materialised. Maybe I wasn't strong enough as a person. Maybe I should have threatened to sue them. I wouldn't do the things Neil Young has done to get a testimonial. I'm not at death's door with no money. I just feel very peeved that, after so many

years, I'm the only player from that squad of sixteen
or eighteen who were eligible to receive a testimonial
but never got one. Now people think that because I
never got a testimonial I must have been a problem
player, but I never was. I got on well with everyone. I
never asked for the world, but I gave everything to
that club.

Occasionally, an article appears in a Sunday newspaper
about the story of Neil Young's betrayal. Such articles rarely
mention David Connor. It upsets both Dave and his faithful
wife, who wrote the letter to David Bernstein pointing out
the anomaly, but it is hard to hold the current board of
directors responsible for a wrong which Peter Swales could,
and should, have righted thirty years ago: 'I don't begrudge
Neil anything. It just annoys me to be totally ignored. Dave
Ewing lived round the corner and they kicked him out of his
house in Platt Lane. He ended up in a nursing home and
there was this big, strong centre-half and he was a sad sight.
He died shortly after. I always felt United looked after their
old players better than City did.'

After Francis Lee became chairman things could have
been different. After all, nobody was better placed to understand what David Connor had given to Manchester City, but
in his time as chairman Lee had more pressing matters to
attend to. Relegation from the premier league, followed by
becoming a laughing stock for hiring five managers in one
season and then the yawning chasm of the Nationwide
League division two were more urgent than the case of a
testimonial for a long-time servant of the club. Nobody was
throwing stones at the administration office windows or
marbles under the hooves of the police horses to demonstrate
their belief in the social justice of David Connor's testimonial
match – and now it appears unlikely that they ever will.

Meanwhile, in 2002, in great pain, David Connor had both hips replaced, a consequence of his years of selfless running in the cause of Manchester City. This is 'the beautiful game' and its ruthless use of the people who make it such.

David Connor is not entirely correct in his assumption that Manchester United treat their old players exceptionally well. David Sadler spent even longer at United than Connor did in his first spell at City and came away with an identical result on the issue of a testimonial game. He did have other compensations, such as a European Cup winner's medal, of course, and four England caps, most of them won in 1970, the year of the World Cup in Mexico. Even though United's star was in the descendant, David played some of his best football in the 1969–70 season. It was no surprise when he was selected by Alf Ramsey to be one of the twenty-eight players who flew to South America and played in the warm-up games before the tournament began. Brian Labone, the centre-half of league champions, Everton, was ahead of him in the queue to play alongside Bobby Moore, as was the familiar presence of Jack Charlton, but David was still only twenty-four and his time would come. What he didn't expect was the manner of his exclusion from the final official party of twenty-two players:

> Ramsey had a terrible relationship with the press right from the word go. It was only ever just about OK and most of the time it wasn't even that. As far as those six of us who were left out, Alf had ironically agreed to help the press by telling them who the six were before the players were told, but because of the time delay in getting the information back to England, it wouldn't be printed until after the players themselves had been told. As players, we were told that at a certain time the squad would be announced at a team meeting.

The previous evening, I came back from training and I had a call from [my wife] Chris, who was very upset, because she'd had the press on the phone to her. Obviously, one of the sports editors back here wanted to get a jump on his rivals and had broken the embargo, so he rang Chris to find out how upset she was that I had been left out of the final squad. She phoned me at the team hotel and told me I was out. I hit the roof and flew in to see Alf, who didn't take kindly to that and, on reflection, I shouldn't have done it, because there was press all around him. I had terrific respect for Ramsey and I thought he was a great manager. When he explained the situation, I knew it wasn't of his making and I understood how it happened. Of course, I told the other five and they weren't too happy either.

Sadler won only one further cap, partly because of the emergence of Roy McFarland and partly because of United's fall from grace. To stop the rot, the United board sacked Wilf McGuinness, brought back Matt Busby to stabilise the club, hired Frank O'Farrell and then fired him after a disastrous 5–0 defeat by Crystal Palace, which was transmitted for the edification of *Match of the Day* viewers just before Christmas 1972. O'Farrell's replacement was Tommy Docherty and David had a strong sensation that his new manager didn't rate him:

When the new season began, it was crystal clear. I had to go back and train in the afternoon with the youngsters. I was suddenly in the wrong squad. He brought in his own men and I could soon see the writing on the wall. Docherty saw it as something he had to do. There had been the talk of Busby's influence ever since he moved upstairs in 1969. Docherty came in to clear out what he thought was the old deadwood and he wasn't going to fail because of Matt's influence upstairs. I didn't agree personally – I thought I was better than anyone he had there and United was my club and I wanted to stay. However, things soon became intolerable. I wasn't playing in the first team, not even in the reserves, and though I had a long contract it was obvious that I would be better off elsewhere.

Bobby Charlton retired at the end of the 1972–73 season, in which United had finished eighteenth in the first division, been knocked out of the FA Cup in the third round and lost to Bristol Rovers in their second game in the League Cup. It must have been a relief to leave this struggling Manchester United, a weak and pale shadow of the club he had joined twenty years earlier. Charlton went to become manager at Preston, after the unlamented Alan Ball Sr had left. He knew how unhappy David Sadler had become at United and offered him a new start in the second division. One thing stopped David from accepting the first offer:

I was next in line for the testimonial. I left in December 1973 and I'd been there over eleven years. This cropped up during the negotiations, but it was very clear from Docherty that I wasn't going to get one – it was an unwritten law that you got them, but not a written one because of the tax situation. If the manager says no it's difficult. Matt was still there and everything that had been said in 1968 and so on … but I had served my ten years and Busby still refused to intervene. I cannot tell you how upset I was. How upset I was personally with Matt. He'd been my father figure all those years.

This is the other Matt Busby, the one you don't read about in the hagiographies, the Busby who had suffered himself from years of exploitation by football employers. He wasn't about to make it easy for the modern generation. His heart remained with the boys who died at Munich. Tommy Taylor and Duncan Edwards wouldn't have come bleating to him, demanding a testimonial. The Busby Babes knew what it was like to play for glory and the honour of wearing the red shirt of Manchester United. Sometimes, when talking to the 1964 team, it is easy to conclude that they felt like a step-family. As far as Busby was concerned, they were there for one reason – to win the European Cup and redeem the suffering of the martyrs of Munich. Once that had been achieved they were of no further use to him. How else can we explain this extraordinary rejection of David Sadler, a faultless professional, as dedicated to the cause of Manchester United as David Connor had been to City?

To avoid the poisonous atmosphere that had enveloped Old Trafford, Sadler signed for Preston, but, like Connor and Young before him, he found it hard to adjust to life at Deepdale:

I went to Preston, though I knew Newcastle, Birmingham and Charlton were interested. I considered going to Charlton and moving back down south, but Chris was working here and we had just had a baby son. It was a major shock at Preston – fish and chips on the coach on the way back from away matches was not what I'd been used to at Manchester United. In addition, the team struggled and we got relegated. I'm sure Bobby would admit that he was an awful manager. He simply never came to terms with it at all. Maybe it was the wrong club at the wrong time. Bobby was an idealist. He played the game like that and he tried to manage like that, but the reality was that it was different in the second and third division. The play was different. It was more physical and, because I'd come from United, I was an open target for both team-mates and the opposition.

Charlton had some good young players coming through the ranks, such as Alex Bruce, Mark Lawrenson and Michael Robinson, but then the financial realities of life as a club in the third division hit home and he was forced to sell. Newcastle bought John Bird and Aston Villa bought Tony Morley. Preston needed the money and they could wipe off the season's debt in one go, but Charlton couldn't accept it and left football management for ever, to be replaced by Harry Catterick. Meanwhile, David Sadler's career continued to spiral downwards:

I got mumps, which was an awful illness in an adult, and that laid me out for nine months. Nobby [Stiles] became a coach there and then I had a decent spell, playing alongside Mark Lawrenson. I thoroughly enjoyed that, but then I got the recurrence of an injury, so by the 1976–77 season I was on the treatment table most of the time. I couldn't train as well, so all I did was to have treatment and play. They did an exploratory operation and I had some options. I could carry on as was, but the fitness levels would drop, but also, eventually, at best I'd have a limp and at worst be in a wheelchair. That didn't please Chris. The other option was to stop playing. I was only thirty-one, but I'd had fourteen or fifteen years and therefore I have no real complaints. I'm sure that was the right decision, because I'm fitter than most these days and I have no regrets about retiring.

He returned to the world of financial services he had last seen as a teenage bank clerk in Maidstone. It was the best he could do, because, although he had paid lip service to the idea of providing for his future after retirement, the reality was that he hadn't done enough, so throughout the eighties he worked in a building society. His first venture into the world of sports agenting proved less than glorious, but now he has set up David Sadler Promotions and, with his column in the *Manchester Evening News* and running the Old Players' Association, David is a respected figure once more at Old Trafford.

John Aston left United two years before David Sadler, but with much the same sense of relief:

> I couldn't wait to get away from United. I'd had enough and it was a troubled time for the club. I'd had my own personal troubles there as well, of course. I remember very distinctly going to pick my boots up in the boot room and thinking I'll never come back here. And I never have. When I was out of the team I felt like I was being pushed out of the club. I had those problems with the crowd and I felt as though I'd been turned on by my own.

Aston was sold to Luton Town because, as he says, 'Busby liked to get you out of the *Manchester Evening News* area.' Luton reluctantly allowed John to train half the week at Oldham, but the arrangement worked out well for club and player and Aston thoroughly enjoyed his time there for five years. The manager was Harry Haslam, whom John Aston Sr knew and liked, and Young John's old United colleague, Jimmy Ryan, was already down there: 'Kenilworth Road had a terrible slope on it and I knew at once I was going to enjoy it, because it sloped just like the way our old school

293

pitch did. Jimmy Ryan said we could pin teams going downhill, so they'd never be able to get out of their own half.' It must have helped that leaving Old Trafford to play in the third division was also financially rewarding:

> Prior to the European Cup, David Sadler and the rest of us lads were on forty quid a week. Then everyone got a £40 a week rise, which doubled my wages. I got a hundred off Luton. Most of the other lads there were on £60, but they didn't know what I was earning. The rumour was I was living off my expenses, but that was only £3 return or something.

Unlike even the canny, thoughtful Sadler, John was one of the few who had seriously thought about the transience of life as a professional footballer and the problems that come with retirement. John had married a local girl in 1969 ,which is why he was so reluctant to move house to live in Luton. He was aware that he lacked much in the way of formal education and underwent a conversion to the attraction of learning when standing in the Sherratt & Hughes bookshop on Cross Street with Jimmy Ryan: 'Jim, who's a well-educated Scottish lad, picks up a poetry book and opens it and he points o ɩ a verse to me and says, "Read that." So I read it, but I d ɩn t have clue what it meant. He explained to me what it meant, and I thought it was the most marvellous thing, and all of a sudden I wanted to read more.' When his children passed the exams for the local grammar school, he and his wife were determined not to uproot the family, which was why he didn't want the life of a peripatetic player, coach or manager, and why he had started a pet food business when he was still training at the Cliff:

> I'd helped out my relative, who had a big pet food

business, and I used to go into the warehouse and help out one or two afternoons a week. My relative died and, with my wife, we bought the business and we've done what they say you shouldn't, and we've worked together ever since. And it's been good. I started my first little business when I was twenty-six or twenty-seven. I worked out that if it flopped, I'd still be playing football, so I'd have the chance to recoup what I'd lost. I'm never going to be a millionaire, but it pays the bills and it gives me a lifestyle I enjoy.

Like Sadler and so many others, it was an injury that eventually drove him into retirement:

It was dead easy to stop playing. I left Luton, where I did well, and went to Mansfield, where it was just awful and I packed it in at the end of that year, but then Blackburn came in for me. I wish now I'd got some compensation. I'd always been a good trainer. I was probably the best at doing the physical stuff at all the clubs I'd been to, but at Blackburn I was always with the kids. I was either the best or the worst, never in between. Sometimes I was just gasping for breath.

Aston had developed an irregular heartbeat, although he made the automatic, but false, assumption that he had no breath left, because he was over thirty and going downhill rapidly. The medical treatment offered by Blackburn Rovers in 1980 attests to the fact that not much had changed since his father had had his broken arm re-set by an inebriated surgeon in a dinner jacket. It wasn't entirely the fault of the football clubs' medical staff, as the National Health Service didn't exactly cover itself in glory either:

There was no medical treatment at all from the clubs. I was sat at home one day and I could see my shirt jumping up and down, because my heart was beating so fast, and I thought I'm sure it shouldn't be like this. I went to the hospital and saw a specialist, because I thought I might need a new valve, but the specialist said there was nothing wrong. He said it was just one of those things. I could take beta-blockers, but he advised me to leave it.

Aston knew when he was at Blackburn that it would be his last club. He was only thirty-two, but he felt old there. The programme notes always described him as a veteran. The irony is that, at the time, he still had that fine mop of thick, black, curly hair. Now he is as bald as Dion Dublin, but his pet food business is thriving and, like all the players whose marriages have lasted, he takes great pride and satisfaction at the way he has raised his family. He has no regrets about leaving the game when he did: 'I just wanted to finish. I was reading those stories in the financial pages about City whizz kids at forty-five and there was me, a veteran at thirty-two. I was desperate to get out and start my life afresh.'

However, like Glyn Pardoe, he is far from enchanted by the experience of going to a football match these days. He works on Saturdays, so he doesn't always get the chance, even if he wanted to take it. And he doesn't now. He went with an Oldham supporter to watch the Latics take on Everton in a cup tie, which was played in an atmosphere of incipient violence. Good humoured banter among crowds has long given way to verbal aggression. He did not enjoy it and never repeated the experience. He candidly admits that he no longer has the same passion for the game that he used to have. The irony is that he is still a United supporter. He looks for the Luton result, because he enjoyed his time down there and wishes them well, but at heart he remains the little boy who collected United programmes all through the fifties. John is well placed to distinguish between supporting a club and dealing with the miseries of life as a professional footballer with that same club. What he remembers best about life there, is what George and David and nearly everyone else remembers – playing in the car park in impromptu games after official training was finished:

> Playing on the gravel on the car park made a great team spirit and the funny thing was, though you got loads of scrapes and knocks, nobody ever got injured. You got cut knees, cut elbows, you got banged up against the stadium walls and there was no quarter asked or given, but it was character-building and we enjoyed it. We called it 'round the back'. It'd start off as five-a-side, and lads would come over and join in, and it'd end up as fifteen-a-side. It was like going back in time to your old school playground.

George was the exceptional talent in those youth team games of 1964 and it seems somehow appropriate that his life after football was unlike any of his contemporaries. As his latest book indicates, most of his life has been lived in the grip of alcoholism and, though many of the other players have had physical ailments – Connor's hips, Pardoe's leg, Doyle's knees – which were the direct consequence of playing football, none, fortunately, have had to struggle with the problem that has beset George. None of them have made (and squandered) the amount of money he has, either, but it was obvious from the time of those games in the Lancashire League that Best's was a prodigious talent. His life has been lived out in the full glare of the publicity that his footballing genius provoked. Today we see him on Sky Sports most

Saturday afternoons, after a liver transplant without which he would have died, looking prematurely aged, a pale shadow of that impish player and good-looking young man.

George Best was the first to mix football and showbiz – a commonplace today but an innovation in the sixties. His impact can be seen in the way the London media tried, unsuccessfully, to create a southern George Best in the Scotsman Peter Marinello, who grew his hair fashionably long and appeared briefly for Arsenal when George was still famous for playing football. George's charisma, though, was natural; it wasn't manufactured. David Meek recalls:

> I was sitting on the team coach with the players as they waited for the directors to join them. Most of the players were playing cards and the girls were all gathered by Best's window and he wasn't playing up to them. He was embarrassed, if anything, and they were getting increasingly hysterical, and this was before he lit up the game with his football. There is something almost animal about his sexuality, yet he also appealed to the mums who wanted to mother him.

In 1968 United bought Willie Morgan, the Burnley winger who clearly thought himself another George Best and, indeed, became unhealthily obsessed with the idea. David Meek was standing in the reception area at Stoke City after the match with United when Willie Morgan came out:

> I said, 'Well played, Willie,' and exaggeratedly he looked over both shoulders and said, 'He's not out yet.' I said, 'What do you mean?' and, of course, he claimed that George was my hero and obviously I'd got him mixed up with Best. So I asked him why he

got so worked up about the comparison with Best. He said the media like to have heroes and they'd chosen George, the implication being that they should have chosen him, and I had to explain that the media didn't pick George. We just followed the public reaction, because that's what newspapers do. It was the public who made George Best a hero and it was the public who decided not to do that with Willie Morgan.

Despite the celebrity that hasn't left him since that night when he destroyed Benfica in the European Cup in 1966, it is somehow comforting to learn that the happiest time of Best's life was around that time when he was twenty years old and playing football with a joyous abandon. It was before the full glare of publicity blinded him, when he gloried in his skills, but still enjoyed the game 'round the back', when his own team-mates tried to get the ball off him by fair means or foul. Bobby and Denis and Shay and Paddy and David Herd were the older, senior players, who carried the expectations of the crowd. His mates were still Fitzy, Young John and David Sadler and they were just thrilled to be playing first-team football and driving their first cars. A night out was a couple of pints with Mike Summerbee wondering if they were going to get lucky and pull and whether Mrs Fullaway would know what was going on and tell Matt, as football club landladies were supposed to do.

As we know, he blew it all in the most dramatic fashion and the waiter who saw him lying next to Miss World on a hotel bed covered with bank notes asked, 'Where did it all go wrong?' George tells the story because it is supposed to induce a laugh. How could it possibly have gone wrong if he is lying in bed with Miss World and literally rolling in money? But the young lad who enjoyed nothing so much as sticking the ball through the legs of Chopper Harris and making ordinary players like him look foolish, would not have laughed at that waiter. Neither do those of us who were around to watch him in the sixties. We know exactly what that waiter meant. It is a tribute to that unique talent that he is as loved as he is after thirty years of self-indulgence and sybaritic excess. Of course, we are grateful to have seen the flowering of the talent, but we also retain the memory of him drunkenly sprawled on the couch on the *Wogan* show in a suit of vomit green and of him staring wild-eyed with terror from the back of a police van on his way to spending Christmas in prison. I wonder whether Connor, Pardoe, Doyle, Sadler and Aston, secure in the warmth of their respective families, would have exchanged their own careers for the video collection and the glory that was Best. Somehow, I doubt it.

CHAPTER TEN

These We Can't Quite Remember

' All political lives, unless they are cut off in midstream at a
happy juncture, end in failure, because that is the nature
of politics and of human affairs,' wrote Enoch Powell in his
1977 biography of the Tory politician, Joseph Chamberlain.
For 'politics' read 'football'. I had originally divided the
twenty-two players into those who 'made it' and those who
didn't, assuming that, as Tolstoy wrote in *Anna Karenina*, 'All
happy families resemble one another, but each unhappy family
is unhappy in its own way.' In fact, this kind of division is
entirely misleading. Nearly all the players who left Old Trafford or Maine Road prematurely (in their opinion) were
unhappy with the manner of their departure, but many of them
recovered to have perfectly rewarding careers in the lower
divisions or in non-league football. Those who remained, as the
previous chapter attempts to demonstrate, did not necessarily
enjoy careers of unbroken happiness, crowned by the affection
of the fans and the gratitude of the club when they made their
way from the stage for the last time. Most of them were so hurt
by what happened that they will never go back. This chapter is
not about the trauma of being asked to leave Manchester
United or Manchester City, but about how the players dealt
with the initial disappointment of the realisation that it was
never going to happen for them there.

The happiest to leave was undoubtedly Dave Farrar, the United centre-half who was 'never mad for a ball'. He wanted to get into Europe all right, but it was as a long distance lorry driver rather than as a footballer, and it was Europe that took him into the business he still works in:

> I was asked to do a job in Germany for an exhibition company. I drove the truck over, then I worked on the site, building exhibition stands. I really enjoyed it and the chippie I was working with persuaded me it was a business worth getting into. I then started doing a lot of continental work – going to Italy every week and so on. I loved that, but eventually the company folded and I asked the boss if there was any chance of work with that exhibition firm in Salford, because I knew he was pals with one of the directors there. That was 1970 and I'm still doing it. I love it, but it did for both of my marriages. They each lasted about seven years, but they couldn't stick the hours. I've been in the business thirty years now.

Despite the two failed marriages, Dave strikes me as a happy, resilient character, who has never given football a second thought since Matt Busby whispered the dreaded words, 'We're going to have to let you go, son,' to be met, surprisingly, by a Homer Simpson-like whoop of joy. Ironically, Dave has become a United supporter forty years after playing for them. He'd like to go to more games, but doesn't like ringing Jimmy Ryan and asking him for tickets.

Alan Duff is also still a United supporter, but after falling out with Matt Busby he went to live with Beryl, his new bride, in South Africa, where he had been offered a contract by Walley Barnes, the former Arsenal full-back, then managing Highland Park:

We didn't really settle out there. I was sent off in their Cup final and Walley Barnes got sacked, so Alex Forbes, who'd been an ex-team-mate of his at Arsenal, took over the manager's job at Highland Park. I started to get interested in a business selling motor cars part-time. We had a little girl called Tania and then Beryl's parents came out to live. At the end of my two and a half year contract, we came back to Manchester on the *Windsor Castle* with Tania, who was six weeks old. I started playing part-time for Rhyl in the Cheshire League when Jack Rowley offered me a two-month trial at Oldham. Meanwhile, I was working for my father-in-law, who was an agricultural machine merchant and I was out on the road doing the selling.

The trial at Oldham never worked out and, playing for Rhyl, he broke his arm twice. Increasingly frustrated by injuries and lack of tangible success, he decided to give up football entirely, moved to Denby in north Wales and took a full-time job. That was when Alan discovered that real tragedy had nothing to do with bad refereeing decisions. Tania was stricken by cancer and she died in Alder Hey hospital at the age of two and a half. There were two other children, sons David and Jonathan, but Beryl and he had started to drift apart and in 1977 they split up and Alan went home to Guisborough. He was in his mid-thirties when he met his current wife, Lynsey, with whom he has a daughter called Nicola, who is fifteen. Together they run the North Skelton Working Men's Club. His FA Youth Cup winner's medal and his precious scrapbook were both lost in a fire which destroyed the house in Denby.

Willie Anderson was one of those who left Manchester United before the age of twenty-one, but still managed to have a happy life. He enjoyed his time at Aston Villa enormously, delighted in the fact that he had gone from playing Central League football in front of a few thousand die-hards to the passion of the first division at Villa Park. More relevantly, it enabled him to play in his native city:

> I played at Anfield twice in a short time, once in the league and once in the Cup and, of course, I also played at Goodison and that meant when I went home I had to get about fifty thousand tickets for everyone. And of course we beat United in the semis [of the League Cup in December 1970, drawing 1–1 at Old Trafford and beating United 2–1 at home].With the team they had, they should have beaten us; on paper they should have killed us, but there seemed to be no heart in the club in those days.

The team that the then third division Villa defeated included Rimmer, Fitzpatrick, Best, Sadler and Aston. Sweet revenge indeed for Anderson. He holds himself entirely responsible for the mistake he made in agreeing to leave Villa Park:

> I was at Villa for six years and then I went to Cardiff, which was the dumbest thing I ever did. I was headstrong. Vic Crowe was the manager and I'd been injured, and I'd worked really hard to get back into the team, but I only ever got one chance as a sub, and then Cardiff came in for me when I was really down. I should have stayed at the Villa, but I was in a bad place and I just took it. I stayed at Cardiff for four years. One summer I went to play in America and as soon as I got there, I thought, 'You know what? This is for me!' I couldn't wait to get back to America full-time.

It wasn't a footballing decision, it was a lifestyle decision, made by many British people who were becoming progressively disenchanted with life in the union-dominated, strike-torn Britain of the late seventies. The quadrupling of oil prices in 1973 decimated the British economy, which was being kept afloat by loans from the International Monetary Fund in return for savage cuts in public services. Uncollected garbage piled up in the streets, dead bodies remained unburied in a union dispute and the electorate voted in Margaret Thatcher. Willie Anderson, delighted to be out of Cardiff, where he was having a miserable time, fell in love with Portland, Oregon:

> It was a struggle at home. The best you could do was to survive, but here you can really live your life. The weather is always better and there's so much to do out of doors. The money was good and I was in a beautiful city. The team was good and I really liked Oregon. Portland Timbers were the Manchester United of our day – we had Peter Withe, Barry Powell, Brian Godfrey – but I fell in love with the lifestyle. They tapped me up every year, but by this time I was married to Vera, a girl from Wrexham, and she didn't fancy it out here. The money out here was so much better that I could play for the season, which is mostly in the summer, and then take the rest of year off. But my wife was an only child and very close to her mum and dad – I couldn't blame her for that. I loved it here and she didn't. I couldn't see myself going back to Wrexham after I retired from football and working in a pub.

Even in the lotus land of west coast America, he maintained the traditional footballer's refusal to face the consequences of retirement which affects all players, except Tony Book, as they approach their thirties:

> I didn't think much about retirement. I didn't want to think about it. I thought I could play forever, even when I was thirty, but as I got older I went into the office side of football – the marketing and promotion of the game – and then I knew that's what I'd do when I stopped playing. When I left the game I took the contacts I'd made working in the office with me and then I worked in radio and now, for the last six years, I've been in cable television. I'm an account executive. I sell air time for commercials.

Even though Willie had been lucky with injuries in that he never had the Glyn Pardoe or the John Clay experience, he still carries the scars of having played professional football for twenty-one years. He has a bad back, which pops out on an irregular basis, and an Achilles tendon problem, which he picked up from playing on artificial surfaces. Jogging hurts him now, so he doesn't do it. After a second failed marriage, this time to a Portland girl, he met and married his current wife, Audrey, who is a New Yorker:

> We met at my best friend's wedding – he's from Manchester. I have five kids – two by Vera – and they are all living in America. My eldest son has a daughter, so I'm now a grandfather, even though he and his partner aren't married. And sometimes I think if I'd stayed at Villa maybe I'd never have got to America.

America was the making of Bobby McAlinden, too, because the rest of football was showing scant interest in him. After City let him go, he had those spells with Glentoran and Port

Vale and another miserable time in South Africa. When he
returned to England he was so disillusioned with the game
that he didn't play football for five years:

> I just went roofing with my brother. I was always a
> naïve, young working-class kid. I never realised all
> the politics and the backstabbing that goes on in
> clubs. Then Stalybridge Celtic came in and asked
> me to go there, and that was all right. I liked
> Stalybridge and I stayed there for a long time,
> part-time, but I was roofing as well, so I was quite
> contented.

Bobby had been born on the same day as George and
displayed some of George's talents, principally a cocky attitude on the field and a love of gambling off it. After the early
teenage years of playing each other in Lancashire League
and Central League and Youth Cup games, the two of them
met up again in Manchester's casinos and in the somewhat
incongruous location of the YMCA, where both of them
went to keep fit. They soon discovered that they enjoyed
each other's company. In 1975, when they were both only
twenty-nine years old, despite scarcely having kicked a
significant ball in years, George was invited by the Los
Angeles Aztecs to play in the North American Soccer League
the following summer. It was George's idea that Bobby go
with him and, despite the lack of a CV to rival those of Best,
Pele and Beckenbauer, Bobby McAlinden abandoned the
roofs of Manchester for the sunshine and palm trees of
Southern California. It wasn't a difficult cultural adjustment
to make. Like Willie Anderson, Bobby quickly settled into
the American lifestyle:

> That first year George and I rented a house together

and the following season we bought a house overlooking Hermosa Beach. Five of us, including George and me, got together and opened a bar. We called it Besties and it did very well, but the Aztecs were bought by new owners and they traded George to Fort Lauderdale and pretty soon all the bar's partners were gone. One was traded to Tampa Bay, another one went off to Oklahoma, so eventually I bought everybody out and I finished up with the bar myself and I had it for twenty years.

Being traded, as they call the transfer system in America, was more of a hazard there than it was in England in the seventies. Then there was still the concept of the one-club player, but since there was no tradition of football-supporting in the United States, it didn't really affect the crowd if the players at their local franchise stayed one year or three. At best, it was a passing entertainment for them, like a circus that comes to town once a year. For the players, it was mostly a matter of following the money and being traded was an occupational risk. George then went off to the San Jose Earthquakes in northern California, while Bobby stayed at the Aztecs for four seasons, until he was thirty-three years old. The coach was Rinus Michels, the former Holland national coach, who used his influence with Johan Cruyff to persuade his national captain to join the Aztecs. Bobby was regarded as less of a capture than Cruyff and was traded to Memphis, Tennessee, which was terrific if you liked country music, but something of a problem if you were supposed to be running a bar called Besties in Los Angeles. He went for the perfectly sound reason that, if he didn't, he wouldn't be paid. He played in Memphis for a year and was coached by ex-Chelsea legend, Charlie Cooke, who had also played for the Aztecs. Cooke wanted him to stay another season, but Bobby had had enough of Tennessee.

Bobby and George shared a taste for most things except booze, which was George's prerogative. Bobby was more addicted to gambling and horse racing, but after being best man at George's wedding to Angie in Las Vegas in 1978 (before the vows were exchanged, he was the only relatively sober member of the wedding party), Bobby met his own wife in a manner which George would instantly recognise:

> She was a flight attendant on the plane I was on when we were flying to San Jose for a game against the Earthquakes. I asked for her phone number and she gave it to me. We finished up getting married two years later in 1979, when I was thirty-three. She found Los Angeles was getting more crowded and expensive and she wanted to move to Oregon. I always said I'd sell the bar when I was fifty. And I did, and after that we moved up to Oregon. That's where we live now. We have some income from properties and my wife has got a couple of antique shops she runs. I keep in touch with football. I'm a good mate of Reidy's. I do scouting for Peter Reid in South America.

Although he was one of the first of that youth team to leave Maine Road, he retains clear memories of his team-mates and the opposition. He is not surprised that only Glyn Pardoe and Mike Doyle became first-team regulars. In both cases, their physical maturity was a huge asset at the age of seventeen or eighteen. Willie Anderson makes much the same point, recalling Alf Wood's physical courage: 'I remember Alf Wood as a really tough lad. He stood out when we were kids, because you could rocket a shot towards goal and he'd head it away.' Alf's courage was not enough to convince

Malcolm Allison that he had a future at Manchester City and when he arrived at Shrewsbury it was to discover that the crowd was quickly on his back:

> The crowd hated me at Shrewsbury, because I played really badly when I got there. Arthur Rowley asked me if I wanted a transfer, but I said no, I wanted to prove my point, and eventually I did. The local paper carried the headline 'Jeers turn to cheers for Alf'. We played at Cardiff on Boxing Day and on the Saturday after, the jeers turned to cheers when I kicked some guy into the stand. I thought Arthur Rowley might take me to Sheffield United when he moved on, but he didn't, and then Harry Gregg came and he said to me he fancied another centre-half and he suggested I move to centre-forward. His plan was to play the new centre-half in the number nine shirt and leave me with the number five on my back. We'd start off the game conventionally and after a few minutes we'd swap round. The centre-half he bought was big Jim Holton. He died before he was forty – he bought a pub and got fat.

Alf went on to become a legend at Shrewsbury. In a recent supporters' poll he finished second to Arthur Rowley as their all-time favourite player. After six years and prodigious goal-scoring feats, including five in one match against Blackburn Rovers, Alf was transferred to Millwall, whose uncluttered style of football presumably matched his own. He spent three enjoyable years playing in one of the least salubrious areas of south London, but living, sensibly, in an attractive house thirty miles away in the Kent countryside, outside Gravesend:

> We used as a reason to leave the fact that my wife

couldn't settle in the south. Everyone did that. The real reason was I challenged the manager, Benny Fenton. I overheard the chairman telling the manager that I'd been doing really well and the manager replied, 'Yes, and we got him for nothing,' and this really bothered me. Eventually I told him I just didn't want to play for him any more. He said, 'Don't be so silly!' I said I wasn't being silly, that's how I felt. We had a big row about money and, although I admitted they had helped me to buy the house, at the end of the year I wanted to leave, so it was easy to say my wife wanted to go back up north, because that would cause the least number of problems.

One free Saturday afternoon six months later, Alf and Joan Wood paid an impromptu visit to Millwall, where they were received with great courtesy in the boardroom, but the crowd who cheered Alf vented their displeasure on poor Joan, whom they held responsible for Alf's departure. She was understandably upset, never having missed a goal or made a bad tackle in her life. As Alf moved on, his combative nature did not diminish:

I signed for Tony Kaye, who had just been made manager at Hull, rather than for West Bromwich Albion, because Don Howe wanted me there, but Hull offered me a better deal and they were both in the second division. I played against West Brom and John Wile and Johnny Giles both whacked me as if by accident. I got my revenge, but it just got worse, because I put my knee up his arse and Johnny Giles caught me, which the ref saw, and sent him off. So then John Wile came back at me again and it got worse still. I can kick people and they go 'ow' and two

days later there's a bruise, but others would leave the
boot in or went over the top. You see it all the time
these days, especially in European games.

Alf continued his tour of the football league grounds of
England after falling out with the Hull chairman over money
because they were supposed to have paid him option money
and they refused. He won his case in front of a tribunal, but
all that could do was to say he must have a free transfer if
they didn't pay up:

> I played in the reserves after that and I was playing
> against York reserves in front of Harold Shepherd-
> son. I took a free kick while everyone was moaning
> and groaning and scored. Harold Shepherdson must
> have been impressed, because Jack Charlton signed
> me within three days for Middlesbrough and I played
> there from November till the end of the season as
> centre-forward, to replace John Hickton. He didn't
> care so much about me scoring, but he wanted me to
> create havoc in the penalty area – which I did.

Alf eventually left Middlesbrough in conventional football
circumstances. In the summer of 1977, the club was due to
depart on a tour to Norway, Hong Kong and Australia:

> Jack had given me a contract to get me through till
> June and said we'd make a full contract in the close
> season. He said, 'We'll chat while we're on the trip,'
> and I said, 'Fine,' because I believed in him and
> trusted him. We were due to leave on the Monday
> and in the Sunday papers the story broke that Charl-
> ton had resigned. The new manager was John Neill,
> who was coming from Wrexham. Harry Gregg asked

me where I was going when I left, because, 'He'll never keep you.' And he was right. The chairman of Middlesbrough told me they'd cancelled the option on my contract, because the new manager wanted to bring his own centre-forward with him, so it was, 'Thanks very much and ta-ta.' Wrexham and Shrewsbury had been local rivals and that's why I think he didn't want me. I used to take the piss out of him.

After Middlesbrough, Dave Mackay offered Alf decent money at Walsall, but he tore his Achilles tendon in preseason training. It proved to be the final injury, from which he never recovered:

I'd run thirty yards and pull up in pain. My biggest asset was my ability in the air and the take-off was off that ankle. I barely played and when I did I was struggling. I got back into the team for the FA Cup in time to play in the fifth round but we lost 4–1 at Arsenal. I was doing nothing and I went to Dave Mackay and apologised. I said, 'If I have an operation now, I'll be out for the rest of the season anyway.' I had a problem, because my children were switching schools so often. My daughter was getting ready to go to secondary school and she'd been to that many schools in the past few years she'd done the same work every time. It was time I called it a day and stayed here. I was thirty-three and I was reaching a stage when I was never sure how fit I would ever be in the future.

The former England Youth centre-half and Manchester City youth-team captain now lives in the West Midlands. The company he owned went into liquidation in January 2002, but he recently set up a simple partnership with his daughter, Samantha, who lives in Worcester. The new company specialises in incentive and promotional items, including T-shirts, calendars and diaries. His other daughter is a keen Manchester City supporter.

Malcolm Allison finished Chris Jones's career at Maine Road as surely as he had ended Alf Wood's. In the summer of 1968, even as the Russian tanks were rolling into Prague, Chris took his pain and anger down to Swindon, reversing the journey taken by Mike Summerbee three years earlier. The vital ingredient for all players is their relationship with the manager and it applies as surely to life in the lower leagues as it does to the well-publicised spats at the top of the Premiership. Unfortunately for Chris, he quickly came to a less than flattering conclusion about the talents of Danny Williams, the manager who had signed him for Swindon Town:

> I thought he was a prat. He dropped me for the League Cup final [against Arsenal, which Swindon famously won]. I had a miserable first year at Swindon. I'd scored eight goals in thirteen games up to the final, but I hadn't played in the quarters or the semis before Christmas. John Smith played and Smith had been out for three months with a hamstring injury, but he played at Wembley for an hour, came off, and Willie Penman, who had played as a sub in the quarters and semis, came on and I was the thirteenth man. That was the nearest I ever got to playing in a Wembley final – sitting in the stand.

Fortunately for Chris, Swindon's exploits made Danny Williams a wanted manager and he left at the end of the 1968–69 season for the greener pastures of Sheffield Wednesday.

Eventually, Chris settled down, but once Dave Mackay became manager he decided he didn't want Chris as his centre-forward, so he quickly moved him out on loan to Oldham, under Jimmy Frizzell, after which Chris signed for Walsall. He was now a journeyman centre-forward, scoring enough goals in the third division to be of interest to the chairman:

> He said to me, 'Chris, you're the only one I can raise any money on and I've got to sell someone to survive through the summer. Will you go to York?' First year I was there they got promotion to the old second division. We had two years there and I formed a very successful striking partnership with Jimmy Seal. We're classed as legendary goalscorers at Bootham Crescent. I played for two years under Tom Johnston and then under Wilf McGuinness. He dropped both of us, played Mickey Cave and Jim Hinch from Plymouth, couldn't decide which of Jimmy Seal and me he wanted to keep as cover, so both of us raced for the door. I get on very well with Wilf, nice bloke, but that was a daft decision. I'd been out injured, having fractured my ankle in a game up in Sunderland, and Sealy hadn't done it for him, and he was under pressure because of results, so he got rid of both of us.

A couple of years before Mike Doyle's ill-fated journey to Spotland, Chris also wound up at Rochdale. His relationship with Mike had not improved over the years. On City's run to their losing League Cup final in 1973–74, they had drawn 0–0 with York City at Bootham Crescent, before winning the replay at Maine Road. Mike was now at centre-back and Chris was leading the York attack. It was still, Chris remarks, 'daggers drawn'. When he arrived at Rochdale for the 1979–80 season, Bob Stokoe, who had taken Sunderland to FA Cup glory in 1973, was the manager of the struggling fourth division side:

> We were at the bottom and Bob was still living in the past. He was a very pessimistic bloke and I'd won player of the year and had been the leading goalscorer the previous year, but he gave me and six others free transfers. I was thirty-four at the time. He let us all go and then resigned, but that was it for me, because his last act was to advise the board not to re-sign any of the players he had let go. The end. A sad and rather strange end.

Like almost every other player of the twenty-two (John Aston and Phil Burrows being rare exceptions), Chris had made no plans for retirement. It's as if the evil day can be postponed by simply not thinking about it:

> In the end we got a guest house business going in York and built it up into a hotel and then lost it. Boom to bust and we went bankrupt. I had to go out selling, but that didn't work out too well either, so I went to night school and got a certificate in education. Now I'm teaching PE and GNVQ vocational studies on short contracts or as a supply teacher.

What distinguishes Chris Jones from most of the others is that he has retained the love for Manchester City which he developed as a kid. Towards the end of our conversation he came out, unprompted, with a line that sent shivers down my spine: 'If they cut my heart open I tell you my heart is Blue. I was always a Manchester City player.' I doubt very much that there are many other players who pulled on the pale blue shirt who would speak so movingly, so fervently and so truthfully. Crowds will forgive players any number of mistakes for a passion like that.

In the spring of 2002, as Ali Benarbia was guiding City to the Nationwide league first division championship, Chris took a party down to Maine Road to watch a comfortable 3–0 victory:

> I said my farewells to the ground. It felt like home. I always go back to the former players' dinners and I like walking down to the pitch by the Kippax and I look at the goals and I remember the times I scored there. During 1963, 1964 and 1965, the Youth Cup side was the best thing that club had going for it, and I left school to help it, and took a job at the gas board to take the chance that one day I'd play for Manchester City. Playing for City was the realisation of a childhood dream.

He also attends the occasional sportsmen's dinner and at one recent evening he saw Malcolm Allison, appropriately enough, across a bar, but he couldn't reach out – metaphorically or physically. The memory of the way Malcolm had manoeuvred him out of Maine Road was still too painful – over thirty years after the event. Then he saw his first mentor, Johnny Hart: 'I went over to him to say hello and Johnny was talking to a group of players and he saw me coming and said, "Chris! How are you, son?" He introduced me to the group and he said to them, "This is Chris Jones. He played for City in the sixties. He could play a bit." And that is an accolade I shall treasure for the rest of my life.'

When Chris joined York City, he rejoined his former youth team-mate, Phil Burrows. York City had become a recognised stop on the travels of former Manchester players, perhaps because Wilf Meek, David's father, was on the board of directors. In 1965, Bobby Cunliffe went there and a year later he was followed by Phil Burrows. When Phil arrived he was twenty years old, living away from home for the first time and York had just been relegated from the third to the fourth division. He went straight into the first team, where he made a big impact, moving from left-half to an overlapping left-back. He was a big fish in a small pond for the first time. His wages went up to £30 a week, which, though not extravagant, was still more than the average working man's wage. The difference between the top of the Football League and the bottom was minimal compared with today's absurd gulf. The diligent Burrows also finished his studies and took a job for three years in a local building firm, so he would be ready for when his football days were over. He was determined to become a quantity surveyor, which was understandable when the pressure of football could be so great:

> The first three years we had to apply for re-election. That takes a great deal of guts just to keep afloat. The manager would be sacked, a new man would come in, get rid of all the players, bring new players in, have a bad season, get sacked and the circle would revolve. It's tough down there. There's England internationals today who could be transferred to Rochdale or Exeter and they would just sink without trace.

The name 'Neville', I believe, surfaced in the conversation some moments later. Phil tried hard to get away from York, but they never told him about the offers that came in for him from other clubs and they retained his registration. Even at the end of the contract, they could offer him terms and, if he turned them down, the club could claim that he was still registered to York and couldn't play for anyone else. Ten years after the George Eastham decision in the High Court, which was supposed to have broken the retain and transfer system which the presiding judge, Mr Justice Wilberforce, had called 'mediaeval', Phil would have had no grounds for redress.

He learned, too late, that both Fulham and Norwich had made bids for him, which York had rejected, as they did to later requests from Wolves and Brighton. His time at York was by no means unproductive. The first three years he was there the club had to apply for re-election at the end of every season, but at the end of the 1970–71 season they were promoted to division three and, in April 1974, they won a further promotion on the same day that Manchester United were relegated from the first division by Denis Law's infamous backheel. In March 1975, nine years after his last visit in the Youth Cup, Phil returned to play at Old Trafford in a league game (which United won 2–1). Despite this success and his award as player of the year, Phil was not happy at York:

> York offered me nothing. The manager was a guy called Tom Johnston and his philosophy was, 'If you love football so much, you'll play for nothing, and besides, you're under contract and we hold your registration.' I asked for a transfer and because we were now in the second division he thought I'd be glad to stay, so he said I could go. He was there for five years and I played every single league game when he was manager and he offered me nothing, just a nominal increase on last year's wage. I went to see the chairman, but he said his hands were tied, because there was a ceiling on wages, but they were playing Villa, United and Sunderland. He did a deal with Halifax for £10,000, but I turned that down. Then

Plymouth came in for me and, even though they were in the old Third Division, which I'd just got out of, I said yes.

He was twenty-eight when he eventually got away and went to Plymouth to play under Tony Waiters who, being a Southport lad himself, had a strong belief in the supremacy of northwestern players. Paul Mariner was a product of this policy. Phil's decision to drop a division was justified: 'In my first year at Home Park we got promotion. Crowds went from 5,000 to 30,000. When we played Blackburn they were top and we were second and I remember we beat them 2–1 in front of 30,000. We played Everton in a cup tie and there were 38,000 there, with 10,000 locked out. It was on *Match of the Day*.'

Waiters was entrepreneurial and imaginative, developing contacts with Bobby Robson and John Cobbold in the similar footballing backwater of Ipswich, a relationship which eventually produced the Paul Mariner transfer. However, his plans for expansion were thwarted by the pay freeze instituted by the government. Plymouth could no longer match his own ambitions and he left to coach the Vancouver Whitecaps, eventually becoming manager of the Canadian national team, which he took to the World Cup finals.

Meanwhile, Phil was thirty years old, but he had never been fitter than he was at Plymouth where, unusually, they trained twice a day. He had settled in the West Country and, when Waiters left, he moved to Hereford United, who had just arrived in the second division, where they played clubs like Burnley, Wolves and Fulham. The last of these, of course, had just signed George, who was currently dividing his time between the west coast of America and southwest London, and so Phil and George met again at the end of their careers, just as Phil had marked George at the very start.

Fulham v Hereford United was covered by ITV's *The Big
Match*: 'It was the famous game where George and Rodney
Marsh tackled each other. In that game I played a poor cross,
Bobby Moore headed it out, Marsh took it on and passed to
Best. I clouted Rodney and tackled Best as he was going
round the goalie and knocked it out for a corner. Best and
Marsh both went crying after the referee.'

Age was catching up with both of them. Phil struggled on
at Hereford until 1980, when he was thirty-four. His leg had
gone, he had lost his pace and his fitness. It was time to call it
a day. Besides, Hereford were on the decline and the supporters' action group was campaigning to remove the manager, John Sillett, and restore Colin Addison, who had taken
them into the Football League. After a career spanning 600
league and cup games, Phil and his family left the attractive,
but somewhat isolated town of Hereford, and returned to
Manchester whence they had come. Elizabeth, his wife, came
from Wythenshawe and Phil from Stockport. They met
before Phil signed professional forms for City. Phil then
spent two years in York, travelling home after the match on
Saturday, after which they decided to get married and set up
house in York. As a reminder of his nomadic life in football,
Phil's first child was born in York, the next in Plymouth and
the youngest child in Hereford. He successfully applied for a
job in Altrincham and he and Elizabeth are now happily
ensconced not too far from Stockport, where he started his
career with the local boys' side. It might not have been the
footballing career he envisaged when he trotted out at Old
Trafford in April 1964, but he's glad he had it and he refuses
to be bitter about the treatment he received at York and
Manchester City.

John Clay's bitterness, such as it is, stems not from the
way he was treated by City as a player, but what happened
after he returned there in an administrative capacity in later

life. On leaving Maine Road within days of the championship victory in 1968, John signed for Macclesfield Town, where he found instant success. It was a side full of seasoned professionals and at twenty-one he was the baby of the team, which went on to win the Northern Premier League in its inaugural season. A number of third and fourth division teams came in for him, but none from the first or second divisions. Through the club he found a job with United Biscuits in Macclesfield, so he decided to work and play part-time. During his second year, however, the injury jinx struck again when he was badly hurt playing against Mossley. He played only a month of the season, though the club went on to win the FA Trophy. Macclesfield, in traditional straitened circumstances, made it clear they couldn't afford to keep him on the payroll, so when he had recovered he went on to play for Witton Albion and then for Rossendale United, a tiny team in the Cheshire League, who had been devoid of success.

Also playing for Rossendale were Fred Eyre, who had been a year ahead of him on the City groundstaff, Dave Wild and John Pearson, the lad from Wigan who had played for England Schoolboys and then for Manchester United youth at the start of the 1964 Cup run, before he was dropped for Best for the semi-final game. That year Rossendale reached the second round of the FA Cup, where they were drawn at home against Bolton Wanderers. The players wanted to play the match at home, because they felt they could win, but the club compromised by opting for a neutral venue at Gigg Lane, which was obviously bigger than the Rossendale ground, but didn't entirely cede ground advantage to Bolton. John scored the first goal that day and a major upset seemed possible, but Bolton equalised just before half-time and, with the help of a Roy Greaves hat trick, Bolton ran out comfortable 4–1 winners.

It was a small triumph for Clay, because towards the end of that season his ankle went again and by now he'd just had enough. He walked away from a training session and never really kicked a ball again. He was still only twenty-four. A few years later, when he was about twenty-eight, Wilf Tranter, who had befriended David Sadler when he first arrived at Manchester United from Maidstone, persuaded him to go along to Wythenshawe Amateurs. Paradoxically, there was a little money there, because it was run by a man who owned fruit machines, so the players were getting paid, which tended to happen when you were an amateur. John went to a couple of training sessions with some trepidation and, sure enough, the ankle gave way. He tried endless cures and endless physiotherapists, but the ruptured tendons of the ankle never healed sufficiently to allow him to play competitive football again. He seemed to be fated. He had the talent to play first-team football at Manchester City for many years, but he lacked the determination that distinguishes the top-class professional, as well as being desperately unlucky with injuries.

He left his dreams of playing football for a living and a job at United Biscuits in Macclesfield to become an estate agent and raise a family. In the late eighties, the estate agency folded, leaving him stranded, and his marriage also disintegrated. He was out of work for over a year before answering an advertisement in the *Manchester Evening News* for a job which turned out to be in the commercial department at Maine Road. His timing could not have been worse. He started in the fag end of the discredited Swales regime, but survived the upheavals when Swales was thankfully and finally removed from power by the Francis Lee/Colin Barlow consortium. Unfortunately, the team fared even worse under the new administration and shortly after Lee, too, was forced out by the hostility of the fans, the club was relegated to division two of the Nationwide League. The club's income was drastically reduced and swingeing cuts had to be made. John Clay was one of the six middle managers who were made redundant. His second departure from Maine Road was, if anything, even more painful than the first. At least in 1968 he didn't take the club to an industrial tribunal, although his claim was settled out of court after the first day. Eight days later the City chief executive, Mike Turner, who had been savaged under cross-examination by Clay's lawyer, hired through the PFA, also left the club. This was the year City finally entertained Macclesfield Town in a league match. John Clay returned to the world of lettings and management, where his job was not at the mercy of disaffected fans and players who couldn't pass straight.

The two final members of that exceptional Stockport Boys side of 1960 who had gone on to play for Manchester City in the Youth Cup of 1964 were the left-back Dave Wild and the right-winger Ronnie Frost. Frost had been an apprentice with Clay, Doyle and McAlinden, had played two matches in the first team during the successful Youth Cup run, but had left the club at the same time as Bobby, in the summer of 1965, to play non-league football at Kettering Town. He never managed to find another league club and eventually drifted out of the game. Until recently, he ran a carpet warehouse just outside Stockport, but despite cropping up frequently in conversation, nobody I spoke to is entirely sure of his current whereabouts, although he is believed to be in Hazel Grove, close to where he was raised.

The Dave Wild story is sadly a tragic one. He had followed a similar path as the others — captain of Reddish Vale Secondary Modern school football team, Westbourne Rangers and Stockport Boys under Frank Aspinall, along with Max Brown, Frost, Doyle, Clay and Phil Burrows, before joining the rising stars of Manchester City under the tutelage of Johnny Hart and Dave Ewing down at Chassen Road in Urmston. Despite his enthusiasm and the fact that he was playing out of position at left-back, he had a poor game against Willie Anderson, who ripped him to shreds, just as Johnny Aston did to Mike Doyle on the other flank. Of all the lads who played in that semi-final, he was the only one never to be offered professional terms, which understandably hurt him badly.

In the small world of non-league football he played for some time under Freddie Pye at Altrincham, before he joined up again with John Clay at Rossendale. It was Dave Wild's goal from the penalty spot, ironically against Altrincham, which brought Rossendale United their famous second round FA Cup tie against Bolton Wanderers. He never got a sniff of another league club, but after playing at a decent non-league standard he decided to become a referee and acquired his badge in his late thirties. He started by running the line and then refereeing in the Northern Premier League, but he had left it too late to progress to the Football League as an official. His devotion to football, however, never wavered and he went on to manage Glossop and Chadderton in the Manchester League. He married Jenny, his childhood sweetheart, with whom he had three children, but the marriage eventually broke down and Dave remarried. When he was fifty years old he was stricken by a tumour on the brain. His old friend, John Buckley, who had lived next door to him when they were growing up and who had been best man at his wedding to Jenny, watched the bitter end:

He was as fit as a fiddle. I was with him the day before he died at St Ann's Hospice in Cheadle. It was a brain tumour, so although I used to go and sit with him when I'd finished work, he couldn't talk. He could understand everything, but it was all one-way traffic. He cried with frustration. He'd sit in his shorts in the lounge and there wasn't an ounce of fat on the man. He was all muscle. He was always strong and fit. When he had treatment at Christies he had four times the regular amount of chemo, because they thought he was so fit his body could take it.

Dave Wild is the only one of the twenty-two who has passed away, although we have come near to losing both George and Bobby Noble. The percentage mortality rate is perhaps no more than we should expect of any cross-section of English society, born in the two years after the end of the Second World War.

There is a small irony that none of the extremely talented Stockport Boys team ever went on to play for Stockport County – and the only one who did was born in Barnsley. Alan Ogley was transferred there in September 1967 and, over the next nine years, achieved justifiable cult status among the County supporters. As Ken Mulhearn became one of the more fortunate goalkeepers to win a first division championship medal, Alan made an immediate impact at Edgeley Park as County rose to second place in the third division by the middle of February 1968. Unfortunately, he tore his cartilage at Leyton Orient and didn't play again that season. Stockport had to put young Brian Lloyd in, and they lost a few vital games, so it is not beyond the bounds of speculation that had Ogley stayed fit, Stockport would have gained promotion in his first season. Ogley had one chance for a return to the first division with Arsenal the following year:

I was having a great season at County and Arsenal approached County to sign me and offered thirty grand. County turned it down, saying they wanted

£35,000 or £40,000. So Arsenal went and signed Barnett from Everton. I didn't know about this till much later. Noble, the writer for the *Stockport Express*, told me, and it really upset me, because they said that if they got a bid for me and I wanted to go they'd let me. I didn't get to know till a lot later. I didn't play at the top level for as long as I should have done. I know for a fact that Malcolm thought I could have done. I blew it, that one incident at Sheffield United. If I hadn't have left City, I'd have played for England. I am absolutely certain.

If Alan needed further proof of the perfidy of football clubs it came at the end of his stay at Stockport. He had been granted a testimonial by the board, because he'd been there nine years, and during the following season he was entitled to it. In 1975, County were in a more than usually precarious financial position and approached Alan, who was the team's PFA representative at the time, to propose that the club pay the players' wages fortnightly, rather than weekly. In fact 'fortnightly' turned out to be code for 'infrequently':

> We had two or three arguments over not getting the wages, but the chairman said he would sign the cheque and we could go to the bank for our wages. Then one Thursday, Terry McCreery walks through the door about half past four and says, 'That's it, lads, you won't be getting your wages today. You'll have to wait.' Now the lads had been through this palaver that many times they just turned round and said, 'In that case we're not playing.' The lads were adamant that if they didn't get paid, they weren't going to play on Friday night.

It was Alan's job to go back upstairs and tell the management what had happened. Jimmy Meadows, who was the manager, in charge for his second spell, explained that the chairman was on holiday in Spain, which wasn't much help to players who needed their wages to pay their mortgages. He returned to the dressing room to explain to the players what had been discussed and they agreed that they would come in as normal, but if they didn't get paid they wouldn't play:

> I drove home to Barnsley and we was sat here about six o'clock at night watching telly and there was a knock at the door and it was a guy from the *Daily Mail*. He said, 'What's all this about you going on strike?' I said, 'What do you mean?' He said, 'Well, you're not playing tomorrow night, are you? You're all on strike.' I said I couldn't deny or confirm. 'I've got nothing to say on the matter. It's private and I can't speak to you.' I said to my wife that first thing in the morning I'd go and see Cliff Lloyd at the PFA, but all over the *Daily Mail* there was this story about Stockport County players going on strike. I said to Cliff I needed help. He said, 'No problem, but you do know you are playing tonight, don't you?' I said, 'Not according to what the lads have said,' and he said, 'I'm telling you, you're playing tonight,' and he warned me of the consequences if we didn't.

Alan drove thoughtfully to the ground, where he found the press was waiting for him in force, along with the players' wages. Someone had clearly been in communication with Dragon Lukic, the chairman, and the wages had mysteriously arrived in cash in brown envelopes. It appeared that this was another victory for the solidarity of the workers in the ongoing class struggle. The downside was that Alan Ogley was then executed. At the end of the season, the option on his contract was not taken up and Ogley was released. Quite coincidentally of course, he was just weeks away from his testimonial match. Like Sadler at United and Connor at City, Ogley discovered that the awarding of testimonials is a custom honoured more in the breach than in the observance. Alan and Diane, his long-suffering wife, were justifiably appalled by the betrayal of his long and faithful service.

When the new season started Alan was playing for Darlington. The family had moved back to Barnsley just before the *contretemps* with County, because they wanted to get the children settled in secondary schools. To minimise the travelling, Alan was allowed to train at Barnsley and travel up to meet the Darlington players on match days. Jim Iley was the obliging manager at Oakwell and Peter Madden at Feethams. However, by the middle of his third season there, even this amount of travelling was tiring, and Darlington were happy enough to pay up his contract. After more than eighteen years, Alan Ogley was no longer a professional footballer. Then came the inevitable problems of readjustment to life in Civvy Street:

The Saturday after I finished playing was the hardest day I've ever known. You know you should be somewhere else, but you're not, and you just have to get into a new routine. We never talked about what I'd do after I retired. Never. I finished in January 1978 and I was paid up till May, so it gave me some time to think about it. Anyway, Johnny Steele told me about the lottery. It had just started up and they needed to take somebody on to collect money from people, so I did that, but I soon realised this wasn't a career. I ended up going down to work at BOC, delivering food for Marks & Spencer for twenty-odd years. Now I'm doing what I should have been doing when I retired – coaching women at Belper and at Doncaster.

This last remark elicited a big laugh from Diane. Ogley was a model professional, always honest and courteous and it seems odd that his career at both City and Stockport should have been abbreviated by two incidents that led the management to regard him as a trouble-maker, because he's anything but that. Although his opinions on current players are as forceful as those of anyone I interviewed, they are made from the standpoint of the model professional, who played for Barnsley for a pittance because he loved the club and not for Leeds United when Don Revie tried to entice him to Elland Road:

I think the attitude of a lot of players today is wrong. All this 'We play too much football' is a load of bollocks. We played seventy games a year. In fact, we'd rather play than train. These people don't want to do that. The hunger's gone. I think a lot of them are greedy and wouldn't have lasted if they'd had to play football when I was playing. There's too much money in the game and I don't think the players are hungry enough. I was playing every year to get a contract for the following year. If Beckham's getting £100,000 a week, where's the fear factor? We'd have played in the local rec. I don't think half of this lot would. I don't blame the players for taking what's on offer. What I do blame the players for is not giving a 100 per cent effort.

It's hard to disagree with much of that.

Ogley's opposite number on the United side, Jimmy

Rimmer, has made few appearances in this book, mostly because, as the youngest player on the field that night in April 1964, his career in the United first team started later than all the others. He was at United for ten years, but made only forty-five appearances, most of them in 1970, when Wilf McGuinness was in charge. He was too young to take over when Busby couldn't decide between Dunne, Gaskell and Gregg, and as soon as Alex Stepney arrived in 1966 the contest was over until Rimmer fought his way in, however briefly. He was, everyone says, unbelievably quiet for a goalkeeper, most of whom are voluble characters, particularly when a goal has been scored which is almost entirely their fault. While self-effacement in a vicar is probably a useful ingredient, it is less helpful in a goalkeeper who should be dominating play in his penalty area. Jimmy got a taste of European action when he played in both legs of the fateful European Cup semi-final defeat at the hands of AC Milan in 1969, but overall he had made only four league appearances that season. His debut had come the previous year in the championship run-in, but he was firmly typed as a reserve to Alex Stepney and he had to leave if he was going to find regular first-team action. Ironically, it was the humiliating defeat to third division Aston Villa (where he was to find his most rewarding days) in the League Cup semi-finals played just before Christmas 1970 which caused McGuinness to be sacked, Rimmer to be dropped and Busby and Stepney to be restored to their traditional positions.

Like Noble, Duff and Kinsey before him, Rimmer felt he had to have it out with Busby. He dreaded going in to see the boss – all the players did. Busby kept his office deliberately dark and uninviting and players who were unhappy at his decision to leave them out of the first team or freeze their wages still needed large quantities of courage to walk up the stairs towards the door that said 'Manager' on it. Like Noble, but not Duff and Kinsey, Jimmy Rimmer got a negative response from his manager. He didn't want to sell his reserve goalkeeper and that was that. As long as Busby remained in charge, Rimmer was going nowhere, because he valued the Southport lad so highly – but he wouldn't play him in the first team instead of Alex Stepney.

Even when Tommy Docherty arrived and was given permission by the board of directors to clear the old guard out of the dressing room, it was of no benefit to Rimmer. For no reason that any United fan could ever comprehend, Docherty started to groom Paddy Roche to take over from Stepney as the first-team goalkeeper. Rimmer had stayed around for ten years out of loyalty, but it had done him little good. For years, he had been told he was too young for promotion to the first team. Now, suddenly, he was too old. It's unclear when the time had been right, but whenever that was, the manager had obviously missed it.

In October 1973, in the face of a shake of the head from the great man who had been moved upstairs, the new manager allowed Jimmy Rimmer to join Swansea City on loan where he did well enough to secure a £40,000 transfer to Arsenal, who had been looking to replace Bob Wilson. According to Alan Ogley, it could have been him, so it was ironic that it should, in the end, have been Jimmy Rimmer. There is some kind of poetic justice in the fact that he was one of the few players to leave Old Trafford who actually furthered his career by doing so, although he worried about it at the time. His old mentor, Harry Gregg, now Alf Wood's manager at Shrewsbury, confirmed that it was time to leave. Docherty's United would have no place for Rimmer and whatever lay in wait for him elsewhere it would have to be better than playing second fiddle to Paddy Roche. Busby later confessed to Rimmer that the only two transfers he bitterly opposed were those of himself and Brian Kidd. Other clubs reaped the benefit of the talent United had nurtured, but failed fully to exploit.

While at Highbury, Jimmy Rimmer won his only international cap, on England's summer tour to the USA, but in August 1977 he was transferred to Aston Villa, where the pattern of his appearances was exactly the reverse of his time at United. Over the six years he was at Villa, Rimmer set up a record by missing only one game in 287 matches. He was a vital part of the Ron Saunders team that won the league championship in 1981 and then went on to claim the European Cup the following year. Just as he appeared in Europe for United without many league appearances to his name, he lasted only eight minutes of the 1982 European Cup final before being carried off injured, allowing the young Nigel Spink to make his debut in the most extraordinary of circumstances.

In 1986, twenty-two years after his youth-team appearances for Manchester United, Jimmy Rimmer's career finished at Swansea. Again, remarkably for a man whom all his colleagues remember as shy and retiring, Jimmy is currently a goalkeeping coach in China, where he has worked with Dalian Shide, the leading club side, for whom Sun Jihai was the star player, and for the Chinese national team. He was invited out there in 1995 for a three-month trial period and has stayed for nine years, during which time the clubs he has been associated with have won nine trophies. No doubt he and Sun Jihai share their memories of Manchester over a dietary drink or two. His marriage to local girl Christine didn't survive the transplant and they divorced in 2003. Christine still lives in Swansea, but Jimmy then married a Canadian woman and now spends his time between Canada and China – a long way from his start in the builder's yard in Southport.

John Fitzpatrick would have longed for a career the

length of Jimmy Rimmer's, though their time at United was almost identical. John arrived on the groundstaff from Aberdeen in August 1961, two years before Jimmy, and although, as we have seen, he made his debut in February 1965, the United side was solidifying with Stiles and Crerand as the irreplaceable wing-halves. With his lank hair flapping and his tackling, which was frequently more suited to the Mel Gibson film *Braveheart*, Fitzpatrick was a caricature of a fiery Scot. When he finally broke into the side it was as the great days were disappearing over the horizon. His longest run in one position came as a replacement for Shay Brennan at right-back, in the season after the European Cup victory. He made twenty-eight appearances that year, twenty the following, and in the troubled 1970–71 season he made thirty-five, so that by any stretch of the imagination he was now regarded as a first-team regular, although he still appeared more often as a right-back than in the wing-half position in which he had been trained.

For all his fierce, some would say wild, tackling, John was constantly plagued by knee problems. After two cartilage operations his progress came to a halt. He played only once in 1971–72 and five times the following year, when he was told by a specialist that the arthritic condition of his knee joints could never be cured. At the age of twenty-six he retired and returned to his native city of Aberdeen, where he still lives and works as a wine importer. On the telephone at least, the vicious Red maniac I remember from my days of swearing at him as he clobbered Colin Bell is the most pleasant and soft-spoken of men. I know he is now fifty-seven and his business is probably not best served by crashing into prospective customers from behind and leaving the imprint of his shoe on the back of their knee, but in my mind the new, improved John Fitzpatrick is fighting with the image of the combative Aberdonian that has been in my head

since the night in April 1964 when he sorted out Bobby
McAlinden.

Despite being at United in the golden mid to late sixties,
John left the club without a medal. In 1990, as United played
Crystal Palace in the FA Cup final at Wembley, David Meek
discovered that Bobby Noble needed to sell his championship medal. Meek alerted Manchester United and the club
bought it to display in the club museum. The financial
relationship between Noble and the club was always
strained. After the club decided there was no point in
renewing his contract in 1969, Bobby asked Matt Busby for
a testimonial game, but Busby, who was soon to be so
unhelpful to the loyal David Sadler, was not about to come to
the rescue of his former youth-team captain and rejected the
request out of hand.

Bobby and his wife, Irene, have differing views on what
Busby did to help them in the nightmare that followed the
crash in April 1967. Irene thought Busby and Jimmy
Murphy came round frequently to the house to give Bobby
money and see how he was getting on, but Bobby thinks
that was Jack Crompton. It's true that United helped him to
buy the club house in Sale after he received £25,000 in
damages from the insurance company of the driver of the
other car, but Bobby is of the opinion that Busby was
always a canny businessman and was just covering his back.
He certainly never arrived with Bobby's 1967 championship
medal. Denis Law brought that to the house: 'Busby offered
me a job in the ticket office, but he knew I'd refuse it. How
could I sit there selling tickets to Denis Law, Bobby
Charlton and Nobby Stiles, when I've just been training and
playing with them?'

Irene thinks a job is a job and, besides, what was the
point of turning it down when he ended up in a dead-end
job anyway? But to Bobby working in the ticket office was

worse than a dead-end job, because of the additional humiliation. Irene explains it by reference to his being only twenty-one at the time and the impossibility of putting an old head on young shoulders, but on reflection he'd have grabbed the job now. He had an offer from Liverpool University to coach their football team, but foolishly he turned that down as well. In June 1969 he started work as a clerk in an engineering works near Old Trafford.

Even the substantial damages he was awarded in 1969 was not much compensation for a football career destroyed at the age of twenty-one and his clinical depression was so severe that he was incapable of using it constructively. In an interview given to the *Manchester Evening News* in May 1972, Irene described the change in his personality in the months after the crash: 'He is violent one minute and placid the next. I never know how he is going to react ... He also began to drink heavily after the crash, as if trying to blot it out of his memory. I keep pleading with him to go and get help for his problems, but it seems he either won't or can't help himself.'

Within eighteen months of the award, Bobby had lost most of the £25,000. A newspaper article in March 1970 even claimed he was on the dole only three months after receiving it. A new car, a haulage business which went broke within four months and a host of new-found, fair-weather friends took much of it and the rest trickled through his fingers. Despite having two (and eventually four) little boys, Irene went back to work to support the family. She had always worked, first at Nettle Electrics, then as a riveter on the shop floor at Reynolds Chains.

At the time of the 1972 interview, Bobby was working on a building site. When I talked to him thirty years later, he was cycling to work in a bakery. The years in between had been hard as he struggled to hold down a series of jobs. In 1975 he was fined for drink-driving and banned for four years. In 1990, when he sold his championship medal, he was working as a security guard at a factory a stone's throw from Old Trafford. You would have thought that one tragedy was enough for Bobby Noble's lifetime, but fate had something even more cruel in store.

Early one Saturday night in December 1994, his twenty-six-year-old son, Grant, a fork lift driver with a firm in Trafford Park, was stabbed to death outside the Station of Sale pub in Hope Road. Three other local men, including Grant's twenty-three-year-old brother, Dean, were treated in hospital for stab wounds, before being discharged. In January 1997, another of Bobby's three remaining sons, Lee, also appeared in court on a drink-drive charge. The court permitted his address to remain a secret when the stipendiary magistrate learned that those whom it was believed were responsible for his brother's murder had been harassing him. It is a tribute to her extraordinary spirit that Irene Noble remains the admirable, indefatigable character she is today, after a lifetime of adversity that would have broken lesser individuals.

The youth-team players of 1964 are all in their mid to late fifties now. Their football careers seem a long time ago. None of them has played the game professionally for over fifteen years. Their lives in football were fleeting in comparison to the allotted life span most of them can expect – and all have had bad times. Many of them found that the game they loved never returned their affection, but none of them regrets making the attempt to earn a living as a professional footballer. For all the betrayals and disappointments, the bitterness that still lingers along with the physical ailments, playing football made them special and they are remembered today with warmth by thousands of people, simply because they appeared in the blue shirt of Manchester City or the red shirt of Manchester United and lived, however briefly, the fantasy we have all harboured.

CHAPTER ELEVEN

Kids Today

I have carried around in my head the mental image of the 1964 Youth Cup semi-final at Old Trafford for nearly forty years. I stood in the paddock that night, between the Stretford End and the cantilever stand, then still in its first flush of youth, with two school friends, marvelling at the fact that the players we were watching were only three or four years older than we were. I remember the excitement in Manchester, the growing conviction that, though our first teams could not be compared, it was just possible that our youth teams were so evenly matched that the lads in blue would be inspired by the palpable sense of occasion and snatch a victory that would re-establish our football cred in school next day. Albert Kinsey's hat trick put paid to that hope.

I knew the teams met again in this competition in the mid-eighties, but when I consulted the record books I was astonished to find that City and United met no fewer than four times in six years in the sixties. In 1961–62 United won 3–0 at the Cliff in round two; in 1963–64 they met in the semi-final; in 1965–66 United won 5–0 at Urmston in round two; and the following year they won there again, this time 3–0 in round four. It was surprising that United won most of those matches so comfortably because the mid-sixties was the start of City's rise to the top under Mercer and Allison, reflected by Allison's belief in nurturing his own talent. Tommy Booth, Tony Towers, Joe Corrigan, Stan Bowles, Derek Jeffries and Ian Bowyer all made it through to first-team status in the years when the youth team performed so relatively poorly in the cup competition.

Results improved when Glyn Pardoe took over in the mid-seventies. They reached the quarter-final in his first year and the final in 1978–79, when they lost 0–2 on aggregate to Millwall. Out of that team came Alex Williams, the goal-keeper whose career was cut short by injury, Tommy Caton who was sold to Arsenal, Nicky Reid, Steve Kinsey and Clive Wilson, all of whom progressed. They reached the final again the following year with the addition of Andy May and Steve Mackenzie, only to lose 2–3 on aggregate to Aston Villa, and the semi-final the year after that. Pardoe's results were truly amazing given the fact that, for all the coaching ability and scouting networks, there is a fair amount of luck involved when teenagers are only allowed two years to compete and it is therefore impossible to construct a side as managers can with a first team of mixed ages.

After 1964, United didn't reach the Youth Cup final again until 1981–82, when the side containing Mark Hughes, Norman Whiteside and Clayton Blackmore lost 6–7 on aggregate to Watford. After their almost yearly battles in the sixties, the two Manchester clubs didn't meet again until 1985–86, when they did so in the final. The teams drew 1–1 in front of 7,602 at Old Trafford, but City triumphed 2–0 at Maine Road, with goals by Boyd and Paul Moulden, to win the benighted trophy at last for the first and only time in their history. Of the United team of Walsh, Gill, Martin, Scott, Gardner, Harvey, Murphy, Todd, Cronin, Bottomley and Goddard, only Gary Walsh, the goalkeeper, and Lee Martin, whose goal won the FA Cup for United in the replay against

Crystal Palace in 1990, prospered briefly in the first team.

The City side of 1986 produced a golden crop of youngsters and will be remembered by those who saw them with the sort of fondness I have retained for Mike Doyle, Glyn Pardoe, Alan Ogley and David Connor. The team which faced United was: Crompton, Mills, Hinchcliffe, Ian Brightwell, Redmond, Thackery, White, Moulden, Lake, Scott and Boyd. Ian Brightwell, Steve Redmond, Dave White, Andy Hinchcliffe and Paul Lake all made it through to regular first-team level. White and Hinchcliffe were capped as full internationals, not exactly with much distinction in the case of Dave White, who will go down as a one-cap wonder. Hinchcliffe, Redmond, White, Brightwell and Lake all played in the legendary 5–1 victory over United at Maine Road in September 1989, a result which made Alex Ferguson, by his own admission, go home and put a pillow over his face. I always thought it was a shame he didn't ask for volunteers to sit on the pillow.

The irony of the youth teams in the eighties was that, although City had by far the better players and the better setup, it didn't help the club, because the first team, the management and the chairman were all so dreadful. In 1983 and 1987 the club was relegated to the second division, gaining promotion in 1985 and 1989. Six months after gaining the last promotion and six weeks after overseeing the legendary 5–1 victory over United, the manager Mel Machin was sacked as Peter Swales brought in Howard Kendall to stave off the prospect of yet another relegation. It was a bad time to be a brilliant youth-team player at Maine Road. Instead of being eased into a winning team as Towers, Corrigan, Jeffries, Bowyer and that generation were, and as Garry Owen and Peter Barnes later slipped into the team of Tueart, Kidd, Hartford, Watson and Royle, the lads of 1986 were flung into first-team action in a desperate but doomed bid to prevent the relegation of 1987. This was no way to nurture that talented youth team and, rather like the country's use of North Sea oil, City wound up squandering their greatest natural resource.

United, on the other hand, had a poor youth system in the seventies and eighties, but the first team managed to survive on the handouts provided by winning the FA Cup by spending freely on Bryan Robson and, triumphantly, Garry Birtles and Peter Davenport. It wasn't until 1991–92, when Glyn Pardoe's last youth team went into battle before his untimely dismissal, that United really produced a youth team to rival that of 1963–64. That season the teams met in round four of the Youth Cup. United emerged victorious by a score of 3–1 and went on to beat Crystal Palace in the final and claim the cup for the first time since Bobby Noble had held it aloft. It was welcomed as evidence that United had reclaimed their birthright, for the belief persists that, possibly because of fading memories of the Busby Babes and the undiluted tragedy of the Munich air disaster, the tradition of youth is more highly esteemed at Manchester United than at any other football club. In the sense that, seven years later, four of the team were in the squad that won the European Cup, it may be said that there was a loud echo of the Best, Sadler, A on side of 1964. Certainly, the class of 1992, the United s e of Robbie Savage, Gary Neville, Beckham, Scholes and Butt, has earned its place in the history of the club by virtue of the value of their image rights, to be found in the overpriced memorabilia clogging up cyberspace and credit card bills.

This book was being written during the second half of the 2002–03 season and, as the chapters were slowly hewn from the block of granite, it became apparent that an unseen hand was guiding the contents of this final chapter. Both Manchester City and Manchester United seemed to have comparably excellent youth sides again and, as each successive round produced the desired result, it became inevitable that they would meet, either in the final, which would make the perfect ending, or in the semi-final, which would at least have the merit of reflecting what happened in 1963–64.

City began their campaign in the third round by beating Wrexham 3–0 in front of 255 spectators at Hyde United's ground, while United triumphed 3–1 away to Newcastle in front of 847. In the next two rounds, United disposed of both Sheffield clubs, while City despatched Peterborough and Millwall. The possibility of another clash of the juvenile titans became even more likely when City impressively beat West Ham United 2–0 and United knocked out Tranmere Rovers 3–1 in the quarter-finals. Unfortunately, the draw kept the clubs apart, United going off to Charlton and City to Middlesbrough, where they drew the first leg 1–1 and were somewhat unfortunate not to have won. United chipped out the same result on an uneven pitch at the Valley, in front of a crowd of 9,074, the highest in the history of Charlton's youth-team matches. The Manchester derby was coming ever closer.

On April Fools' Day 2003, City fell to earth with a bump in front of the 5,790 spectators who packed the main stand. They had all the play in the first half and might have been two goals up at the interval, but, as with all teams who don't score when they are on top, everyone started to feel uneasy and in the middle of the second half a speculative shot from just outside the penalty area by Middlesbrough's talented but tiny number nine, Anthony Peacock, bounced and squirmed past the scrambling Keiren Westwood in the City goal. City could not be faulted for lack of passion, though they could be criticised for lack of brains once the dynamic Willo Flood in midfield had run out of steam in the second half. Only Lee Croft looked the part as he ran tirelessly at the Middlesbrough defence, for whom central defender Andrew Davies was outstanding. With less than fifteen minutes remaining, Croft equalised from the penalty spot to take the match into extra time, but Middlesbrough finished the stronger and it was no surprise to see Davies, in the six-yard box, head the winning goal from an inswinging corner which the goalkeeper should have caught. It was an incredibly deflating moment for the players, the coaching staff and the crowd.

Like City, United allowed their youth team to play the semi-final on the grown-ups' pitch. In the return leg, Charlton didn't prove much of a draw and only 4,427 people dotted the Theatre of Dreams to see United glide through to another final. It was a poor contrast to the 29,706 who had packed Old Trafford for the 1964 match, but the FA Youth Cup isn't the Holy Grail to United any more, not like it was to that 1964 side. Crowds don't watch reserve teams at United the way they did in the fifties and sixties. Those who couldn't be bothered to traipse down to the ground and find a place to park could see the Youth Cup final on Sky Sports. Football has changed and the players' lives have changed with it. The boys weren't playing for professional contracts as the youth sides of forty years ago did. They were playing for endorsements by sporting goods manufacturers.

In the final, Middlesbrough's young side was no match for the older, physically more mature United. Kieran Richardson put United ahead after only four minutes of the away leg, before a miserable 'crowd' of just 1,635, and centre-forward, Ben Collett, effectively won the trophy when he scored the second goal in the last minute. The final match ended in a tame 1–1 draw at Old Trafford, but it was enough to bring United the Cup for the third time in eleven years.

Ironically, ten days after they had surrendered so tamely at home to Middlesbrough in the semi-final, City's Under-19 academy side beat the equivalent age United side 1–0 in a league match. At the end of the season, City's Under-17 side finished top of their league and the Under-19s were second to Nottingham Forest, while United finished a further two points behind City in third place. Had they met in the final, it would have been an interesting contrast between City's pace and aggression and United's rather more stylish pattern of play. Although Kieran Richardson had already made his first-team debut, it was the left-footed midfielder, David Jones, and the right-winger, Chris Eagles, who caught the eye. One thing was for certain. There was no George Best in that side. Forty years is too brief a passage of time to create another like him. In January 2004 United completed a comfortable 2–0 victory over City, both goals ironically the result of unfortunate errors by Peter Schmeichel's son, Kaspar.

We have seen that merely to be a member of the team that wins the Youth Cup has never guaranteed first-team status. Even though eight of the United team of 1964 eventually played first-team football, only three of them had significant careers with the club. Now that the first teams of all Premiership clubs with ambition are dominated by internationals, the chances of the club's own youth-team graduates breaking through are becoming increasingly slight. I'm not at all convinced that the volume of non-British players in the premier league is an undisguised blessing, but I also recognise that if they all disappeared overnight it seems unlikely that they could be replaced by youth-team graduates without a significant lowering of the general standard of play. 'I keep raising the bar for you, don't I?' says a smiling Kevin Keegan to the rueful Jim Cassells, the director of the Manchester City academy.

Cassells played briefly in the A and B sides for both City and United in the early sixties and then later for Bury, before a serious injury caused him to retire from the game at the age of twenty-four and start collecting his coaching qualifications. He now runs a very professional academy, having picked up the pieces in 1997, five years after Glyn Pardoe was sacked and the club was in its traditional tail spin:

> There were no records, no files, no staff, no job description. I was given a Portakabin in the car park and I asked the secretary to contact everyone involved with the youth setup. Ten people showed up. I said to each of them, 'What do you do?' The reply was always along the lines of, 'Don't worry about me. I just need two tickets for City's home games.'

The work at the Platt Lane centre is impressive, but the fact is that City share the facility with the council and the university. At Carrington, the United academy is fully integrated with the outstanding facilities enjoyed by the first-team squad.

The change from the way youth teams were managed forty years ago is the result of the new regulations introduced by the FA when it set up the centres of excellence in the nineties. Schoolboys are not permitted to be signed by clubs if they live more than an hour and a half's driving time away, although all that means is that money changes hands in greater volume and for ever-younger players. The scouting nets are cast wider than ever before, because all the clubs in the northwest compete for Manchester-based youngsters. Indeed, the West Riding of Yorkshire could certainly be regarded as within an hour and a half's drive, too.

Fortunately, there is still a healthy proportion of Manchester-based lads in both teams. As an example, the goalkeeper Keiren Westwood comes from Wythenshawe, Danny Warrender from Blackley, Paul Collins from Droylesden and the impressive central defender, Chinedum Onuoha, lives in Harpurhey. The D'Laryea twins live in Crumpsall, Jamie Tandy in Wythenshawe and the promising striker, Lee Croft, comes from Wigan. Only the midfield dynamo Willo Flood and Paul Murphy, both from Eire, come from outside Lancashire, whereas in the 1964 team, it was just Alan Ogley who came from beyond the Manchester area. Even forty years ago, the United youth team took in Alan Duff from the northeast, Willie Anderson from Liverpool, Fitzpatrick and McBride from Scotland and George from Belfast. In the days of Matt Busby, the club always contained a strong Celtic influence, so the 2004 side compares favourably in terms of local content.

There are, however, many features of youth-team football which have changed greatly. The boys of 2004 don't have to sweep the terraces and clean the boots of the senior professionals. They don't have to knock on the door of the first-team dressing room and wait for permission before they can enter. The days of landladies, lunch at the UCP paid for with luncheon vouchers and snooker halls and bowling alleys in the afternoons are long gone. Landladies are now called family accommodation providers – FAPs for short (the dead hand of American or possibly New Labour nomenclature is everywhere apparent). Everything is much more tightly structured, with the emphasis on coaching rather than matches, and advice given (though not necessarily heeded) on diet and lifestyle.

Both City and United have an identical working week for the sixteen to nineteen-year-olds who form the basis of the Youth Cup teams. On Monday morning they go to college, the courses ranging from A levels for the academically gifted to car maintenance for those who might find it useful on that rare occasion when the Ferrari breaks down on the M60. In 2002, the City youngster Andrew Tunnicliffe was offered a place at Oxford University. He didn't take it up, but he was bright enough and the fact that he left Maine Road with that opportunity, Cassells believes, means his staff have done an equally good job with him as they have with Shaun Wright-Phillips. Of the current crop, the D'Laryea twins are taking A levels. At United, Dave Bushell is the head of education and welfare: 'It's a rubbish title, because I'm head of nothing. Mostly I look after boys off the field. I'm the youth development officer.' He believes the intake is getting more academic because there are more boys coming through who have five GCSEs at A to C level, although that may be the result of what broadsheet news-papers call 'grade inflation' every August when the exam results are released.

College finishes at 11.50a.m. on Monday mornings, after which the first years are ferried to Carrington or Platt Lane, but the older ones invariably drive their own cars. Thereaf-ter, the week is split between training and learning. On Tuesday, the boys arrive at 9.30a.m., start training at 10.30a.m., train until lunch and again in the afternoon, although they are free to go from about 3.30 or 4p.m. Wednesday is all-day training and Thursday is all-day col-lege, which is supposed to allow the staff the day off to compensate for the Saturdays they all work, but it doesn't always happen that way because the staff look after other ages than just the sixteen to nineteen-year-olds. On Friday, the boys have a light training session in the morning, practis-ing set pieces, and the afternoon is free, although sometimes that's when they get their financial advice and media training. Well, somebody has to teach them how to say, 'We'll treat our opponents with every respect.' After all, you can't just make up the clichés that are as vital a part of their footballing education as dyeing their hair a grotesque shade of yellow. Saturday, of course, is match day and then they get Sunday off, unless they need treatment. It's a full week, but it's one that the lads of 1964 would have regarded as if it were a luxury cruise.

Of course, the money has changed because society has changed. You can't imagine any current 'scholar', as the lads are termed (much, I would imagine, to the horror of anyone who has actually won an academic scholarship), appreciating the fondness with which Chris Jones describes the crisp ten shilling note he remembers as his first expenses payment after he had signed amateur forms. The academy rules lay down that the lads shall receive a minimum of £75 a week in their first year, £90 a week in their second year and £115 in their final year. The lads of 1964 were desperate for the security of a professional contract. Now, the competition between clubs for the best schoolboys is so fierce that few will take up their scholarship without the guarantee of a professional contract – and that is likely to be in the range of £20,000 a year, which they can start to receive when they are still nineteen years old. Wayne Rooney's wages went from £90 a week to £9,000 a week as he graduated to the first team during his second year on Everton's books. He is an exceptional talent, but his success both as a player and a cash cow re-emphasises the belief many parents have that their own offspring can provide similarly. The money is a lure to the parents as much as to their sons. In most cases, the father becomes the son's agent (and press agent) and the bigger the financial incentive, the more likely the father is to pressure the son into signing for a particular club.

Tom Doyle was terrified lest his son Mike should sign for a club other than Manchester City. John Clay's dad was a Blue and the day his son signed for City must have been one of the happiest of his tragically short life. Alan Ogley's dad earned £18 a week down the pits, but he wouldn't take Don Revie's car because his son wanted to play for Barnsley. Phil Burrows and Dave Connor and Alf Wood were all warned against signing professional forms by their fathers. 'Get yourself a trade, lad,' they said with one voice. Football was a chancy business and all they could see ahead was the dole queue, not the sexy girl in the sports car.

Connor worked in an accountant's office all day and went to Urmston for training on Tuesday and Thursday evenings. Chris Jones worked for the gas board, Alf Wood helped to build Piccadilly Station and Phil Burrows worked for a quantity surveyor. The problem today's boys have is how to spend their spare time, but the lads of 1964 had none. Dave Bushell has been involved in schoolboy football all his working life:

> You have to love the life and live it. Do you just want to play football or do you really want to be a footballer? Do you want to be a professional? You need a lot of self-discipline to do the right things. To go to bed, to rest at the right times, to not eat too much pasta. Even though you need the right amount of pasta and carbs, you can eat too much of it. You won't burn off all the fat. Do you want to go out at night? Can you manage with going to the pictures once a fortnight instead of trying to go three times a week? How many times do you need to go to the Trafford Centre? Why don't you just go to bed? Why don't you practise lying down for two hours in the afternoon and listening to a CD instead of driving your new car? 'It's boring,' they say. Well, once you learn how to deal with the boredom you've got a chance of becoming a professional footballer.

For all the talent and dedication, they still need luck to make the transition. Principally, they need the luck to avoid injury. United prospect Danny Webber is a case in point. He was thought to have the right temperament, but he suffered badly from injuries. He went out on loan to Watford, performed admirably at Vicarage Road, but then dislocated his shoulder. He struggled back to fitness, played in a Senior Cup match, scored twice and within ten minutes of the second goal going in he was stretchered off with a broken ankle. Luck works the other way, too. Someone else's injury or misfortune can be your lucky break. It certainly was for Gary Neville, who went from being a substitute for the United reserve team in August 1995, to replace David May who was playing poorly at right-back. At the end of the season, Neville was playing for England in the European Championships and, to the incredulity of football supporters nationwide, he has kept his place.

The general increase in professionalism at the bottom of the ladder – improved scouting networks, coaching and social adjustment – has, ironically, come at a time when the pool of talent, though fiercely fought over, is getting smaller. As a cricket lover, I bemoan the sight of lads playing football in the parks during the summer when they should be playing cricket, although what I am seeing is apparently a mirage. The scouts tell the academy director that there are fewer and fewer talented boys to be seen. In fact, there are fewer boys actually playing football. The rival attractions of satellite television, the computer and video games have cut a swathe through the numbers of boys who just want to play football all day as the sixties boys did. Where do they play? Think of the cars in your street. It's not possible to play where we played. Boys as young as seven or eight would leave the house after breakfast in the summer holidays and 'play outside' until it was dark. Few parents would now be so blasé about allowing their children out of their sight for that length of time. The boys who emerge as footballers now are manufactured, rather than natural players.

When United professionals played those competitive games 'round the back' on the gravel, it was a return to the rough and tumble of the school playground and the bomb site. Now they want schoolboys to experience the manufactured excellence of grass like billiard tables. Look at the pitches the Spurs double-winning side of 1961, the Law, Best, Charlton side of 1967 or the Lee, Bell, Summerbee side of 1968 were made to play on. From November to May the only grass to be seen was down the wings. The goalmouths were either wet or dry mudheaps. The balls were like canon balls (a coroner recently suggested that Jeff Astle's untimely death was the result of heading the old leather ball which, when wet, could dent your head). The shirts felt like wearing a wet towel after you'd been running for ten minutes and the referees permitted the sort of tackles that would be taken to the European Court of Human Rights today. Players used to eat steak and chips before a match and yet we produced some of the best footballers in the history of the game in these conditions. Scotland produced Crerand and Mackay, Law and Dalglish, Baxter and Bremner. For all the advances in medicine and nutrition, for all the admirable athleticism in the game today, for all the fact that old football looks slow and boring, whom would you rather watch? George Best or Nicky Butt? Don't bother to send the answer on a postcard.

We live in a society that values different things than those that were prized by the children of austerity. We produce different children from those who grew up as baby boomers. Kids today see a society that places value on material possessions, on physical appearance, on tabloid celebrity. We shouldn't condemn them for wanting trivia. We are the society who created those conditions. We didn't want to stand up for the national anthem after a movie finished, we wanted all the things our parents couldn't have because they were too busy fighting Hitler or finding a job. We wanted what the advertisers told us would make us richer, healthier, sexier, happier. It was all nonsense, but our children believe it because we have not disabused them sufficiently. We have the football and the footballers we deserve.

And yet, and yet ... At the end of Alan Bennett's play *Forty Years On*, the retiring headmaster delivers a closing panegyric, bemoaning the death of the England he loved and the traditional English values he cherished:

> Once we had a romantic and old-fashioned concep-
> tion of honour, of patriotism, chivalry and duty. But it
> was a duty which didn't have much to do with justice,
> with social justice anyway. And in default of that
> justice and in pursuit of it, that was how the great
> words came to be cancelled out. The crowd has found
> the door into the secret garden. Now they will tear up
> the flowers by the roots, strip the borders and strew
> them with paper and broken bottles.

Forty Years On opened at the Apollo Theatre on Shaftesbury Avenue in October 1968, just five months after Manchester City won the league championship and Manchester United won the European Cup with teams composed of mostly local young players, certainly entirely English in City's case and British in United's. 1968, when Bennett was mourning the death of English civilisation, was the apotheosis for my generation of football as the manifestation of the symbiotic relationship between football clubs and their supporters. By this measure of achievement 1968 was undoubtedly the greatest season in the history of Manchester football. *Plus ça change, plus c'est la même chose* as they all say in all the best Premiership dressing rooms these days.

End Credits

Manchester United

Jimmy Rimmer 1967–72 (45 appearances, 1 as sub, 0 goals)
Lives in Canada. Goalkeeping coach to the Chinese national side.
Other clubs: Swansea 1973 (17 appearances, 0 goals); Arsenal 1974–77 (124 appearances, 0 goals); Aston Villa 1977–83 (229 appearances, 0 goals); Swansea 1983–86 (66 appearances, 0 goals)

Alan Duff (0 games, 0 goals)
Back near Guisborough, north Yorkshire. Runs the local working men's club.
Other clubs: Highland Park (South Africa); Rhyl (Cheshire League)

Bobby Noble 1965–67 (33 games, 0 goals)
Still lives in the same house in Sale. Has done various jobs. Currently works in a local bakery.

Peter McBride (0 games, 0 goals)
Believed to have returned to live in Scotland. No longer in touch with Manchester United.

Dave Farrar (0 goals, 0 games)
Lives just outside Altrincham. Works in the exhibition stand business.

John Fitzpatrick 1964–72 (141 games, 6 as sub, 10 goals)
Returned to live in Aberdeen. Works in the wine importing business.

Willie Anderson 1963–66 (10 games, 2 as sub, 0 goals)
Sells air time for a local television station in Portland, Oregon, USA.
Other clubs: Aston Villa 1966–73 (231 appearances, 36 goals); Cardiff City 1973–77 (126 appearances, 12 goals); Portland Timbers 1976–81

George Best 1963–73 (466 games, 178 goals – third equal with Dennis Viollet in United history, after Bobby Charlton and Denis Law)
Still a national celebrity, even with a transplanted liver.
Other clubs: Stockport County; Cork Celtic; Los Angeles Aztecs; Fulham; Hibernian; Fort Lauderdale Strikers; San Jose Earthquakes; Bournemouth

David Sadler 1963–73 (326 games, 7 as sub, 24 goals)
Runs David Sadler Promotions. Has a column in the *Manchester Evening News*.
Other clubs: Preston North End 1973–77 (105 appearances, 3 goals)

Albert Kinsey 1964 (1 game, 1 goal)
Believed to be living in Australia.
Other clubs: Wrexham 1966–73 (253 appearances, 80 goals); Crewe 1973–75 (32 appearances, 1 goal)

John Aston 1964–71 (164 games, 21 as sub, 27 goals)
Lives in Ashton. Runs a pet food business.
Other clubs: Luton Town 1972–77 (174 appearances, 31 goals); Mansfield Town 1977–78 (31 appearances, 4 goals); Blackburn Rovers 1978–80 (15 appearances, 2 goals)

Manchester City

Alan Ogley 1964–67 (57 games, 0 goals)
Lives in Barnsley. Worked for BOC for twenty years delivering for Marks & Spencer. Now coaches local ladies' team.
Other clubs: Barnsley; Stockport County; Darlington

Mike Doyle 1965–78 (551 games, 7 as sub, 40 goals)
Lives in Ashton. Worked for Slazenger but recently retired because of knee problems.
Other clubs: Stoke City; Bolton Wanderers; Rochdale

Dave Wild (0 games, 0 goals)
Deceased
Other clubs: Altrincham; Rossendale United

John Clay 1967–68 (1 game, 1 as sub, 0 goals)
Lives in Swinton. Works in lettings and management.
Other clubs: Macclesfield Town; Witton Albion; Rossendale United

Alf Wood 1963–66 (32 games, 1 as sub, 0 goals)
Lives in the West Midlands. Runs a promotional company with his daughter.
Other clubs: Shrewsbury Town; Millwall; Hull City; Middlesbrough; Walsall

Phil Burrows (0 games, 0 goals)
Lives near Stockport. Works as a quantity surveyor for a national building company.
Other clubs: York City; Plymouth Argyle; Hereford United

Ron Frost 1964–65 (2 games, 1 goal)
Believed to live in Hazel Grove. Owned Ron Frost Carpets warehouse.

Max Brown (0 games, 0 goals)
Not traced.

Glyn Pardoe 1962–76 (374 games, 2 as sub, 22 goals)
Lives in Cheshire. Works at the National Nuclear Corporation.

Chris Jones 1966–68 (6 games, 1 as sub, 2 goals)
Lives in York. Works as a supply teacher.
Other clubs: Swindon Town; Oldham Athletic; Walsall; York City; Rochdale

Bobby McAlinden (1 game, 0 goals)
Lives in Seaside, Oregon, USA. Works in real estate.
Other clubs: Glentoran; Port Vale; Durban City (South Africa); Stalybridge Celtic; Los Angeles Aztecs; Memphis

David Connor 1964–72, 1974–75 (152 games, 13 as sub, 10 goals)
Lives in Heald Green. Manages local sports centre.
Other clubs: Preston North End 1972–74

Index

Bacuzzi, Dave 188, 196
Bailey, Roy 274
Ball, Alan 277, 278
Ball, Alan Sr 283, 284
Banks, Gordon 223–4
Banks, Tommy 250
Barnes, Ken 285
Barnes, Peter 341
Barnes, Walley 210, 302–3
Barnett, Laurie 31, 113
Barnsley Boys 100–1
Barnsley FC 102–4
Batty, Mike 116, 118, 170, 171
Beatles, the 179, 231
Beckenbauer, Franz 278
Beckham, David 1, 330
Bell, Colin 129, 227, 253, 254
Benfica 184, 200, 218
Bennett, Alan 353
Bernstein, David 272, 284, 287
Bernstein, Sidney 58–9
Berry, Johnny 31
Best, George 5, 34–5, 53, 89,
    150, 352
  celebrity status 177, 184–5
  Chelsea match (September
    1964) 177–8
  effect on women 123, 298
  first team 121, 122–3, 137–8,
    152
  and Glyn Pardoe's broken leg
    258–66
  homesickness 42, 95
  international debut 137
  life after football 297–300
  on Mike Doyle 21
  and Phil Burrows 320–1

physique 120
playing in America 307–9
social life 178, 180
Youth Cup team 1, 3, 12, 13,
    14, 15, 19, 22–3, 137,
    138, 217
Birmingham City 91
Birtles, Garry 342
Bishop, Bob 34
Bishop Auckland FC 44
Blackburn Rovers 74, 295–6,
    320
Blackpool 60
  FC 10, 73, 116
Blanchflower, Danny 136
Bolton Wanderers 38, 70, 74, 99,
    322
Book, Tony 267, 268, 277, 285,
    306
Booth, Tommy 272
Bowles, Stan 222, 251, 252,
    253–4, 281
Bowyer, Ian 281, 341
Box, Mick 42
Boyle, Harry 40
Brand, Ralph 193, 197–8
Bremner, Billy 114
Brennan, Shay 122, 150, 152,
    201, 207, 210, 334
Briggs, Ronnie 120
Bristol Rovers 102
Brown, Allan 262
Brown, Max 9, 196
Bryceland, Tommy 169
Buckley, John 175, 325
Burnley FC 66, 97–8, 122, 123,
    131